REFLECTIONS

On the Magic of Writing

DIANA WYNNE JONES

REFLECTIONS
On the Magic of Writing

Greenwillow Books

An Imprint of HarperCollinsPublishers

Reflections was first published by David Fickling Books (UK) and edited by Charlie Butler.

Several titles mentioned in this collection were published under alternate titles in the US: *Black Maria* was published as *Aunt Maria* and *Wilkins' Tooth* was published as *Witch's Business*. In addition, *Dark Lord of Derkholm* and its sequel *The Year of the Griffin* were published in the UK as adult titles but in the US were young adult books

First published in 2012 by David Fickling Books, a division of Random House Children's Books, a Random house Group Company. First published in 2012 in the United States by Greenwillow Books. The right of Diana Wynne Jones to be identified as the author of this work has been asserted in accordance with the Copyright, Designs and Patents Act 1988. All rights reserved. No part of this book may be used or reproduced in any manner whatsoever without written permission except in the case of brief quotations embodied in critical articles and reviews. Printed in the United States of America. For information address HarperCollins Children's Books, a division of HarperCollins Publishers, 10 East 53rd Street, New York, NY 10022. www.epicreads.com. The text of this book is set in Garamond. Book design by Sylvie Le Floc'h.

Library of Congress Cataloging-in-Publication Data

Jones, Diana Wynne, author. Reflections : on the magic of writing / by Diana Wynne Jones. pages cm
Summary: "This collection of more than twenty-five critical essays, speeches, and biographical pieces written and/or chosen by Diana Wynne Jones will be required reading for the author's many fans and for students and teachers of the genre. Reflections includes insightful literary criticism alongside autobiographical anecdotes about reading tours (including an account of the author's famous travel jinx), revelations about the origins of the author's books, and thoughts in general about the life of an author and the value of writing. The longest autobiographical piece, "Something About the Author," details Diana's extraordinary childhood and is illustrated with family photographs. Reflections is essential reading for anyone interested in Diana Wynne Jones's work, fantasy, or creative writing. With a foreword by Neil Gaiman, introduction and interview by Charlie Butler, bibliography, and index." "Various threads run through this collection, but by far the strongest is that of the need for fantasy in all its many facets and its value for children and adults alike. It is my hope that some of these items will be of use to people."—Diana Wynne Jones. "Her writings assembled in one place tell us how she thought about literature and the reasons for literature, about the place of children's fiction in the world, about the circumstances that shaped her and her own understanding and vision of who she was and what she did. It is ferociously intelligent, astonishingly readable, and as with so much that Diana Wynne Jones did, she makes each thing she writes, each explanation for why the world is as it is, look so easy."—Neil Gaiman"—Provided by publisher. Includes bibliographical references and index.
ISBN 978-0-06-221989-3 (hardback) 1. Jones, Diana Wynne—Authorship. 2. Children's stories—Authorship. 3. Fantasy fiction—Authorship. I. Title. PR6060.O497Z46 2012 823'.914—dc23 [B] 2012018080

12 13 14 15 16 CG/RRDH 10 9 8 7 6 5 4 3 2 1 First Edition

Greenwillow Books

Contents

Foreword

It was easy, when you knew her, to forget what an astonishing intellect Diana Wynne Jones had, or how deeply and how well she understood her craft.

She would certainly strike you when you met her as being friendly and funny, easygoing and opinionated. She was a perceptive reader (I had the enormous pleasure of spending a week with her at the Milford Writers' Workshop, hearing her opinions on story after story) but she rarely talked about stories technically. She would tell you what she loved, and she would tell you how much she loved it. She would tell you what she didn't like, too, but rarely wasted breath or emotion on it. She was, in conversation about stories, like a winemaker who would taste wine, and discuss the taste of the wine and how it made her feel, but rarely even mention the winemaking process. That does not mean she did not understand it, though, and understand every nuance of it.

The joy for me of reading these essays and thoughts, these

reflections on a life spent writing, was watching her discuss both her life and the (metaphorical) winemaking process.

She does not describe herself in this book, so I shall describe her for you: she had a shock of curly, dark hair and, much of the time, a smile, which ranged from easygoing and content to a broad whorl of delight, the smile of someone who was enjoying herself enormously. She laughed a lot, too, the easy laugh of someone who thought the world was funny and filled with interesting things, and she would laugh at her own anecdotes, in the way of someone who had simply not stopped finding what she was going to tell you funny. She smoked too much, but she smoked with enthusiasm and enjoyment until the end. She had a smoker's chuckle. She did not suffer fools of the self-important kind, but she loved and took pleasure in people, the foolish as well as the wise.

She was polite, unless she was being gloriously rude, and she was, I suppose, relatively normal, if you were able to ignore the swirls and eddies of improbability that bubbled and crashed around her. And believe me, they did: Diana would talk about her "travel jinx," and I thought she was exaggerating until we had to fly to America on the same plane. The plane we were meant to fly on was taken out of commission after the door fell off, and it took many hours to get another plane. Diana accepted this as a normal part of the usual business of travel. Doors fell off planes. Sunken islands rose up beneath you if you were in boats. Cars simply and inexplicably ceased to function. Trains with Diana on them went to places they had never been before and technically could not have gone.

She was witchy, yes, and in charge of a cauldron roiling with ideas and stories, but she always gave the impression that the stories, the ones she wrote and wrote so very well and so wisely, had simply happened, and that all she had done was to hold the pen. My favorite essay in this book describes her writing process and shows the immense amount of craft and care that went into each book.

She made a family, and without her family she would not have written. She was well loved, and she was well worth loving.

This book shows us a master craftswoman reflecting on her life, her trade, and the building blocks she used to become a writer. We will meet, in these reflections, someone who has taken the elements of a most peculiar childhood (are there any non-peculiar childhoods? Perhaps not. They are all unique, all unlikely, but Diana's was unlikelier than most) and a formidable intellect, an understanding of language and of story, a keen grasp of politics (on so many levels—personal, familial, organizational, and international), an education that was part autodidactic but in which, as you will learn here, C. S. Lewis and J. R. R. Tolkien both lectured for her, even if she was never quite sure what Tolkien was actually saying, and then, armed with all these things, becomes quite simply the best writer for children of her generation.

I am baffled that Diana did not receive the awards and medals that should have been hers: no Carnegie Medal, for a start (although she was twice a runner-up for it). There was a decade during which she published some of the most important pieces of children's fiction to come out of the U.K.: *Archer's Goon*, *Dogsbody*, *Fire and Hemlock*, the Chrestomanci books . . . these were books that should have been acknowledged as they came out as game changers, and simply weren't. The readers knew. But they were, for the most part, young.

I suspect that there were three things against Diana and the medals:

First, she made it look easy. Much too easy. Like the best jugglers or slack-rope walkers, it looked so natural that the reader couldn't see her working and assumed that the writing process really was that simple, that natural, and that Diana's works were written without thought or effort or were found objects, like beautiful rocks, uncrafted by human hand.

Second, she was unfashionable. You can learn from some of the essays in this volume just how unfashionable she was as she describes the prescriptive books that were fashionable, particularly with teachers and those who published and bought books for young readers, from the 1970s until the 1990s: books in which the circumstances of the protagonist were, as much as possible, the circumstances of the readers, in the kind of fiction that was considered Good For You. What the Victorians might have considered an "improving novel."

Diana's fiction was never improving, or if it was, it was in a way that neither the Victorians nor the 1980s editors would have recognized. Her books took things from unfamiliar angles. The dragons and demons that her heroes and heroines battle may not be the demons her readers are literally battling—but her books are unfailingly realistic in their examinations of what it's like to be, or to fail to be, part of a family, the ways we fail to fit in or deal with uncaring carers.

The third thing that Diana had working against her was this: her books are difficult. Which does not mean that they are not pleasurable. But she makes you work as a reader.

As an adult reader coming to a Diana Wynne Jones book I expected to reread great chunks of a book as I reached the end, all puzzled and filled with brow-crinkling "How did she do that?" and "Now wait a minute, I thought . . ." and I would put it together, and then see what she had done. I challenged her on this, and she told me that children read more carefully than adults did and rarely had that trouble—and indeed, when I came to read Diana's books aloud to Maddy, my daughter, I discovered that they weren't ever problematic or even hard. All the pieces were there for you. You just had to be paying attention to everything she wrote, and to understand that if there was a word on the paper, it was there for a reason.

I don't think she minded not having the medals. She knew how good she was, and she had generations of readers who had grown up reading and loving her work. She was read, and she was loved. As the years went on and the readers who had discovered her when young grew up and wrote about her, talked about her, wrote fiction influenced by her; as magical fiction for children became less unusual; as her books sold more with each year that passed, Diana knew that what she had written had worked, and found its readers, and that was all that, in the end, mattered.

I am a handful of years too old to have read Diana's books as a boy. I wish I had—she would have been one of those people who formed the way I saw the world, the way I thought about it and perceived it. Instead, reading her, it felt familiar, and when, in my twenties, I read all of Diana's books that I could find, it felt like I was coming home.

If, like me, you love Diana's fiction, and you wish to learn more about the person, who she was and how she thought, then this book will enlighten you. But it will give you more than that. Her writings assembled in one place tell us how she thought about literature and the reasons for literature, about the place of children's fiction in the world, about the circumstances that shaped her and her own understanding and vision of who she was and what she did. It is ferociously intelligent, astonishingly readable, and as with so much that Diana Wynne Jones did, she makes each thing she writes, each explanation for why the world is as it is, look so easy.

—Neil Gaiman

Reflecting on *Reflections*

By the time I first read Diana Wynne Jones I was already an adult—but that doesn't matter. Many of her readers encounter her later in life, and those who know her as children tend to stick with her into adulthood. That is one of her qualities: her books change and grow as you do.

It is a testimony to the impression Diana makes on her readers that so many have a "How I first came across Diana Wynne Jones" story. Mine is not especially dramatic, but in retrospect our accidental encounter feels providential. When I was a young lecturer, one of my jobs was to sit for an hour each week in a far-flung office in a far-flung corner of my university, ready to offer course advice to any students who might come seeking it. No students ever did come, and I would pass the time by reading. One week, finding myself accidentally bookless, I browsed through the room's many cupboards (it was a storeroom at heart, not office at all) and found there a copy of *Charmed Life* by a writer called Diana Wynne Jones. The name was familiar, but I knew nothing about her. And so, having almost an hour to fill, I sat down and began to read.

That was my first Diana Wynne Jones, and from the opening page, with its mysterious Edwardian-but-not-quite milieu and its paddleboat accident (as shocking and excitingly peremptory, in its way, as the angry rhinoceros in Dahl's *James and the Giant Peach*), I was hooked—by the twistiness, the wit, the superabundant imagination, and the emotional wisdom. These were among the qualities I came to associate with Diana long before I met her in person or began to write about her work. I soon learned to value others, too, and it may be worth enumerating them.

First, there is her range. Diana wrote books for young children, for older children, and for adults. She wrote picture books, chapter books, full-length novels, poetry, plays, and nonfiction. She wrote fantasy, science fiction, romance, farce, and satire; and she wrote books that looped the loop, refusing to be confined within any generic box. She could handle outrageous comedy, but also turn on a sixpence and evoke subtle shades of desire, grief, loneliness, bliss, and love, and do so in prose that never strove to draw attention to its own virtuosity. She could also, as this volume attests, turn out a pretty mean academic essay when she set her mind to it.

Her range is equaled by her stamina, shown not just in producing so many books over such a long period (more than forty books in forty-one years)—something other writers have done only by sticking to a winning formula—but by keeping her art so fresh. No book of hers is simply a rehash of a previous one. In some cases she has invented, or reinvented, entire genres. Edith Nesbit wrote urban fantasy, but not like

Archer's Goon. C. S. Lewis wrote about alternative worlds, but not like the Chrestomanci books. And J. R. R. Tolkien, for all the depth and tenacity of his imagination, would never have come up with the strange loop that is *Hexwood*, or with *Deep Secret*, or the Dalemark quartet.

Diana Wynne Jones was a prodigiously creative writer. This is true not only in terms of the number and range of books she produced, but also in her ability to load every rift with ore. Some of her stories involve mundane situations or everyday phrases, seen from new angles and stretched out to reveal their latent absurdity. Elsewhere you will find a rich idea lying apparently unregarded in a single line. *The Merlin Conspiracy*, for example, features a short conversation with an elf. Diana created elves in a wide variety of models and moral orientations, by the way, but this elf is relatively benign, even though he irritates Roddy Hyde (who has a herb that enables her to understand elfish), because he insists on practicing his broken English on her like an earnest foreign tourist: "I need learn!" This is funny enough, but perhaps the most memorable thing about the elf is the way he explains his appearance and disappearance into an earthen mound with the throwaway sentence, "Space is as a folding screen to the little people." So much is suggested by that one phrase that many novelists would have been tempted to extrapolate a novel from it. But so little is made explicit that it remains in the mind like a grenade with the pin already pulled—a phrase whose potential is all the more powerful for being unrealized. What does it mean, for space to be "like a folding screen"? Diana was a writer abundant in ideas: realms and islands were as plates dropped from her pocket. But she also knew her craft and knew that sometimes being prolific is a matter of knowing when not to speak.

Then there is her magic. No one does magic like Diana Wynne Jones. In the course of her books she runs the gamut of magical styles, and demonstrates that she knows quite a frightening amount about the technicalities, too. She has a sure instinct for the way magic works: totem magic, social magic, transformation magic, and the rest. Some of her spells are grand, formal affairs, like the climax of *The Merlin Conspiracy*. Others are casual, like the way Sophie in *Howl's Moving Castle* unwittingly charms the hats she decorates, simply by talking to them: "You have mysterious allure." Sometimes, as in *Fire and Hemlock*, she keeps you guessing as to whether any magic has taken place at all. At others she shocks you with something startlingly and undeniably magical, as when the eponymous villain of *Black Maria*, who until this point has primarily used the powers of suggestion and social manipulation, turns her nephew into a wolf.

Diana's humor is of course everywhere. Her books are full of verbal wit, but she rejoices too in physical comedy, and in the spectacle of people acting in absurd ways that appear to them to be the height of good sense—a tendency she laughed at but also recognized as an aspect of the human condition. Everyone will have favorite images from her books: Wizard Howl covered with self-indulgent green slime; the conga of alien magicians and witches in *A Sudden Wild Magic*; Chrestomanci giving the gods flu in "The Sage of Theare"; the giant sentient toffee bars that drape themselves over the radiators in *The Ogre Downstairs*; the *Importance of Being Earnest*-style multiple revelations of identity and relationship that feature in several of her final chapters. Then there is her satire—nowhere packaged more conveniently than in *The Tough Guide to Fantasyland*, a book that it is almost impossible not to quote from (and I resist the temptation here only because Diana quotes from it herself in two pieces in this book).

"The world is not enough," Diana once said, and for her this was true. Her imagination shuffled universes like cards, or bent them into origami shapes. It was not enough for her to invent parallel worlds. She invented multiple multiverses: the worlds of Chrestomanci, of *The Homeward Bounders*, of *Deep Secret* and *The Merlin Conspiracy*, of Dalemark, of *A Sudden Wild Magic*, of *The Dark Lord of Derkholm* and *Year of the Griffin*, of *The Game*—each has its own geography and ecology, its own politics and fashions, its own rules of physics, its own magic. Some are linked to our own world through having split off from it at earlier points in history; others are connected in different ways, or not at all. Diana never insists on surplus exposition, but her worlds have a conviction and a coherence that communicate themselves immediately. As she once put it:

You have to know enough about a world to be able to show things in the foreground that bring the background with them. You must have it firmly enough in your mind so that it all hangs together. You don't have to say that there are wild beasts in the wood, so long as you have got the right setup where there might be.

All her worlds have that thought-through, *felt* quality. The same applies to her characters: she takes seriously the advice that she gives aspiring writers in an article in the present collection, that whatever appears on the page about a character, the author must know many times more again—about his or her appearance, past, taste in clothes and music. Diana was adamant that such knowledge did not need to be set down explicitly but that, with people as with physical locations, if the writer knows what she is talking about, her knowledge will communicate itself. The description Virginia Woolf gave of her method in *Mrs. Dalloway* is no less applicable to Diana:

> *I dig out beautiful caves behind my characters: I think that gives exactly what I want; humanity, humor, depth. The idea is that the caves shall connect and each comes to daylight at the present moment.*[1]

This is true; but one of the many ways in which reading Diana does not resemble reading Virginia Woolf is that Diana gives her readers waymarks by which to navigate her text, Homeric epithets that conjure a character in a minimal number of words. What reader of *Fire and Hemlock* will forget that Polly's granny's house smells of biscuits, for example, and the way that this comes to symbolize the homely, reliable, sweet but highly nutritious nature of Granny herself? How potent a symbol are Chrestomanci's flamboyant dressing gowns, denoting both wildness and yet a certain physical indolence? How irritatingly recognizable are helpful people who, like Joris in *The Homeward Bounders*, are always ready to reach into their jerkins and find some desired item with a "Why, as to *that*!" Yet none of these is a caricature or simply a collection of catchphrases. We never doubt that behind each surface lies a system of complex and beautiful caves.

Diana's books have many subjects and many distinctive themes: language, imagination, storytelling, the recognition of talent in oneself, the ability to look beyond the obvious. If there is one that sums up the rest, however, perhaps it is that of empowerment—although I doubt whether Diana would have cared for the word. It is true that she also has a kind of affection for put-upon officials and for adults swept along by the tide of daily responsibilities. Their desire for respect, or at least feeling that they are not being positively laughed at, is one she treats with sympathy: one thinks of the anguished Sempitern Walker in *A Tale of Time City*, the earnest Rupert Venables from *Deep Secret*, or the harassed Wizard Corkoran in *Year of the Griffin*. But if there is a question of sides there can be no doubt that Diana is on the side of the powerless, the ones who have decisions taken and imposed upon them by others. And this, of course, usually means that she is on the side of children. As she has said, she aims to "provide a space where children can relax and walk round their problems and think 'Mum's a silly fusspot and I don't need to be quite so enslaved by her notions.'" In a Diana Wynne Jones book, no orthodoxy or authority is above question. She is no nihilist—indeed, she has strong views about the responsibilities of the children's author—but she is nevertheless one of the most thoroughly transgressive writers around.

All these qualities—her imaginative fertility, her range, her stamina, the breadth of her human sympathy and understanding, her command of plotting and of the other technicalities of the writer's craft, along with her unquenchable curiosity about life and people—have given Diana a unique place, not just in literature for children or within speculative fiction, but in modern literature generally.

Diana did not write in a way that drew attention to her writing; she was more interested in the story that she wished to tell. However, anyone who met Diana or heard her speak will know that, for all the qualities evident *in* her work, she was also a keen thinker *about* writing. Her *Tough Guide to Fantasyland* is a piece of literary criticism disguised as a guidebook, and her fiction is shot through with insights into the power of words and the importance of their judicious deployment. *Fire and Hemlock* has important things to say about influence and originality, while "Carol Oneir's Hundredth Dream" and *Archer's Goon* make telling points about writer's block. Besides these oblique contributions, however, she produced numerous essays and articles, as well as giving talks at conventions, schools, and conferences. The current volume gathers together much of that material. The wife, mother, and sister of professional academics, Diana was nevertheless ambivalent about the technical language of literary criticism, but as this volume demonstrates, she was a talented critic with important insights into her own work, that of other writers, and the creative process.

Diana's essays and talks in this volume were written during the years from 1978 to 2008 and are arranged in a running order chosen by Diana. This is not strictly chronological but does reflect the development of her ideas. As she points out in her preface, in a collection such as this it is inevitable that certain anecdotes and experiences are mentioned more than once, since she recounted them to different audiences in various articles and talks. A recurrent topic is Diana's childhood, a time when she learned the strangeness of human behavior and the arbitrariness of power, and when (living a life of neglect and emotional abuse with her two younger sisters) she began to craft imaginative worlds for her own benefit and theirs. Here too we see her beginning to piece together her ideas about the nature and purpose of fantasy, as symbolized in the two gardens kept by her parents—one dull and quotidian, the other magical, bee haunted, and securely locked. These symbols and experiences appear at various times throughout the volume, as does evidence of her early love of fantasy, epitomized in her preference for the "Piper at the Gates of Dawn" chapter in *The Wind in the Willows*, which was censored by her mother as being too fanciful. Given the occasional nature of the pieces in this volume, we have performed only a minimum of editing, leaving such reiteration of material as there is to speak naturally within its varying contexts. We hope that the result will be a cumulative appreciation of the role these ideas and experiences held in Diana's thought.

For all their autobiographical content, the pieces in this volume are primarily concerned with writing. Some are about the art and craft of writing in general, and contain either observations about Diana's writing life, or else practical advice to those who might wish to take up the profession. These include "The Children in the Wood," "When I Won the *Guardian* Award," "A Talk About Rules," "Answers to Some Questions," "A Whirlwind Tour of Australia," "Some Hints on Writing," "Characterization: Advice for Young Writers," and, in a more oblique way, "Our Hidden Gifts." Two others, "The Halloween Worms" and "A Day Visiting Schools," deal with the adventures and misadventures that can happen to authors engaged in the tasks attendant on the professional life of a children's writer, such as making school visits. In Diana's case, such visits were always potentially charged with danger, due to a notorious travel jinx.

Another group of pieces focuses on Diana's own work, either in general ("Creating the Experience," "The Value of Learning

Anglo-Saxon," "Freedom to Write") or else relating to specific works, as in "The Origins of *The Merlin Conspiracy*" and "The Origins of *Changeover*." "Two Kinds of Writing?" explains Diana's move into writing for adults with *A Sudden Wild Magic*, and includes some surprising thoughts about the differences between children and adults as readers. "The Heroic Ideal: A Personal Odyssey" is her most extended piece of analytical self-criticism and is a fascinating account of the ingredients that went into the making of *Fire and Hemlock*. Ideally, it should be read in tandem with "Some Truths About Writing," a partial palinode for the earlier piece, which provides an alternative approach to the perennial question of where ideas come from, from a writerly rather than an academic perspective.

Apart from reviews Diana did not write much criticism of the work of others, but when she did so her major preoccupation was with the art of constructing and telling stories. "The Shape of the Narrative in *The Lord of the Rings*" is a sharp analysis of Tolkien, partly inspired by attending his lectures on plot construction as a student in the 1950s, while another of her lecturers is the subject of "Reading C. S. Lewis's Narnia." "Inventing the Middle Ages" describes the storytelling techniques that fascinate her in writers of the medieval period, many of whom haunt her own fiction through their example. Her work as a reviewer is represented here by a review of Mervyn Peake's *Boy in Darkness*.

This book contains an interview Diana gave just a few weeks before her death. She was still very much interested in all the questions discussed in this volume, and still finding fresh ways to answer them. Besides its content, I hope that this interview captures something of how much *fun* a face-to-face conversation with Diana Wynne Jones could be.

Finally, this collection includes pieces by two of Diana's sons: an address given at her funeral ceremony, and a radio talk. Both show how her magical writings permeated and strengthened her family bonds. Together, the pieces in this book allow us to view Diana's mind through various shades of enchanted glass and to enjoy its rare combinations of subtle thought and lucid expression, seriousness and humor, rootedness in the world and boundless imagination. They are not only valuable in themselves, but also serve as a *vade mecum* for anyone wishing to read—or perhaps reread—Diana Wynne Jones's stories and novels. And that is a journey well worth taking.

—Charlie Butler

Preface

In 2009 I was told I had cancer. In 2010 I was told I had only a few months to live. Laura Cecil, who has been my agent ever since my first book for children was published, then felt it was time that we sorted out all my manuscripts in order to donate them to the archive Seven Stories. Since my handwritten first drafts often differ substantially from the printed book, she expected this would cast light on my working methods and so be of interest to future research.

We set to work. (The amount of dust that accumulates upon papers stored for up to thirty years in an unopened drawer surprised us both.) We discovered many things, some of them very odd, and, among them, a pile of the various lectures, articles, and reviews I had written between 1978 and 2008. These were, quite accidentally, stored more or less in chronological order, and as I looked through them, I realized that they provide a fairly complete picture of my growing ideas and convictions about writing for children, writing, and fantasy generally. They move from a discussion of Tolkien's narrative, to reflections on my aims and methods, and then to efforts to describe and chart the creative process itself. Some items made me laugh as I reread them. People, I thought, might enjoy these. Then it occurred to me that this collection could amuse and interest students too, and might also be useful to teachers of creative writing and tutors of university courses on children's literature and fantasy, of which there are now many.

Curiously enough, almost none of these items was spontaneous. Except for "The Children in the Wood," which is an early meditation on the needs and habits of children, all the rest were requested by bodies in America and Australia as well as in Scotland, Ireland, and England. Nearly all these requests were for something amusing but serious in intent, which might lift the tone of an otherwise solemn conference. For instance, "Inventing the Middle Ages" was written for a conference at the University of Nottingham where contributors discussed the dialects of a number of small regions, the influence of the Vikings, the meter of medieval poetry, and suchlike topics. The organizer said she hoped I would approach the Middle Ages from an entirely different point of view, and I did my best to comply with this.

It is in the nature of such a collection of writings that certain facts and ideas tend to get repeated, although I hope not too often. As I do when writing a book, I tried, in each lecture or article, to present people with something different from what had gone before. In the process I found my own thinking expanding.

Some of the shorter items were requested by magazines for children. "When I Won the *Guardian* Award" was written for a children's group in Rochdale, and likewise, I think, was "The Halloween Worms." "Some Hints on Writing" and "Characterization: Advice for Young Writers" were both requested by the BBC for an educational website. The letter on the advantages of studying Anglo-Saxon at university is included because most people still do not believe how many highly respected writers have been inspired by learning the language and literature of that time. And, though I found I had written many reviews, I have only included one: of *Boy in Darkness*, by Mervyn Peake. I felt this was necessary as it is an account of the way even the most baroque fantasy can be directly relevant to ordinary life.

Various threads run through this collection, but by far the strongest is that of the need for fantasy in all its many facets and its value for children and adults alike. It is my hope that some of these items will be of use to people.

—Diana Wynne Jones
November 2010

The Children in the Wood

Written around the year 1981, this brief, personal story about narratives is, Diana says in her preface, one of the few articles she wrote that was not commissioned. Instead, she says, it is a "meditative" piece.

From my window I can see a steep stretch of woodland, which is really the garden of a big terrace of flats. I have watched it for five years now. It is full of children who appear to be mad. A group of girls totter down the slope. Each is wearing a skirt of her mother's and holding a homemade crown onto her head. Every so often, they all stop and shake hands. Further along, another group of girls wanders among the bushes. Some bushes seem to terrify them. They clutch one another and scream. But they seem quite unaware of the bush beside them where three boys are crouching, armed with guns, and do not even look when one boy throws up both arms and dies. The girls in crowns seem equally unaware of four other boys struggling on their bellies up the gentle slope toward them. These boys seem to be in the last stages of exhaustion. One of the four dies as the girls pass, and the others roll back down the slope. The rest of the wood is full of similar groups. They are there day after day, tirelessly and all apparently insane.

Of course we all know at once that each group is playing a different game of Let's Pretend. But anyone who watches this wood, or anywhere else where children habitually play, will quite soon notice a number of things, all of which ought to have great importance for anyone who is interested in writing for children.

The first thing is how *often* children play these kind of games. It seems to be something they need to do. You can see they need to, because they are all so happy. The second group of girls is only pretending to be frightened. None of the groups are quarreling or crying—only screaming, dying, or ignoring one another. The next most important fact is that the children are all in groups. In five years watching this wood I have scarcely ever seen a child obviously playing this kind of game alone. Solitary children do not act mad. He or she may be wandering in the wood imagining things, but it will not show. Acting out a Let's Pretend game does seem to be a social act. I am sure that it is when I see how sexist the various games are. None of these children seem to have heard of women's liberation. The girls say, "Let's pretend we're all queens," and the boys, "Pretend we're soldiers"—and though I haven't a notion why the other girls are screaming at bushes, they are not playing with the boys. It really does seem as if Let's Pretend games are children's way of practicing being a girl or a boy—as they see it—as well as learning how to behave in a group.

You can see this is true when a quarrel breaks out. All the quarrels in the wood happen—with someone in tears and someone else bleating, "I'm not play-ying!"—when the children are trying to play a game like hide-and-seek or building a tree house, which does not involve make-believe. The rules allow both sexes to combine in these games. And it is hopeless. All children under about thirteen are so *bad* at cooperating. I watch them in exasperation, each one running about as if they were the only child there, without the slightest notion of how to get together with the rest. They really do seem to need some sort of Let's Pretend to make them combine. And the thing which seems to allow them to get together is the thing which makes the games seem so mad to an onlooker: they at once seem to enter a sort of enchanted circle, where they are in control and nothing outside matters.

Now a book is another form of this enchanted circle. Any book, whether realistic or fantasy, is a self-contained world with the reader in control (if you do not like the game the writer is playing, you can always stop reading). My feeling is that children get most from books which work along the same lines as they do—in other words, by Let's Pretend. I am not saying that a fantasy needs to ape children's games, but I do think it should be not unlike them in a number of important respects. Above all, it should be as exciting and engrossing as the games in the wood. I aim to be as gripped by a book I am writing as I hope any reader will be. I want to know what happens next. If it bores me, I stop. But a book has an additional asset: it seems to be real. If you say in a book that a certain thing is real, then in that book it is real. This is splendid, but it can also be a snare. I find I have to control any fantasy I write by constantly remembering the sort of things children do in their games.

Notice, for instance, that the children in the wood are very wisely not pretending too many things at once. They say "Pretend we're all queens," or "Pretend we're explorers," and part of the point of what follows is to find out what this entails. In the same way, I find it works best to suppose just one thing: Pretend you are a ghost, or Pretend your chemistry set works magic, or Pretend this dog is the Dog Star. Then I go on to explore the implications of this supposition. Quite often, I am totally surprised by the result.

I also bear constantly in mind the fact that pretending is a thing most usefully done in groups. It is done to show you how to get on with one another. When I write a book, it seems useful to extend the group to include both sexes, so that both girls and boys can enjoy it, but I do not find I can completely ignore the one-sex nature of the games in the wood. Oddly enough, this means that if I want a neutral character, not particularly girlish or boyish, I have to use a boy. A neutral girl would strike most girl readers as a tomboy. Otherwise, it is obvious that all other characters in a fantasy ought to be very real and clear and individual, and to interact profoundly—real, colorful people, behaving as people do. For instance, the first three girls who the ghost observes in *The Time of the Ghost*, strange as they are, are all drawn from life. One of them was me.

The third thing I bear in mind is the peculiar happiness of the children wandering in the wood. They are killing one another, terrifying one another, and (as queens) despising one another and everyone else too. And they are loving it. This mixture of nastiness and happiness is typical of most children and makes wonderful opportunities for a writer. Your story can be violent, serious, and funny, all at once—indeed I think it *should* be—and the stronger in all three the better. Fantasy can deal with death, malice, and violence in the same way that the children in the wood are doing. You make clear that it is make-believe. And by showing it applies to nobody, you show that it applies to everyone. It is the way all fairy tales work.

But when all is said and done, there is an aspect to fantasy which defies description. Those children in the wood are going to grow up and remember that they played there. They will not remember what they were playing, or who pretended what. But they will remember the wood, and the big city all round it, in a special, vivid way. It does seem that a fantasy, working out in its own terms, stretching you beyond the normal concerns of your own life, gains you a peculiar charge of energy which inexplicably enriches you. At least, this is my ideal of a fantasy, and I am always trying to write it.

The Shape of the Narrative in
The Lord of the Rings

First published in 1983 in J. R. R. Tolkien: This Far Land, *edited by Robert Giddings (Vision Press), this article was also reprinted in Diana's 1995 collection* Everard's Ride, *published by NESFA Press.*

When I say "narrative," I do not mean simply the plot. I mean considerably more. Plots and their shapes—the bare outlines of stories—were something I know J. R. R. Tolkien himself was interested in. When I was an undergraduate, I went to a course of lectures he gave on the subject—at least, I think that was the subject, because Tolkien was all but inaudible.[1] He evidently hated lecturing, and I suspect he also hated giving his thoughts away. At any rate, within two weeks he succeeded in reducing his substantial audience to myself and four others. We stuck on, despite his efforts. He worked at it: when it did appear that we might be hearing what he said, it was his custom to turn round and address the blackboard. Dim inklings alone reached me of what he meant, but these were too fascinating to miss. He started with the simplest possible story: a man (prince or woodcutter) going on a journey. He then gave the journey an aim, and we found that the simple picaresque plot had developed into a quest story. I am not quite sure what happened then, but I know that by the end he was discussing the peculiar adaptation of the quest story which Chaucer made in his "Pardoner's Tale."

As you see, Tolkien did not give away half of what he knew, even about plots, and I suspect he never talked about narrative at all, but it is clear from *The Lord of the Rings* that he knew all about narrative as well. The plot of *The Lord of the Rings* is, on the face of it, exactly the same simple one that he appeared to describe in his lectures: a journey that acquires an aim and develops into a kind of quest. But the bare plot is to any writer no more than the main theme of a sort of symphony which requires other themes added to it and the whole orchestrated into a narrative. To shape a narrative, you have to phase the various incidents and so control their nature that you set up significances, correspondences, foretastes, and expectations, until your finished story becomes something else again from its simple outline. Tolkien does this orchestrating supremely well: so much so that, by various narrative sleights-of-hand, he almost reverses the normal flow of a quest story, or at least makes an adaptation of it every bit as peculiar as the one he described in his lectures, and nobody ever notices. It continues to fool me even now, though I think I can see what he is up to.

The Lord of the Rings is organized in movements, just like a symphony, but with this difference: each movement has an extension, or coda, which reflects partly back on the movement just completed, and partly forward to what is to come. This coda is highly characteristic of Tolkien's method, and it becomes increasingly important as the narrative proceeds. You always have to watch what happens in these codas. And yet they, and the movements which precede them, in no way interfere with the story, the actual events being described, which appears to march steadily forward and to unfold with the utmost clarity and regularity. This limpid tale of events is one of Tolkien's major achievements, when you consider all the other things he was doing too. However, one thing he was *not* doing was striving to put it all in elegant language. His manner is at all times prolix and a little threadbare. The most he will do is to attempt a rough appropriateness. When he is dealing with Hobbits, he is chatty and a little arch: "If Frodo had really wanted to write a book and had had many ears, he would have learned enough for several chapters in a few minutes" (I, 167).[2] In more awesome places, he uses a hackneyed high style: "Then his wrath blazed in a consuming flame, but his fear rose like a vast black smoke to choke him" (III, 223). It is symptomatic, I think, that he at all times overworks the word "suddenly." To take the most random sample: "Suddenly he knew in his heart . . ." (I, 225); "Suddenly the lights went out" (II, 197); "Suddenly the silence was broken" (III, 127). As I know well enough myself, "suddenly" is a word hard to avoid in this kind of narrative. For Tolkien, as D. S. Brewer points out,[3] was writing a Romance in the old sense of the word. A Romance, unlike a novel, does not aim to draw attention to the way it is written. Tolkien was far more concerned with the matter of his narrative than its manner, and he only exercised his undoubted gift for language in inventing names, particularly names of places—which is again exactly in the tradition of a Romance. I always wish that Tolkien's many imitators would notice how comparatively modest his language is, and not insist on writing their stuff in translationese.

The first movement of the narrative lasts until the flight from

Bree. Here, along with the chatty manner, we are in a cozy Hobbit world not very far removed from that of fairy tales and nursery rhymes. Hobbits have that prosaic fubsiness one associates with a certain kind of children's story. And they are agreeably greedy and, above all, secure. But there is more to it than that. Throughout this section, Tolkien, like Lewis Carroll before him, is drawing heavily on the landscape round Oxford where he lived. Just as, I am sure, the chessboard view of three counties from White Horse Hill suggested *Alice Through the Looking-Glass*, it surely also gave rise to the Shire. But Tolkien took a leaf out of William Morris's book too, *The Well at the World's End*, and drew on the whole Upper Thames Valley. Here there are stuffy willow-choked flats, Wychwood, rivers like the Windrush and the Evenlode, the Rollright Stones, the long barrow called Wayland's Smithy, plow land and orchards round Didcot, the Seven Barrows, Thames water meadows, and the austere landscape of the chalk downs. And he used them all: there is even a real place called Buckland. Three other things he did not use here, though they are immensely important in the rest of the book, are the Thames itself; the old prehistoric road called the Ridgeway, which is probably the oldest road in Britain, leading from east to west (like the way to the Grey Havens), sometimes as a cart track, sometimes as broad as a motorway, and at other times vanishing in a valley; and finally a strange Oxford phenomenon, whereby the streets of the town are at times filled with a scent of distant flowers, for hours on end, as if one were smelling Heaven somehow. This is in a manner setting a thief to catch a thief, since I lived in Oxford for many years too and tend to use these things as well, but it is not important to know about them. I only draw attention to them to point out this first of Tolkien's narrative sleights-of-hand: by writing of things which were home to him, he contrives to give the reader a sense of home and security too.

But he is about to do something much more complicated than Carroll or Morris. He opens with a party. A burst of fireworks and fun. And here at once he surreptitiously introduces three major themes. The first, and by far the most important for the rest of the book, is the pressure of events which have happened long before the story opens. Later, this pressure comes from the far-off heroic past; but here it is underplayed, deftly, and seems merely to be a hangover from Bilbo's former mad journey. Which of course brought the Ring into Bilbo's possession. The Ring, whatever else it does, always brings the tragic past into the present. But at this stage Gandalf, in a pedagogic way in keeping with the homely tone, simply makes Bilbo give the Ring to Frodo and retire into the past himself.

But make no mistake. Undertones of the heroic and of the chivalry of Medieval Romances are being firmly introduced too, in the other two themes. One of these is the Quest itself. Because of the beguiling domesticity of the Shire and Tolkien's manner at this point, you are lulled into thinking of it in fairy-story terms: the hero journeys to a confrontation and receives supernatural help on the way. Of course the hero wins. And yet it starts with a party, like the best-known of all high romances, the stories of King Arthur. A Quest nearly always begins with the King feasting in Camelot. Enter a damsel or a churl demanding a boon. In this case Gandalf, and the Quest is delayed, but the pattern is there. And you should remember that, though a lot of quests, like that of Sir Gareth, prove the hero a man, a great many, like Gawain's with the Green Knight or that of the Grail, do no such thing. Furthermore, the title of the most famous collection of Arthurian Romances, Malory's, is *The Death of Arthur*. In fact, You Have Been Warned— although you need only feel a little uneasy at the moment.

For his third theme, Tolkien also drew on romances. The poet of *Gawain and the Green Knight* calls King Arthur "sumquat childgered"—i.e., rather boyish. Froissart too regards this as the most chivalrous aspect of real knights (and so did Kipling later). Sir Percival is traditionally naive to childishness. And so are the Hobbits who set out on their journey. So you have a notion here which at once reinforces the prevailing nursery-tale atmosphere and contradicts it: it is cozy, but it is also heroic.

It seems reasonable to mention these things because it is quite certain that Tolkien had them at his fingertips. The marvel is that he was capable of handling them, just as he did with the Oxford landscape, so that it is not necessary for the reader to know them in order to get the message. The message is a fourth theme, also thoroughly traditional, which these three come together to suggest: people have gone downhill from the heroic days. Now it is ordinary people who have to cope as best they can.

So Bilbo plays his practical joke and vanishes. Frodo lingers, even after Gandalf has reappeared and introduced seriously for the first time the deep notes of the distant past. It is typical of this movement that the history is Hobbit-oriented and concerns Gollum as much as Sauron and Isildur. Frodo, with what we are meant to consider dramatic irony, repudiates Gollum. The lingering ensures that, as Frodo and his companions set off, autumn is coming on, with all that can imply. We are meant to take the point that local changes of season are cosmic in origin,

but attention is on the domestic landscape through which the
Hobbits journey. This is so solidly persuasive that Tolkien is
able to introduce the Ringwraiths with the lightest of touches.
A few words, and they are spine-chilling. A black figure *sniffing*
for you. They are childhood nightmares and gaps in the order
of things, just with that.

Then a new theme enters, as the Elves intervene in their
remote way. Their songs are of departed glories, which are still,
it seems, things to conjure with. It is the past-history theme
again, but it has a powerful woodwind nostalgia. It begins—
just—to suggest that the coming autumn is a season of Middle-
earth, not only of the year. But the scene is still so firmly local
that all you get at this stage is a sense of yearning, both for
the past and for the Sea-crossing of the future. The present is
detached from the Elves. The story has begun to spread a little
in time, and a little in space too.

Anyway, we are briskly back again to the domestic, with the
matter of the mushrooms and the adventure-story excitement
of the river crossing and the escape through the Hedge. The
Hobbits muddle through, until they get into real trouble with
the sinister Old Forest. This too is wonderfully spine-chilling
by reason of being only just removed from a real wood. Even
Old Man Willow is solidly a real willow tree. And once again
they need rescuing, this time by Tom Bombadil. By now, it
looks as if the fairy-story pattern, of travelers being saved
from their own errors by supernatural intervention, is here to
stay.

I find Tom Bombadil supremely irritating myself. I am well
aware that he is a chthonic figure seen from, as it were, knee
high, and I can see his presence here is important, standing as

he does between earth and sky in the first truly open country, but I am always glad when he is dismissed by Elrond. It is a relief to have him distanced with high-sounding names as Iarwain, Forn, and Orald. As Bombadil, he is perverse and whimsical. He is the quintessence of the nursery story gone wrong, as it does from then on. Tolkien was quite right to put him in, but I wish he hadn't. He was quite right because here, in the haunting country of the Barrows—which was still domestic to Tolkien, though not perhaps to his readers—dead history, with all its wasted heroism and lingering evil, literally comes up and grabs the Hobbits. The Barrow-wights, however, are not strictly this: they are spiteful ghosts. All the same, this is where Tolkien does, briefly, confront you with the scale of his narrative. Tom is near eternal. The bones in the Barrows are so old their deeds have been forgotten. The present is represented by the Hobbits, apparently neither very noble nor very effectual. Around them the landscape first opens, then closes to lead them to death's door, and from the dead they acquire a knife that will be important later. It is a notable piece of foreshadowing, which ends in their rescue by Tom.

This is really the last time they are rescued in this way. That comforting pattern, and the movement, ends with their doings at Bree, which is, not insignificantly, a town half of men and half of Hobbits. Men are now going to enter into the picture. The nursery tales, despite the cozy inn scene, are done with. And—this is an example of Tolkien's ability to use surreptitious themes from elsewhere—Frodo, like Adam and Eve and all the failures of fairy stories, has come there under a prohibition: not to put on the Ring. Which he proceeds to disobey. The fact that he puts the Ring on while singing a nursery rhyme only underlines the fact that such things are now inappropriate. And the movement ends with the same thing as it began.

The coda to this movement is very short but packed out with adumbrations: a journey of hardship over a desolate landscape, toward a hill topped with fires. While purporting simply to carry on the story, this section does all manner of things. It spreads the narrative considerably in space, and in time too. The past reappears in two forms, first as the petrified Trolls, harking back to Bilbo's adventures, and then, far more potently, as the Black Riders. It now becomes clear that the Ringwraiths are not simply terrifying but that they can harm the living. That they could win. We should remember here that Bilbo's victory over the Trolls had been almost by luck. Frodo is almost not lucky. And, when they race to the Ford and it appears that even an Elf-lord has limited powers, your doubts increase, although you still hope for the supernatural rescue that the main movement has led you to expect. It comes, after a fashion, in the confusion at the Ford. This confusion, considering Tolkien's ability everywhere else to present landscapes and events with total clarity, must be deliberate. It must look forward to the profusion of doubtful events to follow. I do not think it comes off at all, but it does provide a wonderful introit to the ordered peace and measured debate of the next movement.

Rivendell is the Last Homely House of *The Hobbit*. But of course it is no such thing. It is under threat from Mordor. You realize this and cast your mind back, uneasily trying to find someone or somewhere that is safe and homely. Bree? Tom Bombadil? No, not even him. And the Ringwraiths were in the Shire too. Even before the debate begins, you become aware that the only defense can be some form of attack. But this is not for Frodo to decide: he has reached his limited objective. The narrative stops short and reassembles itself by means of the debate.

Tolkien performs several remarkable narrative feats here. One is of course the retrospective doubts cast back on the earlier illusion of security. But the one which amazes me most is the fact that the debate is not in the least boring. It could be. Milton, in a similar situation, almost is. But there are so many questions by now raised that need answers, and so many new people to present—Gimli, Legolas, Boromir, Strider in his new role as Aragorn, Elrond revealed as truly half Elf, Gandalf acquiring new stature, and news of Gollum's escape—that I find my attention truly riveted. For the first time, the major themes enter undisguised, and you are made aware not only of the depths of past history, but also of the huge spread of the land affected by it. You are shown a divided kingdom now reduced to a few outposts, once again threatened and likely this time to dwindle away. Elves, Dwarves, Men, and Hobbits are all likely to go down with it. A solution is propounded: destroy the Ring.

And this is the other amazing feat of narrative: you are told, this early on, exactly what is going to happen. And you are still in doubt that it will. Each of the Fellowship of the Ring says exactly what his intentions are, and yet you do not believe they will do as they say. Each time I read it, I am still pained and shocked when the Fellowship divides later on. I am still in doubt that the Ring will be destroyed, or what good it would do if it was. It seems to me to need some explaining how Tolkien got away with it.

The main answer, I think, is the depth and variety of the history he invokes in the course of this movement. I suppose it is a commonplace that he took over the idea of the inset histories and legends from the Anglo-Saxon poem *Beowulf*, in which each inset vaguely echoes the action in the poem's present and each is progressively more doom laden, but I am not sure if it is realized how thoroughly Tolkien adapted the notion to his own purposes. *Beowulf* uses the things purely for atmosphere. Tolkien uses his histories that way too, but only secondarily. His primary use for history is as a motive power, pushing his present-day characters into certain actions, to bring about the future. He presents us with triple measure: Elven history, mostly as hints and songs, immeasurably old and indicating the Elves are a dying race; that of men and Dwarves, both of whom have more than once flourished heroically and then been decimated by the power of Sauron; and Hobbits, who have existence rather than history. All (except for the Hobbits) are united by owning rings of power and are united again in their opposition to the One Ring. Thanks to the Elves, there is a huge time span here, showing a continuous falling off. Elrond says, "I have seen three ages in the west of the world, and many defeats, and many fruitless victories" (I, 256). The effect of this, on top of the first movement's suggestion that only ordinary folk are left to cope, is to present the Fellowship, once formed, as a thread-thin company. It is as narrow in numbers and space as the present moment is in time. Against the past weight of failure, its only hope seems to be to hang together.

If this picks up and amplifies the earlier suggestions in the Shire that the present is small and ordinary, so does the nature of the Quest, now properly revealed. It is to be a negative one, a raid to destroy the enemy's inmost defenses. It can only be made by beings so insignificant that the chances of success are minimal. It is destructive. It does not suggest renewal. Or does it? I have heard *The Lord of the Rings* stigmatized as simply a goodies v. baddies story. Insofar as this is true, it is of course a very modern story. Romances, fairy tales, and even *Beowulf* do not have baddies the way we do, the way Sauron is. But it is more original than it is modern, now that Tolkien has shown his hand, because it is really about people in time. It concerns the present, fully conscious of the past, injured by it, in fact, pressing forward to make the unformed future. And of course the present is very small compared with both; mere instants. Tolkien makes the outcome dubious, if not equivocal, by having his Fellowship set off in winter—a time of ill omen, of traditional heroism, and of hope too, since spring is to follow—and then by cunningly organizing his narrative in its later stages, so that the issue is continually in doubt, just as the future always is.

The coda to this movement is, very characteristically, the start of the journey. Through more of Tolkien's meticulously visualized country, the Fellowship sets out. There is a strong sense that this is the nitty-gritty, the real stuff, because the landscape is now harsh and strange and because the proper Quest has been determined. In fact, not insignificantly, this is only partly true. This section serves mainly to lead into the next movement, which is a double one, bringing us hard up against endurance of two kinds.

First comes the achievement of the Dwarves, heralded by the entry into Moria. The finding and opening of the gate is pure magic. I wish I could have written it. But once they get inside, I am never as impressed as I could wish. True, we have majestic evidence of Dwarves' industry, and proof that their legends at least did not lie—and this tacitly reinforces the rest of the histories we have been given—so that when we come upon the long-dead Dwarves, it should strike us cold as evidence of the latest heroic failure. But I never find it does. I just feel the easy regret one feels on being told someone one didn't know had died. I suspect that Tolkien has here slipped over into the goodies v. baddies, adventure-story mode. The Orcs, when they appear, do not have personalities as they do in Volume II. They are just the enemy. And then, sudden and shocking, comes the demise of Gandalf. Tolkien must have meant it to be so. I am sure he wanted to impress us with the fact that there is always the unforeseen disaster, and I am sure too that he wanted an ominous foreshadowing of the Lair of Shelob and the Paths of the Dead, but it won't do all the same. Who or what is the sudden Balrog? Up it pops, and down it goes again, taking Gandalf with it. For all that, the sense of loss is real, and leads in admirably to the second part of the movement, the sojourn in Lórien.

Oh good, you think, we are at last going to plumb the mysteries of the Elves! Legolas has been there for some time now, hinting at these mysteries, and yet, since he is one of the Fellowship, kidding you that Elves can be human and approachable. This is not the case. Tolkien lets you see much, but still leaves the Elves almost as mysterious and alien as they were before you saw Lothlórien. They are genuinely not human. Their concerns seem other, even when they help. The reason seems to be their intense, abiding melancholy. The nostalgia shown earlier by the Elves in the Shire, and then, in a more restrained way, by Elrond, swells here into a huge woodwind theme. The Elves are dwindling, we are told. The Dwarves awakened evil and forced many Elves over the Sea. This could be the explanation, but it is not really. You get the real reason by hints, which you pick up mostly subconsciously: the Elves, by reason of their apparent immortality, are widowed from history. They are forced back on their own, which is merely living memory, unimaginably long. Tolkien conveys quietly, without ever quite centering your sights on it, the immense burden immortality would be. He uses women to do it: the Morning Star, Arwen Evening Star, and Galadriel herself. I daresay women's lib could make destructive points here, but it is entirely appropriate in a Romance, in which women are traditionally mysterious and a little passive. He is drawing on all the stories of Elf women loving mortal men, and quietly pointing up the concealed consequences: when the lover dies, the immortal woman grieves forever. Women are generally more often widowed than men. But this stands for the situation of all the Elves. When they enter the temporary brawls of history, they pay for it by having to endure its horrors forever. So they are forced for the most part to stay withdrawn among their yellow trees, never dying, but never quite coming to maturity either. The yellow trees vividly express their state. Are mallorns the yellow of spring, or autumn? Both, but not summer or winter. I find them profoundly saddening.

The Elves have wisdom, by a sort of natural compensation, but this can be an equal burden. Galadriel does, in her aloof way, enter history, but she has to do it in full knowledge that she is helping to end the Third Age of the world. You come away from Lothlórien with two pieces of hidden knowledge: a sense of a doomed age, and the fact that every gift exacts its price—sometimes a terrible one.

By now you should be well aware that putting on the Ring exacts its price. This is what happens to end the coda to this movement, just as it ended the coda to the first movement. It has become a pattern now: another stage in the journey, down the Anduin this time, ending in Frodo's putting on the Ring again. Because of the pattern, you are half expecting another last-minute rescue. So it comes as a real shock when this does not happen and the Fellowship breaks up. Lothlórien fools us to some extent, by appearing to awe and tame Boromir—though it is never *said* that it has—and the Great River fools us too. The Fellowship appears to be sliding united along its current to a single end. But you always have to watch Tolkien with water. He never uses it unmeaningfully. Pools and lakes mirror stars, and hold hidden things. This Anduin has contrasting banks and, moreover, reeks of history. In a way, it *is* history, and the Fellowship is going with its current, to break up in confusion at the falls of Rauros. It is worth pointing out that when Aragorn later uses the same river, he comes *up* it, against the current, changing a course of events that seems inevitable.

The other water is of course the Sea. This has been sounding dimly in our ears throughout the book, but in Lothlórien it begins to thunder. Does it suggest loss, departure, and death? Certainly. But since water is always life to Tolkien, it must also be eternity. Eternity, we must not forget, is by its nature both all time and no time at all. It is quite a feat to invoke the Sea so far inland. The effect is to end the movement with two symbols: a line of scattered figures with the ocean at their backs, confronting the ringed Eye of Sauron. The Eye, which also comes out into the open in Lothlórien, is an absolutely spine-chilling expression of evil—the more so because we never see more of the enemy than that. But it is possible to see the Eye, among its various significances, as the eye of the storm, the self-contained here and now, which the present has to pass through before it becomes the future.

Volume II inaugurates what might be called the great choral movement. The scene widens enormously and the numbers of both enemies and friends suddenly multiply by hundreds. The scale of the story, which Tolkien has unobtrusively been preparing us for, is now shown to be immense. It also involves a fiendishly difficult piece of double and treble narration. I know from bitter experience how difficult it is, when your narrative divides into two or more and both parts happen simultaneously, to decide which part to tell when. But Tolkien's narrative makes it more difficult still, because Frodo's part of the story is plotted to run counter to Merry and Pippin's, to narrow where theirs expands, to flow uphill as it were from the main course of events, so that not only does their Quest seem bound to fail, but you are in doubt as to whether this is what the narrative is really about.

If Tolkien agonized at all about how to do it, it does not show. He solved it characteristically by adopting a pattern: he will tell the positive side first, and the negative second. So he succeeds, apparently carelessly and politically, in flinging a huge double and treble twist of narrative across a huge area of land. He fools us a bit, of course, as usual. He represents the destruction of the Ring throughout as the thing of real importance, whereas it is only half of it. The act of destruction must be accompanied by the act of creation—in this case the mustering of allies to Minas Tirith to found a new Gondor. But he represents that as a desperate rearguard action. Indeed, some of his point is that such desperate defenses are unintentionally regenerative. But, from the mere fact of devoting half his narrative to it, he gives away its importance.

First, however, he devotes himself to the Ents, the Riders of Rohan, and to Saruman. The first and last of these have been so firmly foreshadowed in earlier parts of the narrative that one receives them almost with recognition, like a theme emerging from the orchestra, or prophecies fulfilled. Rohan, though it has been mentioned, is like a new theme entirely—which is as it should be. Against all three, the power of Mordor is slowly defined as the true great evil. I do not think that it could have been suggested so strongly in any better way. Mordor is never actually present, but always there in the searching Eye.

Orcs, on the other hand, representing Mordor and Isengard, are very much there, in numbers, splendidly solid: "his aching head was grated by the filthy jowl and hairy ear . . . Immediately in front were bowed backs and tough thick legs going up and down, up and down, unresting, as if they were made of wire and horn" (II, 55). And I think it a stroke of genius to have the Elvish for Orc be *Yrch*, like an expression of disgust in itself. These Orcs serve the double purpose of presenting the might of Mordor and Isengard and of getting Merry and Pippin to Fangorn—I do like things to pull their weight. Here are the Ents. I remember reading a review of *The Two Towers* when it first came out, in which the reviewer could not take the Ents. Walking trees! He indignantly concluded Tolkien was trying to foist a children's story on him as serious literature.

He was not far wrong, in a way. Here in Fangorn, Tolkien is echoing the Forest outside the Shire. He is also echoing the childish innocence of the first movement, deliberately and with a difference. Treebeard and his fellows are innocents. I am always impressed by how simply and completely Tolkien expresses this innocence. Like Mordor, Treebeard has eyes:

These deep eyes were now surveying them, slow and solemn, but very penetrating. They were brown shot with a green light. Often afterward Pippin tried to describe his first impression of them. 'One felt as if there was an enormous well behind them, filled up with ages of memory and long, slow, steady thinking; but their surface was sparkling with the present...' (II, 66)

As I said, take note when Tolkien talks of water. The well of the past contains truth, but it stops short at the present. In this, it is like the Hobbits of the Shire, but unlike the Elves, whose pools reflect stars. The Ents, however, unlike Hobbits, who are pragmatic and capable of growth, are grown up and complete as they are. They are hard to budge toward the future. It is a measure of the seriousness of the situation that the Ents are actually persuaded to move, and even then they only move against the lesser evil of Saruman. They are one of the things which will not survive long in a new age. You are meant to feel, and you do, that is a pity: they embody the mature innocence of the Third Age. But you have to look for real help to the Riders of Rohan, the comparative newcomers, who have yet to make history.

Rohan and its grassy plains have been foreshadowed too, in a way, in the Barrow-downs, so that the new theme when it emerges seems entirely in keeping. But here, instead of Tom Bombadil between grass and sky, it is Gandalf who suddenly reappears, with something of the same force. This too is not unheralded, both by Galadriel's Mirror and by the previous pattern of the narrative. Gandalf disappears; sooner or later after that, the Ring is used; sooner or later, after that again, Gandalf reappears, a spearhead for the allies, just as the Ringwraiths are for Mordor. Gandalf's coming to Rohan ought to make one certain that Frodo will put on the Ring again in Mordor.

The Rohirrim are purely Anglo-Saxon. Tolkien lifted them entirely from his study of Old English—even their horses, I suspect, come from the legendary first Saxons in Britain, Hengist and Horsa. They have the Old English heroic culture complete. Tolkien does a delicate job here of differentiating them from Aragorn, who is at once both rougher and more sophisticated, coming as he does from a far older culture. For, as I said, these are a people without a past to whom we should look for the future. If you doubt this, you should contrast the passive roles of the Elf-women with that of Éowyn and the active part she plays, albeit disobediently. But before the Riders can do anything, they have to put their own house in order. Théoden, King of Rohan, has to cast off evil counsel and the weight of age, and then to fight in Helm's Deep—all of which involves such bewildering coming and going that I always have twinges of incredulity about the stamina of Shadowfax. I also have twinges of doubt, as I am sure you are intended to, about the reliability of Rohan, despite their nobility. I go very Welsh, and when the men of Minas Tirith later say, "Rohan will not come," I shake my head and mutter about perfidious Albion.

Tolkien, as a Welsh scholar, may have had this reaction of mine in mind too. Certainly he is once again performing one of his sleights-of-narrative: for the thing at the back of his mind must certainly have been the way the Saxon King Harold had to march north to fight one invasion force in 1066, before rushing south again to fight the Normans, who were the real threat. Again, there is no need for the reader to know this. It comes over very clearly that the Rohirrim are having difficulty disentangling themselves from their own pressing present. Quite early on, you are asking, can they do it in time to be of use to the future?

Parallel to this in time at least, Frodo and Sam and the noxious Gollum are creeping toward Mordor. This is the section foreshadowed in the coda to the first movement, but the landscape is now far more luridly depressing. Vividly in tune with the negative nature of their Quest are the marsh pools containing images of dead people. Again, watch Tolkien with water. What is history now? Similarly, the only virtues they can exercise are negative: endurance, and forbearance toward Gollum. Everything is sterile, for all their heroism. Tolkien begins asserting their heroism from here on, and it obviously exists, like the positive love between Frodo and Sam, but the negatives are so overwhelming that you sense impending failure.

Therefore you feel relief as well as surprise when they run into Faramir and his guerrillas. It is like coming out into the sun. Tolkien does wonders of suggestion here: the landscape is meticulously southern and the ferns are brown with winter, but the herbs Sam uses to cook with are all evergreen, and so is the cedar he makes his fire with. This has to be deliberate.

About the same time, the others are meeting the futureless Ents and the pastless Rohirrim: Frodo and Sam meet those who have a long past but also obvious potential for the future. But notice that, when Tolkien typically reinforces his point with water, Frodo and Faramir are both behind the waterfall at the time when they spare Gollum in the pool. But at the time you ignore that hint and realize simply that here is hope, and a potent force for good. You discover that Mordor has only yet spread patchily in Ithilien.

Be that as it may, as the others make their successful onslaught on Isengard, Frodo and Sam also attack a tower, by way of Cirith Ungol and Shelob. This section has been heavily foreshadowed in the Barrows and the mines of Moria, with their unavailing heroisms, and the weight of that makes this one more horrible. It is horrible enough on its own. The indecisions of Sam make it worse. And finally, despite Sting and Galadriel's aid, while the other Hobbits triumph in Isengard, Frodo is taken prisoner, an exact reversal of their respective positions at the beginning of the movement. This reversing is part of the deliberate counterplotting of this whole section.

And now we turn to the marvelous city of Minas Tirith, in nearly the final swatch in the plaiting of this huge penultimate movement. We already admire the place because of Faramir, with whom, in a brief episode, Tolkien has succeeded in dissipating the impression left by Boromir. It adds to the sense of marvel that Minas Tirith is not degenerate and cynical after all. The city has been kept before us one way or another since the Council of Elrond, so that, along with the surprise when we come to it at last, there is a sense of familiarity, as of a hidden theme related to all the others finally emerging from the orchestra. Something of it has been suggested too in the episode back in the Shire when Fatty Bolger is left alone to deal with the Black Riders, and the Hobbits sound their alarm. We are told that the horn "rent the night like fire on a hilltop. AWAKE!" (I, 188). And again in II when the watchfires of Rohan surround the Orcs. Now the beacon fires spring alight round the city as Pippin rides up with Gandalf. The effect is to give Minas Tirith distinctly Christian associations—and why not, since Tolkien has used everything else in our heritage?— because you think at once of "Christians awake!" and that bit of a hymn "How gleam thy watchfires through the night," which not only adds to the stature of the city, but, as we shall see, casts a little Christianity on Frodo and Sam too.

But it would be daft to see Minas Tirith as Jerusalem, bravely fronting evil. It owes far, far more to the doomed city of Atlantis. With it, Tolkien is working another sleight-of-narrative. Atlantis was very old, wonderfully civilized, and built in a series of terracelike rings. And it was inundated before the dawn of history. By deliberately using and knowing that he was using Atlantis as a model, Tolkien again ensures that the reader gets the message without needing to know: Minas Tirith is doomed. And, as the muster of Mordor proceeds, you cannot see how, even if Rohan comes, that could make much difference.

Rohan is preparing to come. So is Aragorn. In an action heralded in the Barrows, in Moria, and again in Shelob's Lair, Aragorn sets out with his Grey Company to take the Paths of the Dead. Aragorn is of course, as the descendant of the Kings of the North, preeminently qualified to summon those faithless dead in there and make them keep their word at last. But this episode, terrifying as it is, repeats such an often-adumbrated scene that it almost carries the weight of an allegory: you can take the failures of the past, much as Tolkien has by now taken most of Western literary heritage, and force them to do at least some good toward the future. Tolkien would deny this. He says irritably in the foreword to the second edition of *The Lord of the Rings*, "I think that many confuse 'applicability' with 'allegory'" (I, 7), and maybe he is right. And watch out. Strewn all around this section are striking examples of the fey or doomed utterance. Aragorn himself says, "It will be long, I fear, ere Theoden sits at ease again in Meduseld" (III, 46). Halbarad says in Dimholt, "This is an evil door, and my death lies beyond it" (III, 59). And in the midst of the battle, the Black Captain himself says, "No living man may hinder me!" (III, 116). This sort of thing has also been heralded, when Aragorn warns Gandalf against entering Moria. Because of that, we are prone to believe these sayings. Then notice that not one of them comes true in the way it suggests. Theoden is killed and never sits in Meduseld. Halbarad is not killed in the Paths of the Dead, but a long way out on the other side. And the Black Captain is hindered by a Hobbit and killed by a girl. Since the bringing about of the future is what this movement is concerned with, we should be troubled.

For, you see, the battle which ought to be final, in which the forces of good throw everything they have at Mordor, is no such thing. It is a magnificent battle, though. One of Tolkien's gifts is being able to rise to the largest occasion. I wait with bated breath every time for Rohan to come, or not come, and sing as they slay. But when it is over, the enemy is still working on Denethor and Mordor is not destroyed. So, in a pattern which is now familiar, there is a coda to this huge movement. By now these codas are definitely forming an "afterward" and looking to the future. In this one, Faramir and Éowyn find healing and love, and the other protagonists debate, in a way that echoes the Council of Elrond, and like that Council, resolve on an act of aggression: they will attack Mordor as a diversion for Frodo. So are we to suppose that this whole movement has been a huge diversion?

Only then does Tolkien take up the story of Frodo and Sam. This is what might be called the slow movement, drear and negative and full of tribulation. Although it is odd that the positive side of the action is compounded of killing and politics, and the negative of love, endurance, and courage, this is how it seems to be. Tolkien insists that the first is valueless without the second. Odd, as I said, particularly as the slight Christian tinge given to Minas Tirith definitely reflects on Frodo, who is now displaying what one thinks of as the humbler Christian virtues; and because the careful plotting of this movement, to make it in most ways the antithesis of the preceding one, keeps bringing, to my mind at least, Clough's poem "Say not the struggle nought availeth." The force of that poem is that, even if you are not succeeding in your own locality, someone somewhere else *is*.

Anyway, as one side enters glorious Minas Tirith, Frodo and Sam creep into Mordor, its antithesis; and with them Gollum, a sort of anti-Hobbit. This ignoble trio are the only ones likely to succeed. And they fail. Make no mistake, despite their courage, and their wholly admirable affection for one another, and Frodo's near transfiguration, their action is indeed negative. At the last minute, Frodo refuses to throw the Ring into the

Cracks of Doom and puts it on instead. Their almost accidental success is due to a negative action both Hobbits performed in the past. Frodo, not lovingly, spared Gollum's life. Sam, not understanding Gollum's loneliness in the marshes, threatened him and turned his incipient friendship to hatred. So Gollum bites off Frodo's finger and falls with it and the Ring into the Cracks of Doom.

Now what are we to make of this? I have of course put it far more baldly than Tolkien does, but it is there for everyone to read. I think the explanation is suggested in the very long coda to the entire story which takes up nearly half the last volume. Most writers would have been content to stop with the destruction of Mordor, or at least after the shorter coda of rejoicing and the celebrating of Nine-Fingered Frodo that follows the fall of Mordor. But Tolkien, characteristically, has a whole further movement, which now definitely is "and afterward . . ."

Before we try to make sense of it, let me draw your attention to another aspect of Tolkien's narrative skill: his constant care to have each stage of his story viewed or experienced by one or other of his central characters. He had to split them apart to do it, but it is a great strength of the narrative, and one not often shared by his imitators. Each major event has a firm viewpoint and solid substance. Things are visualized, and because Hobbits are present, eating and drinking gets done. The overall effect is to show that huge events are composed of small ones, and as was signaled at the beginning, that ordinary people can get forced to make history—forced by history itself. By this stage of the narrative, however, the idea is being proposed in a different form: even the smallest and most ignoble act can have untold effect. And thank goodness for Gollum.

Well, yes. But remember that Gollum only did for Frodo what the Dead did for Aragorn. And indeed much of this coda of codas is concerned with shrinking the scale again, back to the Shire, where the now battle-hardened Hobbits make their bit of personal history by dislodging Saruman, and the Hobbits of the Shire settle down with a happy sigh to draw quietly aside from the path of history. As Tolkien has been unobtrusively pointing out all along, if it were not for such folk, there would be nothing worth doing heroic things for. But we are being lulled again. We must not forget the Sea, nor the very clear statements that an age of the world is passing. Tolkien was not cheating about that—it proves to have passed—but only suggesting that the next age *could* be an age of Sauron. And remember Sauron was never really precisely *there*, unlike all the other characters. Before we are prepared for it, the woodwind nostalgia theme is swelling again, to drown everything else. Sam is saddened to find his actions not remembered. A mallorn tree grows in the Shire. Frodo is ill and finishes writing his history. And at length it becomes evident that the destruction of the Age entails the passing of Elf rings too, along with Galadriel, and Gandalf, whose nature has been concealed in his name all along. And Frodo too. Frodo has become Elvish, quite literally. By his not-doing, however heroic, he has widowed himself from history, just like the Elves, and must now go off upon the Sea like the rest.

Tolkien works his final sleight-of-narrative here. He was perfectly aware of the Germanic custom of ship burial, in which a dead king was floated out to sea in a ship. Crossing the Sea is represented as a matter full of sadness, and Cirdan the shipwright is given many attributes of a priest, but the passing of Frodo is never represented as other than a permanent voyage. So the ending is heartrendingly equivocal. You can see it as Frodo moving into eternity, or into history—or not. You can see it as a justification—or not—of the negative side. In fact, we are experiencing the proper mode of Romance, which was signaled right from the start. The values of the people who wrote Romances never seem quite the same as our own. This kind of equivocal ending where winning and failing amount to the same, Arthur passes to sleep in a hill, and a gift exacts its price, is exactly what should have been expected. You Were Warned. For good measure, you knew that life never comes round to a happy ending and stops there. There is always afterward. But such was the skill with which this narrative was shaped that you could not see the pattern, even when it was being constantly put before you.

Yes, there really was nothing about narrative that Tolkien didn't know.

Two Kinds of Writing?

The American fantasy author Emma Bull produced a literary magazine/ fanzine in the 1990s titled The Medusa: The Journal of the Pre-Joycean Fellowship. *This article was published in the first issue in 1990. In the journal, Diana was described as "the author of quantities of excellent books, all of which should be read by discriminating adults, on trains, with shameless enthusiasm and the occasional audible giggle."*

With very minor changes, the article was also published in the British science fiction magazine Nexus, *issue one, April 1991.*

I write what is often called speculative fiction. Usually I write it for children, but recently I wrote a novel specifically for adults.[1] This was something I had long wanted to do—really ever since I discovered that quite as many adults read my books as children do; and several grown men confessed to me that, although they were quite shameless when it came to hunting through the juvenile sections of libraries and bookshops, they still felt incredibly sheepish on a train reading something that was labeled Teen Fiction. Why? I wondered. The assumption underlying their sheepishness seemed to be that teenage fiction counts as just close enough to adult fiction to be seen as regressive, whereas if they are seen reading a children's book, that counts as research. In neither case are they assumed to be *enjoying* the book for its own sake.

Silly though this seemed, it struck me as hard on them. So when I was asked if I'd like to try my hand at an adult novel, I most joyfully agreed. To my great surprise, writing it and, after that, receiving the comments of an editor revealed all sorts of additional hidden assumptions about the two kinds of writing. Most of these were quite as irrational as the shame of a grown man caught reading teenage fiction. They ran right across the board, too, and affected almost everything, from the length of the book to its style and subject matter. And nearly all of them—this was what disturbed me most—acted to deprive me of the freedom I experience when I write for children. Furthermore, when I thought more deeply about these assumptions, I found they reflected badly on both kinds of writing.

To take the most obvious first: I found myself thinking as I wrote, "These poor adults are never going to understand this; I must explain it to them twice more and then remind them again later in different terms." Now this is something I never have to think when I write for younger readers. Children are used to making an effort to understand. They are asked for this effort every hour of every school day, and though they may not make the effort willingly, they at least expect it. In addition, nearly everyone between the ages of nine and fifteen is amazingly good at solving puzzles and following complicated plots—this being the happy result of many hours spent at computer games and watching television. I can rely on this. I can make my plots for them as complex as I please, and yet I know I never have to explain them more than once (or twice at the very most). And here I was, writing for people of fifteen and over, assuming that the people who read, say,

Fire and Hemlock last year have now given up using their brains.

This is back-to-front to what one usually assumes, if one only looks on the surface, but I found it went much deeper than that. At first I thought it was my own assumption, based on personal experiences. Once when I was doing a signing, a mother came in with her nine-year-old son and berated me for making *The Homeward Bounders* so difficult. So I turned to the boy to ask him what he didn't understand. "Oh, don't listen to *her*," he said. "*I* understood everything. It was just her that didn't." It was clear to both of us that his poor mother had given up using her brain when she read. Likewise, a schoolmaster who was supposed to be interviewing me for a magazine explained to me that he had tried to read *Charmed Life* and couldn't understand a word, which meant, he said, that it was much too difficult for children. So he didn't interview me. He was making the surface assumption that children need things easy. But since I have never yet come across a child who *didn't* understand *Charmed Life*, it occurred to me that he was making the assumption about *himself*. But it was a hidden one, and when I came to write for adults, I realized that it was something all adults assumed. I grew tender of their brains and kept explaining.

This makes an absurd situation. Here we have books for children, which a host of adults dismiss as puerile, overeasy, and are no such thing; and there we have books for adults, who might be supposed to need something more advanced and difficult, which we have to write as if the readers were simpleminded.

Anyone examining this rather surprising assumption will see that it comes all tangled up in at least one other one: that books for adults are supposed to be *longer*. Everyone appears to know this. There are jokes about the fifth book in the trilogy—for longer seems to mean "lots" as well—and it would probably startle most adults to discover that an average children's book picked at random from my shelves (it happened to be *To Tame a Sister*, by Gillian Avery) runs to 260 pages of very small print, that T. H. White's *The Sword in the Stone* is only a few pages shorter, and that Arthur Ransome's series of thirteen books average 350 pages each (and, by the way, *The Sword in the Stone* is first in a set of four). Nevertheless, in spite of knowing this, when I came to write for adults, I found myself assuming I was writing something *long*. It was very exasperating. Though the finished book is actually slightly shorter than *Fire and Hemlock*, it carries in it, despite my best efforts, all the results and implications of this hidden assumption.

A long book, it follows, is going to be read in bits. Therefore you have to keep reminding your readers of things, even if they do use their brains. Some adult writers trust their readers so little that if they have, say, a hero with blue eyes who comes from Mars, they call him "the man from Mars" every time they mention him, and interlard this with "the blue-eyed man from Mars," or occasionally "the man with blue eyes." I swore a great oath not to do this, but it hovered, and I had to fight it. Hovering over me also was the notion "This should be the first in a trilogy" (which is another way of having things read in bits), and I kept worrying that I was not only bringing the book to too definite a conclusion but that I was also obliged to set up a world in great detail in order to be able to use it again. Now, having come to my senses and started to think about these assumptions, I ask myself why. A book should conclude satisfactorily; to leave the ending for the next volume is cynical (*and* annoying for readers). And as for having my world there in detail, it was when I realized that I was actually being deterred from considering the sequel by the assumption that adults have to be reminded of the plot and action of the First Book between the lines of the Second Book—this despite a host of really good ideas—that I began to feel this was absurd. When I wrote *Drowned Ammet* I did not feel it necessary to recapitulate *Cart and Cwidder*. It would have been largely irrelevant anyway. I took the usual course of those who write for children and relied on my readers having the *nous* to pick up the situation as they went along. So why should I assume adults are different?

The answer seems to be: because publishers do. It was around this area that I began to run foul of the assumptions of my would-be editor as well as my own. A "long" book naturally entails various kinds of padding. Apart from the kinds I've already mentioned, the most obvious form of padding is description—whether of the galactic core seen from the vertiginous skin of a spaceship, or the landscape passed through on the quest. Unfortunately, descriptions are where children stop reading, unless something is being described as an essential part of the story. I agree with them. I have long ago discovered that if I know what a given scene looks like in exact detail I do not need to describe, because it comes over in the writing, in phrases and not as a set piece. But I knew the assumption was different for adults. I used my usual method, but I added a hundred percent more describing. The would-be editor objected. "Too short" and "I don't get enough of a sense of wonder" were the phrases used. I bit back a retort to the effect, "But you *should* get a sense of wonder if you stop to imagine it!" Adults are different. They need me to do all that for them.

Perhaps the difference is merely that they need me to do different things. I started writing for children at a point where all but a few children's books were very bad and inane. So inane were they that my husband used to fall asleep, when reading aloud at bedtime to our young, after a maximum of three sentences. The resulting outcry convinced me not only that I could do better myself, but also that it was imperative to put something in the books for the benefit of adults who had to read them aloud. I always do this, which is what makes me so amazed that I think of adults as a different animal when I come to write a book especially for them. But—and it is a big but—I am always aware that the different thing I am doing for the *children* is writing something that can be read aloud. This has nothing to do with subject matter: it is purely a matter of the cadence of a sentence. If a sentence can't be spoken with ease, then you rewrite it. When I started the adult novel, I thought, "Oh, good. I don't need to think of that. What freedom!"

Oddly enough, this revealed another hidden assumption. Adults expect a more "literary" turn of phrase. This does not necessarily mean more polysyllables—though as a lover of words I seized the chance to use those—but simply the kind of sentence that does *not* reproduce the way we all speak. It has hanging clauses and inversion and is long—and here was a terrible discovery: more clichés lurk in those literary turns than ever appear in any spoken kind. For the sake of freedom from forms of words that others had overworked, I had to go back to assuming that this, too, was going to be read aloud.

But I came out of a billow of turgid sentences still assuming that writing for adults gave me more freedom, for instance, in the way I could tell the story. I could split my cast of characters up and flip from one to another. I could have a short section on Tod, outcast on Earth and bewildered by it, followed by a longer account of Flan, who is in a pocket universe having a nervous breakdown, and then jump to Zillah accompanying a centaur into an alternative world. Everyone concerned with children's books assumes that children have trouble with this kind of narrative method and I got gleefully to work. Then I realized that this freedom was equally illusory. Adults may expect this, but it is also the narrative method of *Doctor Who*, and anyone who can follow *Doctor Who* can follow this in their sleep.

But there really *is* greater freedom in writing for adults, you will be saying. What about the actual content of the story? All of sex, violence, politics, and the arcane skulduggery of science or mage craft would be mine to use. Yes, despite the fact that I had used all of these in *Power of Three*, I did assume I had this freedom. I did. The measure of that freedom can be seen from my saying with increasing uneasiness as I wrote, "This isn't like any adult speculative fiction I ever read!" My would-be editor echoed this exact phrase, dubiously, and followed it with, "And you seem to be mixing science fiction and fantasy here." Oh dear. These are simply not problems writing for children. The new and different thing is welcomed. Numerous teachers and librarians refuse shelf space to writers like Enid Blyton, on the grounds that they always write the same book; and as for the mixing of genres—well, there *is* only the one and that is books for children. For children, if I want to send a decrepit starship full of witches to a quasi-monastery in another adjacent universe, no one turns a hair. But adults are handicapped by terminal assumptions about what goes with which genre. If they think I am writing fantasy, then my belligerent witches must go on a quest armed only with swords and spells and either on foot or horseback; and if what I am doing is to be science fiction, no one aboard my starship is allowed magic, but only scientific principles not altogether yet proven, such as an ability to travel faster than light.

Does nobody find these unspoken assumptions absurd? There is another: sex. Contrary to most popular belief, children's books concern themselves vastly and outspokenly with sex, for two main reasons: first, because children are so frequently abducted and raped; and second, because children have to spend so much of their lives dealing with the sex life of their parents—particularly when those parents are divorcing. True, scenes of explicit sex between adults are not much use to children—it affects them rather like the drunk across the street affects you when you happen to be cold sober and in a hurry—but most of them can't wait to grow up and try it. But when such scenes are an essential part of the story, no one makes any bones about putting them in. They run the whole gamut, too, of human emotions, through rapture, tragedy, and comedy, and all the smaller emotions besides. Now when I came to write for adults, I assumed I had the same freedom, and more. And this surface assumption of mine fell foul of another underlying assumption as soon as my would-be editor read the book.

My witches were invading a place full of polite and largely innocent quasi-monks. Apart from the fact that they were all witches, each woman was as different from the others as may be a real person in her own right. So, as usual, I sat down and thought carefully, "Now what would *really* happen, to this real woman in this situation? And to this and these real men?" The answer is various on both sides: a lot of guilt, a lot of pressure from inside and outside the group of women, and an awful lot of whoopee at some point when enough people relaxed enough. In the course of it two-thirds die, two get badly victimized, one falls into a clinical depression, one gets blackmailed, everyone's judgment goes askew, and one woman runs away and nearly gets her small child killed. The assumptions I had ignored came out in my would-be editor's response: "It's all so *nice*." I said, "I beg your pardon?" The reply was, "Well, most writers would take this opportunity to make everything miserable and tragic—and you had one pair fall in love." I had. It seemed to me that they would, those particular ones. In fact, they did it without any help from me. "Now what's going on here?" I thought. I am assumed to be writing fantasy. Therefore, it seems, where adults are concerned, one must only write of sex in fantasy in a tragic and elegiac way. People are not supposed to behave in the way that people *would*. Oh no. Surely this is only one editor's aberrant assumption? But I fear not.

This kind of thing cuts down the freedom one ought to have when writing for adults to a point which I find claustrophobic. It gets worse when I realize that there were certain sorts of story which I didn't even consider. To take two examples, I knew I couldn't write anything like Vivien Alcock's *The Monster Garden* or Philippa Pearce's *Tom's Midnight Garden*. *The Monster Garden* is simply a rewrite of *Frankenstein*, in which a modern girl called Frankie (!) accidentally grows some protoplasm from her father's lab into a *creature*. As in all children's books, nothing turns out as you'd expect (which is part of the beautiful freedom of this branch of writing), but this plot is unavailable for adults because everyone knows it's been done before. Adults are supposed to be sophisticated about this. In that case, would someone tell me why people keep writing the one about the female warrior with the map in the front? Or why *Frankenstein* is a no-no, while everyone is free to reuse *The Lord of the Rings*? The rationale of these assumptions escapes me.

Tom's Midnight Garden is a branch of time-travel writing (loosely related to that of Dickens in *A Christmas Carol*) in which a ghost from the past takes a lonely small boy to explore the house and countryside as it was in his grandmother's day. It is most elegantly and exactly done and rightly a children's classic, but what adult would accept a plot like that outside Dickens? This really raises the whole large question of time travel, which I will reserve for a later date, only pointing out here what seems to be the hidden assumption: adults can only accept time travel on a fairly gross scale. Time travel up or down a generation or so is only allowed for breeding purposes (either with one's mother or one's niece). Otherwise one has to go back to, say, Roman times or *way* back to our origins—and then only when provided with plenty of anxious archaeological explanations. Personally, since I like more modest time trips better, I think this is a pity.

In fact, it is all a pity. Every hidden assumption I discovered seems to be felt as a law, or a rule, or an absolute difference between two branches of writing, and I cannot see they are any such thing. They shackle the speculative fiction written for adults and reflect badly on that written for children—since the final hidden assumption has to be that as fiction written for adults is so puerile, how much more so must fiction written for children be? This, I know, is not the case. But let no one argue that these hidden assumptions about writing for adults are not there. I assure you they are. I felt every one of them like a ball and chain when I tried to do it. I think it is high time people started examining them in order to free the wealth of good stories cramped under this load of old iron. For, when all is said and done, it is telling a good story, and telling it well, that is the point of both kinds of writing.

When I Won the *Guardian* Award

Diana Wynne Jones won the prestigious Guardian *Children's Fiction Prize (then known simply as the* Guardian *Award) in 1978 for* Charmed Life. *Since 1967, the* Guardian *has given an annual award for the best children's book written by a British or British Commonwealth author and published in the UK during the preceding year. A panel of authors, along with the reviews editor of the* Guardian's *children's books section, judges the award.*

When I won the *Guardian* Award for *Charmed Life* (in 1978 I think it was), I was exceedingly astonished—and also very, very pleased. The reason for both these feelings was that the judges were all writers themselves. There is nothing more flattering than having your book liked by people who do the same thing as you do—because, surely, they must be the hardest to fool *and* the hardest to please. They know how to do it: if *they* think you've done it right, then you have.

It turns out that I was right to feel that way. If I'd known then what I know now, I'd have been even more surprised and flattered, because people who have won this award were always asked to be one of the judges for next year. I have been doing that. As soon as I got home from a book fair in Rochdale, books began to arrive, stacks of them, two nearly every day. It was better than Christmas. The rest of my family began to get rather envious. Until, that is, they saw the books. Then they said things like, "I wouldn't read that lot if you paid me!" and turned away.

I thought they were being a little unreasonable. After all, as I well knew, it takes a lot of time and a vast amount of effort to write a book. You ought to do people the courtesy of deciding you don't like a book *after* you've read it at least. So I read diligently—luckily I read fast—three or more books a day. And it did impress me what a lot of time and what a vast amount of effort these writers had put into their books. I felt I couldn't be so unkind as to dislike *any* of them. I wrote long, long notes on each book, pointing out to myself all the good things these authors had done.

Well. Armed with this heavy stack of kind remarks, I went to London to meet the other writers on the panel. The judging began.

"Now what about this book?" said the chairperson. "*Fairies at the Bottom of the Garden*, by Selina Slime?"

And all hell broke loose.

"Disgusting! Horrible! *Terrible!*" shouted the writers. "Are people still writing such things? *No marks!*"

"Then how about this beautiful historical romance?" asked the chairperson. "*In the Hands of Crusoe's Cannibals?*"

"Dreadful!" yelled the authors. "Nobody gets to eat anybody."

"Then," said the chairperson desperately, "how about this lovely description of how it feels to be a child at a bad school— *Hero of the Slum*, by Sylvester Glum?"

By this time I had realized that my kind notes were just hiding my true feelings, and I began yelling with the rest. "Revolting! Who's this Glum trying to fool?!"

"Terrible do-gooding book!" bawled all the rest.

"Then what about this charmingly poetic—" began the chairperson.

"NO!" we screamed. "Tear it up!"

In short, we were utterly ruthless, terribly noisy, and quite right. There did finally come a book at which we all screamed "YES!" even louder. And started reading bits out and howling with laughter and interrupting one another to say what the best bits were. And it was a terribly good book.

But when I was on the train, going back home, I did think, "Good heavens! I wonder what they all screamed about *my* book?"

Reading C. S. Lewis's Narnia

This commentary on The Chronicles of Narnia *was originally delivered at a conference on C. S. Lewis. The article has also been published on www.amazon.com as "The Magic of Narnia."*

Before my student days I knew C. S. Lewis merely as the author of *The Screwtape Letters*. These were read out at morning assembly in my school, and very whimsical and condescending I found them, feeding you Christianity by pretending to speak as a devil—though I had to admit this was very good as an idea.

Judge my surprise when I went up to Oxford and discovered that this devil's advocate was a small, pear-shaped man with a mighty, rolling voice and quite formidable learning. His lectures were called "Mediaeval Prolegomena"—a title, you might think, to put anyone off. In fact, he filled the largest lecture hall to overflowing every week, discoursing from memory about the underlying beliefs of the Middle Ages with such vision, humor, and total clarity that his audience became excited enough almost to cheer.

Quite soon after, I had the splendid experience of discovering Lewis's Narnia books when my own children did.

The excitement I remembered from his lectures was there, and the learning, and the clarity. There was also a measure of the whimsy I knew from *The Screwtape Letters*, but here it pulled its weight, since it was coupled with an outflowing of the imagination which gripped me and my children alike. The books are all surprisingly short. But an immense amount happens in each, apparently leisurely, yet with all the crowding action you are never in doubt what is going on. You can *see* everything that happens, so that surprisingly young children— one of mine was only two—can understand every incident. This is despite the fact that Lewis mines material from his own huge learning, drawing on theology, Renaissance geography, myth, folktales, medieval writings, and even earlier children's books, and through this he contrives to talk of the obscurer movements of the human mind in the face of faith. I marveled and learned from it.

The Lion, the Witch and the Wardrobe, Lewis said, started with his vision of a faun walking in the snow beside an old-fashioned streetlight. It begins a little stiffly (and this stiffness never leaves his child protagonists) because he is feeling his way, and does not really take off until the advent of the lion, Aslan, with whom Lewis discovered he could tap in to deeper tragedy and triumph. For me, this was his major discovery: that you can invoke the whole range of human thought and feeling by beginning from one simple, clear scene. But Lewis himself asserted that it was the talking animals that truly fascinated him. He has a field day with these in *Prince Caspian*.[1] By this book he is totally assured, and the pace and scope of the story are breathtaking—myths mingle, alternate worlds clash, and you get a profound sense of the changes history brings.

That was *almost* my children's favorite, but the one they put top was *The Voyage of the Dawn Treader*,[2] where Lewis plunders medieval and Renaissance travel tales to give a limpid, episodic account of Caspian's journey to the ends of eternity. My children's best-loved episode was where Eustace gets turned into a dragon. They liked it that he got what he deserved.

This is a major theme in the Narnia books: you get what you earn. If your misfortune is undeserved, then you can overcome it with help from Beyond. *The Silver Chair* is all about this. The only thing my children liked about this one was gloomy old Puddleglum. They were uncomfortable with the almost overt expression of sexual seduction and they did not get the other point Lewis is trying to make: that moral and physical dangers you have been warned about are not always easy to recognize when you actually meet them.

My favorite is *The Magician's Nephew*. This is how to write a prequel. I admire the way Lewis contrives an explanation of that solitary street lamp in Narnia by shamelessly borrowing from E. Nesbit—and improving on her—to do it. I am utterly overwhelmed by the Wood Between the Worlds, including the way the kids nearly forget to mark their home pool; and the sheer, magical invention of things like the toffee tree, which arises purely from logically following through a magical premise, taught me a great deal about how magic should work. And *The Horse and His Boy* is a lesson in how to slot a sequel in at right angles, as it were. This happens during the time of *The Lion, the Witch and the Wardrobe*, but it starts from another country (Calormen) and works back into Narnia. I never could get on with *The Last Battle*, though. Reading it as an adult, I recognized Antichrist and the Apocalypse and too readily knew everyone was dead. But this was my nephew's favorite because—as he told me at length—it is so exciting and, when you think everyone is dead, they all come alive again. No, not in heaven, he insisted. For real. Well, this is the magic of the Narnia books for you.

Creating the Experience

This article about writing for children was published in The Times Literary Supplement *on July 11, 1975. Diana originally titled it simply "Experience."*

Before writing a book for children, I tell myself this: you are trying to give children an experience they can accept and enjoy. You may also offer help, advice and information, but this is no use without mutual understanding. What you are primarily offering is your book as an experience.

Then I can start producing the experience. It is always something of an experiment. The field is so vast that I never want to do the same thing twice. But look at the possibilities. An experience is an action *combined with* the thoughts or sensations of the person performing it. Now, since the experience in question is a book, this gives me at least three sets of thoughts (or sensations) involved with the action: first I have what the characters in the book think of the action; second, what I as the writer think of it; and third, what the reader makes of it all. It is open to me to combine any of these with the action in all manner of interesting ways. I could, for instance, do as W. E. Johns does with splendid success and cut out my own thoughts entirely. If you read a Biggles book you, as the reader, are in the closest possible relationship with the characters, grown men as they are, and Johns works skillfully at keeping you that way by presenting you with an action hectic with spies and airplanes. You get a very vivid experience.

But if I want to write about ordinary children doing ordinary things, as I did in *Wilkins' Tooth*, it would be a mistake to do it the Biggles way. I might enjoy a loving re-creation of childhood—though I doubt it—merely because I am not a child. But to children it would not be an experience at all. "We *know* all about that," they would say. "Nothing *happens*." This cry is never a simple demand for an adventurous plot, but a criticism of the method. If I am going to produce action which is ordinary, then I must stop in myself and combine my thoughts with the action to complete the experience.

The situation I tried stepping into in *Wilkins' Tooth* is a normal one—children out on their own, as they are in the playground or in the holidays. Their only safeguard is a constant cry of "It isn't fair!" Their world is within but beyond that of adults, remote and lonely and echoing as the magic void where they find themselves after breaking Biddy's spell. From it, you appeal to adults in vain. "Help!" says Jess on one occasion. "I beg your pardon?" says the adult. These adults who impinge do so because they are too eccentric to be part of their own world.

Now, push the reader directly against this situation and it is appalling. And it is all too familiar to most children. Yet I am wanting to remove their major prop by suggesting that this cry of "It isn't fair!" is just not adequate. So I tried to make the situation acceptable in the way children make it acceptable to themselves—by finding it funny. Children are always laughing, jeering, and joking. For them, laughter is not a way of dismissing things. They learn by it. Laughter staves off the fear, horror, or bewilderment they might feel so that they can come to grips with the facts. Treat the facts that way in *Wilkins' Tooth* and you can make a fantasia on the notion of justice—"It isn't fair!" leads to a tooth for a tooth, which in turn leads to the secretive nastiness of witchcraft—and might even suggest the halting operation of mercy.

Further possibilities open up. If you treat a thing as funny the way children do, you have a ready-made bridge to fantasy. Kids tell dreadful punning jokes, every one a pocket fantasy: *Q. What lies on the seabed and shivers? A. A nervous wreck.* Poor thing. And if I am combining my own humorous thoughts with the action, why should I not, through this kind of fantasy, use the thoughts of the characters in the book in the same way?

I really enjoyed doing just this in *The Ogre Downstairs.* Thoughts figure as magic, and magic is a metaphor for thoughts. The basic idea is a kind of pun: what possible alchemy can make a set of people only yoked together by a remarriage start liking one another? Take alchemy to be magic chemistry, and there it is. The magic does all the usual things, like making people able to fly, or small, or invisible, because these things have the sort of dream-symbol quality I needed. The book is meant to function like a dream. You participate in a violent action full of hate and fury, but you are naturally horrified when Johnny pours blood about and tries to land the Ogre one with the vacuum cleaner. Books, like dreams, let you have your experience and reject it too. If I cast a fantastical-comical light over the action, you can accept it that more readily. But I was handling a situation basically more appalling than the one in *Wilkins' Tooth*, one that needs serious things said, and the magic metaphors proved wonderfully useful here. Metaphors can be distant from their referent, as the toffee bars and the dust balls are distant from the children's thoughts, but they can also be so close as to surface into the real thing. I surfaced twice, when what I was saying seemed too important to be left to chance: once when Caspar literally puts himself in Malcolm's place; and again in the "cloak of darkness" section[1] to make it clear that invisibility stands for thought. Johnny becomes all thoughts—violent ones. Thought is something no one can see, but it initiates most action.

The beauty of writing for children is that they admit to violent thoughts and accept that one violent emotion leads readily to another. Anyone knows this who has looked at a group of hilarious children and predicted, "There'll be tears in a minute." Hilarity is on the way to tragedy, and tragedy is close and frequent among children. Now tragedy entails awe. Children's books deal much and splendidly in the awesome, and children love it. Possibly what they love is the nubbin of tragedy, modified by fantasy and its sting removed by laughter. For adults, this usually leads to sentimentality, but children are largely impervious to sentimentality. They acknowledge emotion simply.

In *Eight Days of Luke* I was experimenting in pushing the reader close to a tragic experience by laughing at it. David is in a situation I think most appalling of all—living with relatives who are not interested in him, but who justify their neglect by demanding his gratitude. I have made them funny, but the situation itself is not funny. David has to work out his loveless salvation for himself. His reaction summons up Luke. Luke is Loki,[2] a magic metaphor used this time not solely to represent David's thoughts but as a vehicle for awe. On a mundane level, he is amoral violence. If you accept him for what he is, as David does, you are willy-nilly hunted out by more awesome things. You are open to learn. The dreadful relatives mistake Luke's nature and are not open to learn anything but anger. They get Mr. Chew.[3] David moves among the entire pantheon, to Valhalla, and thence to discover real sympathy.

Because you cannot rely on children having read anything, my notion was to let the Norse legends I used make their own impact. I dissolved the action into a series of images in the latter part of the book to set the reader face to face with the awesome. At the World-tree David cheats his fate by learning from it. Stupid little girls help. At Wallsey, Cousin Ronald sees a bunch of yobbos and one-armed bandits. His is the comic view diminished. You no longer need that much, since David is dimly aware of the hall of the great dead opening onto a mundane fairground. I wanted to show how the awesome leads both to and from everyday life. The gods themselves are the big thoughts that stalk through ordinary actions, as much a part of experience as the days of the week—which of course these gods literally are.

After this I could go on to remove the action from ordinary life and see what happens then. As I said, the possibilities are boundless.

Fantasy Books for Children

A short piece on the lasting impact of fantasy, this article was commissioned by The Good Book Guide *for an introduction to the Fiction and Fantasy section of* The Good Book Guide's *annual selection of children's books in 1991–2.*

The Good Book Guide *is a subscription-only journal for everybody who wants to know about and buy books published in the UK. It was founded in 1977 to offer an informed, independent selection of outstanding books.*

Writers of fantasy for children have a heavy responsibility: anything they write is likely to have a profound effect for the next fifty years. You can see why if you ask ten adults which book they remember best from their childhood. Nine of them will certainly name a fantasy.

If you inquire further, you will find your nine adults admitting that they acquired many of the rules they live by from this book that so impressed them. This may not necessarily mean rules of morality—though it may—but wider things like what ways of behaving are wise, or unwise; or how to spot a person who is going to let you down; or what frame of mind in which to face a disaster; or possibly the way you look at life in general. For instance, when I discovered Brunhilde[1] from an antiquated retelling of Norse legends and found that she was a warrior, I was intensely excited: now it didn't matter anymore that I was born a girl.

This excitement is something all nine adults are likely to confess to, whatever else the book gave them. The book endowed them with experience which they could not get any other way, by speaking to them in a way and at a level that touches the roots of the imagination. They will also probably say the book made them laugh or cry, or both. Good. The emotions are very important. You need to acknowledge their power at the earliest possible age. It is the only way to get the rest of life straight.

As you see, it is a heavy responsibility. I think all writers of fantasy know this, but do not dwell on it. Their aim is to give children an *experience*.

The Value of Learning Anglo-Saxon

On August 30, 1991, The Times Literary Supplement *published a commentary debate on the future of Old English. The critic Valentine Cunningham, who is a professor of English Language and Literature at the University of Oxford, called for an end to the compulsory teaching of Anglo-Saxon in the Oxford English course. Opposing him was medievalist J. A. Burrow, Diana Wynne Jones's husband.*

That same day Diana wrote this letter to the editor of The Times Literary Supplement. *Although there was correspondence on the topic for the following three issues (mostly supportive of teaching Anglo-Saxon), Diana's letter was not published.*

Dear Sir,

As a writer, I resent Val Cunningham's implication that learning Anglo-Saxon is a dead loss to all writers. I would like to put a writer's case for being forced to learn Anglo-Saxon as part of a degree in English.

Forced is the word. I would not have chosen to learn it; I did not take to it; and I frequently fell asleep with my face on the library blotter trying to learn paradigms. In addition, when I was an undergraduate at Oxford, Anglo-Saxon texts were not taught as literature but as exercises in translation and as mines for fearsome problems called "cruxes." So it says volumes for these texts that the actual things written in Anglo-Saxon came blazing through all tutors' attempts to quench them.

Take *Beowulf*—a large poem that is thrown at you. Laboriously you realize that its writer has signaled that he is giving you an epic, a promise he proceeds to fulfill in fluid and clangorous language through linked episodes, some of them closely attentive to the hero, some ranging outward into history. Even before it had dawned on me that I was studying a masterpiece nobody had told me about, I found I was learning from it *as a writer*. I can safely say that this anonymous poem taught me more about how to orchestrate and shape a narrative than any writer of more recent date. By this I mean the "novelistic" or *engineering* part of writing: when to devote detailed attention, when to slide over, how to thunder and how to restrain, and where to do it; and of course how to dovetail a narrative into the rest of history and make it relevant. It was a privilege to watch someone from so long ago doing all this so consummately well.

I do not think you gain the same sense of privilege from reading a translation. You certainly miss out disastrously on the shorter poems, like the cloudy and emblematic "Dream of the Rood," where part of the point is that terms from older battle epics are transferred to Christian use; or the hints and allusions in "Widsith" or "The Wife's Lament." I forget which of the "Wanderer" or the "Seafarer" was a "set" text for us to study. I read them all avidly, realizing that here was the origin of the queer, sideways narrative manner of the Border Ballads—and again learned.

Oddly enough, the main thing I learned was that Anglo-Saxon (like the Ballads) is still very much with us today: it is English in all sorts of ways. Take "The Battle of Maldon," where the leader, Byrhtnoth, is the first recorded example of winning the toss and putting the opposition in to bat on a perfect pitch; or, on a more serious note, take the prose of Ælfric and Wulfstan. A lot of the words are different, but the basic sentence and the basic paragraph, the sinews and engineering of it, are precisely as in modern English. And because the Anglo-Saxon vocabulary was not large, you can watch these prose writers doing much with little. They use every device possible of the rhetoric that Val Cunningham appears to believe was invented by the Renaissance or somewhen—and these of course are the stock in trade of any writer. Reading Ælfric and Wulfstan slowly in the original, I gained more knowledge of—for instance—how to build a paragraph, than I ever did from the mannered stuff in *Tristram Shandy*.

This is all personal, but I would like to add that I am by no means the only imaginative writer to be inspired by being made to learn Anglo-Saxon. There was a whole generation of us, and others after that. It seems hard on future writers, if they are not to be put to this enabling experience somewhere.

Yours sincerely,
Diana Wynne Jones

The Halloween Worms

This comic article shows how Diana Wynne Jones could find humor even in the roughest circumstance, and how incidents from her books were always returning to haunt her.

This is a true story, even though it came out of a book. You see, what I write in my books and think I have made up has a creepy way of coming true. I noticed it first over *The Ogre Downstairs*. When I wrote that book, we were living in a new house with a flat roof and almost no stairs. The roof turned out to dissolve in rain, the lavatories every so often flushed boiling water, and we had an electric fountain in the living room, because the builders had got confused about which were electric cables and which were heating pipes. I was so sick of that house that I invented a quite different one for *The Ogre Downstairs*—a tall, thin house with lots and lots of stairs.

Now I live in a tall, thin house with lots and lots of stairs. I didn't do it on purpose. It came about by accident, in an awful hurry. But the house is almost exactly like the house I put in that book.

After that, things out of other books started coming true too. It was quite frightening. Imagine meeting the most sinister baddie you have ever invented (or thought you had invented), and hearing him say exactly the things you had put in the book for him to say. That happened. I asked other writers whether anything like this had ever happened to them. "Oh, yes," they said. "Isn't it creepy?" It was. I decided that in the next book I wrote I would put in so many things from real life that it couldn't come true because it had happened anyway. Ha, ha. I decided to write about my schooldays.

The book was called *Witch Week*. It takes place in a very old-fashioned school at Halloween. The thing about writing a book is that, whatever you mean to do, you find the book takes on a life of its own from the first page onward. The school in this book turned into a sort of redbrick Disneyland castle as soon as I started to write, and the headmistress was almost a monster. But one bit I firmly put in from my schooldays, and that was the custom that certain pupils had to sit beside the Headmistress at High Table every lunchtime and make polite conversation. The rule was that you had to wait until the headmistress started to eat and then use the same eating implement as she did. And she always used a fork. For everything. People were forced to eat runny rice pudding with forks. It was like a medieval torture. I was very bad at eating with a fork, and I was also very bad at polite conversation, because the mere sight of the awful food we used to have seemed to inspire me to describe it, out loud. "Fishes' eyes in glue," I used to find myself saying. "Dead daffodils and mashed caterpillar."

I put all this, exactly, in the book. The girl in it finds she can't stop describing the food as she sits beside the headmistress. But, in the way books do, something took over and made that dinner a bit different from the ones I used to have. There are grand visitors, so the High Table gets given a starter. The girl looks at it, and it seems to be worms in custard. Really, of course, it is seafood cocktail. And the rest of the book got less and less like my schooldays. They were all tearing about in the nights just before Halloween, some of them riding broomsticks, and the rest of them causing the most peculiar bumps in the night, and there were all sorts of goings-on in the washrooms.

The book had not long been published when I got an invitation to attend a reunion—not a school reunion, that would have warned me off; but a reunion of people who used to come to the conference center my parents ran when I was a child. It was to be the weekend of Halloween, because that was half term and everyone was free. So we said we would go.

The place was out in the country and extraordinarily hard to find. We drove round and round, and we didn't find the driveway until it was getting dark. It was a very long driveway. The first thing that warned us what we might be getting to was a set of dim, white goalposts looming out of the dusk. Then we drove round some dark trees and found huge, dark buildings ahead. There were battlements and towers. A castle? No. The last sunset came through one of the buildings and showed that it had pointed church windows, vast ones. A ruined abbey then? All the buildings were quite dark and absolutely quiet, but there was one dim orange light, low down, shining through a pointed window. We parked the car beside it and stuck our heads through a pointed door. There was nobody there, nothing but a vaulted stone corridor leading into darkness. But there was a smell. One sniff and we knew what that building was. It was a school. I don't know what makes the smell of a school always so unmistakable, any more than I know what makes the smell itself—old socks and chalk? Tests and timetables?—but it is always the same whether the building is new or old. But there was no one there. We didn't like to barge in, in case we had come to the wrong place, so we walked round the outsides of the huge, churchlike buildings, trying to find someone to ask. Owls hooted. Bats fluttered against the last brown sunset, just like the start of the creepiest horror story you have ever read, and we never found a soul. So we went round again, back to the dim orange light.

There, suddenly, there were a few people, so suddenly that I began to feel they had been laid on by magic. They were all people that I hadn't seen for at least twenty years, and that was very creepy. They all looked just the same, except they looked as if they had made themselves up to look old by powdering their hair and painting on wrinkles and sticking white beards on their faces. But they were all very friendly, and shortly we found ourselves being ushered into the grand reunion dinner. That took place in the great dining hall, which was like the biggest cathedral I had ever seen, all pointed arches stretching away into darkness. It turned out that very few people had been able to attend the dinner, so there were only ten or so of us at the High Table, which was so big that you had to shout to the person beside you. And winds blew out of the dark part of the Great Hall, bringing the school smell in gusts, like the scent of dead schoolboys. It was half term, we were told, so all the pupils had gone home.

But it was also Halloween, so, naturally, the first thing we were given to eat was a bowl of yellow stuff with little, pink, wriggly things floating in it. "Worms in custard!" I thought, peering at the stuff in the candlelight. "Seafood cocktail!" shouted the person on my left. "How delicious!"

I managed not to describe the worms out loud, but they were awfully hard to eat. That was followed by daffodil buds and shoe soles, with little yellow flowerpots someone told me were Yorkshire puddings. And all the while the winds blew, bringing the ghosts of schoolboys out of the dark hall. Just the place for things to go bump in the night, I thought, wishing we were not staying the night.

The room where we were to sleep was along corridors, up bare, splintering stairs, along more corridors, through a long room with rows of baths in it, side by side, through another long room with two rows of little tiny washbasins—here, beside each washbasin, hung the boys' towels, each neatly folded square, and the boys' sponge bags, each exactly four inches away from the towels (obviously they didn't clean their teeth while they were at home)—and then along another corridor, through a neat, neat study, and finally up a fourteen-foot ladder to a sort of loft with three beds in it. I don't know why the school bothered with beds. They were exactly as hard as the floor, except that each bed had a hair shirt on it stuffed with what felt like a gorse bush. You got bruised every time you turned over. And I did a lot of turning over because, soon after midnight, it was borne in upon me that those worms— seafood, I mean—had disagreed with me horribly. By two in the morning, I knew I was going to be sick.

I tried to put it off. I didn't know where to be sick, and whatever it was, it had to be down that fourteen-foot ladder in the dark. But being sick is something you just can't put off. I had to get up. Somehow I found the hole in the floor and fell down the ladder. Then where? The study was far too neat. I blundered out into the corridor and ran along it. There was a door I hadn't remembered at the end of the corridor, and it would only open when I backed off and ran at it like a bull. I shot out into the place with rows of washbasins. I was desperate by then. But I couldn't mess up all those neat towels, and the boys would probably be made to clean it up after me. Rows of dim baths now. No, the baths didn't seem the proper place either. I held my hand over my mouth and ran on. Showers. No. Help! Then another door which I had to butt open with my head. And there at last I found a door which I could just see was labeled SENIOR BOYS ONLY. By that time I was too far gone to care and I burst through that door. I don't know what the place was—it was too dark—but I do know that as soon as I went in, it started to fill with water. Water was up round my ankles by the time I was ready to back out.

Then I had to bump and barge my way back to the ladder and climb back up to the loft. I lay down on the gorse bush feeling I never wanted to move again. But the moment I lay down, I found I was going to be sick. Up I leaped. Down the ladder, through the study, along the corridor, through the door that wouldn't open, past the washbasins, past the baths . . . I did that eight more times. Those things were either worms or they were the fingers of little boys. Each time, the only possible place I could find was SENIOR BOYS ONLY, and each time I went in, it filled with water again. I was still charging back and forth when it began to get light. I was still doing it when the other eight guests started getting up and wondering whether they were allowed to wash in the little washbasins.

"Must you run?" one of them shouted irritably at me as

I sped wearily past. "Someone was running and banging all night!"

"That was me!" I croaked, and made it to SENIOR BOYS, which began to fill with water again at once. It wasn't meant to flood, I could see now. Water was gushing in from under the linoleum, probably just to spite me. No doubt the ghosts of little boys— all of whom were missing at least one finger—were laughing heartily.

I didn't want breakfast. By then, all I wanted was to get away from church windows and rows of washbasins. I left as soon as I could, and didn't feel happy until I was back home in our tall, thin house with lots of stairs, and only one washbasin, with the towels hung up anyhow. Here the windows are square and there is nothing to go bump in the night. . . .

There was a tremendous knocking at the front door.

I opened it to find a lot of people made up to look old. They had powdered their hair and stuck gray beards on their chins and painted wrinkles on their faces. One was a witch, one was a high priest, one was a devil, and the others were probably goblins. "Trick or treat!" they all shouted as I opened the door.

I had forgotten it was Halloween.

A Day Visiting Schools

This account was put together from nearly a hundred school visits. Everything in it happened more than once. Diana wanted to highlight that this shows that an author's life is not always a happy one.

A condensed form of this article was published with the title "The Other Half" in the Horn Book Magazine, *September/October 2008. This title refers to the fact that these school visits kept Diana going for the other half of the time, in which there was never any problem with the children.*

Morning

I have been asked to arrive at 10:30 without fail to spend the morning with one class of children. After driving eighty miles and hunting all over town, I reach the school at 10:29. The school is being rebuilt. There is no door and no one to ask. I force my way under scaffolding and get in through a hole in the wall. An angry lady in glasses rushes down the corridor at me. "You can't come in here!" I explain. She says she is the school secretary and *she* has heard nothing about my visit. "You'd better wait in the staff room," she says. "The Head's got the whole school in singing practice until 11:00. I *would* offer you a coffee only the water's cut off at the moment."

The staff room is like an airport lounge. I sit there for half an hour until a breathless teacher rushes in. She says, "You'll be starting in twenty minutes. That gives you less than an hour to get round the whole school."

I say, "But you told me I'd be with just one class."

She says, "Yes, but since you're *here* . . . You won't mind, will you? It's all arranged."

There follows a breathless rush round the classrooms. The children crowd to ask questions and try to show me their writing in the few seconds available. Each demands two autographs, one to keep and one to swap. The teacher says wonderingly, "I'd no idea they'd be so interested. Is there anywhere I can get hold of your books?"

Dinner

The kitchen ladies have decided I would prefer a pilchard and lettuce. They have kept it in a hot cupboard all morning because there are chips with it. They fetch it out, lukewarm, wilted, with the chips turned to a pile of kindling. So they freshen it up by pouring a large ladleful of gravy over everything. "There!" they say proudly.

Afternoon

I have been asked to come at 1:00 to spend the afternoon with sixty children. I arrive in pouring rain and the only person I can find is a dinner lady, who eventually finds a child to take me to the staff room. The Head is there. He wrings my hand until the bones crack. "I haven't read any of your books, of course," he says. "Can you sit quietly in that chair by the wall—we're having a staff meeting."

I sit quietly through the staff meeting. At 1:30, a teacher springs out of the dispersing staff. "I've got great news for you!" she cries. "We've given you the whole school for the afternoon."

I say, "But you told me sixty children."

She says, "You won't mind, will you? It's all arranged." And she sends me out to queue in the rain until someone opens the hall.

It is *not* all arranged. The only children present are half of one grumpy class who stare and say, "Who's she? Why are we here?" The other classes have not been told. While they are being fetched, the teacher says, "You'll have to arrange the hall the way you want it. I'm not used to this." I spend half an hour dragging chairs about.

At last several hundred children rush into the hall, accompanied by shouting teachers. When the children are seated, the teachers turn in a body and start to leave the hall. I recollect that it is illegal for me to be left in sole charge. "Where are you all going?" I ask. They do not admit they are going to the staff room to put their feet up. They say, "You don't need us."

"Yes I do," I say. "You might want to follow this talk up." They look puzzled at this. Resentfully, they find chairs. One stands up and takes revenge. "This lady," he announces in a sickly voice, "knows all about magic." Half the children recoil. The rest look round for my conjuring kit.

I stand up and explain, after which I do my best with the short time remaining. The children, once they understand why we are all here, become keenly enthusiastic. Those who do not get a question in are near tears. The teachers bear me a further grudge for this. At the end, they hasten me off the premises, saying, "We *would* offer you a coffee, but the water's cut off just now."

My Very Worst School Visit

I arrived with the county children's librarian. We were met by a teacher in the playground who said, "Go away. The careers interview is canceled." We explained and got as far as the entrance. The Deputy Head met us there, saying, "Go away. We don't need any supply teachers today." We explained again and eventually reached a classroom where six depressed children sat dotted about among empty desks. "The rest have gone to Latin," the teacher explained. "You won't mind. You wouldn't want them to miss Latin, would you?" I clenched my teeth, smiled politely, and started trying to cheer up the six depressed children. I had barely spoken two sentences when the Deputy Head reappeared, saying, "Everybody out of here at once. We're on strike."

I had, I may add, come three hundred miles to visit that school.

Writing for Children:
A Matter of Responsibility

This article reveals Diana's developing awareness that since young and impressionable minds were reading her works, she owed them a sense of responsibility.

I have just read a book which—the writer declares in a postscript—would not have been written at all had he not, as a child, chanced to read that chapter of *The Wind in the Willows* called "The Piper at the Gates of Dawn." Those who have not read it can probably gather, just from the title, the sense of wonder, and of magic half heard and half out of sight, in this chapter. The writer I am speaking of, who is an adult, writing for adults, found it influenced him for the rest of his life. And this sort of thing has happened to a lot of people, not just those who went on to become writers themselves. Most adults, in fact, if you question them, will admit that there was this marvelous book they read when they were eight, or ten, or maybe fifteen, that has lived in their minds ever since. It may be a book by Rosemary Sutcliffe, Joan Aiken, Enid Blyton, or even Arthur Ransome. The important thing about it is that it has entered this person's consciousness at a time when ideas were still forming, waking their sense of wonder and forcing their ideas in a new direction—enlarging their imagination, in fact—and, by the mere fact of always being in their mind from then on, has influenced that reader's entire personality. Permanently.

Anyone who writes for children has to bear in mind that one of *their* books might have this effect. It is quite a responsibility. I want to discuss this responsibility and—particularly—the ways in which it can be abused.

One adult I questioned said that John Masefield's *The Box of Delights* would have been his always-remembered marvelous book, but for the fact that when he thought of it he always remembered that at the end it turned out to have been only a dream. Quite right. This is cheating. It is giving a feast of the imagination with one hand and taking it away with the other. It is as if Masefield's nerve failed and he said at the end, "You needn't bother to believe this." But in doing so he had abused the responsibility he had by suddenly grinding the reader's nose into a sober, waking life where the wonders he has just been telling you simply do not count.

If the wonders are going to be with you for the rest of your life, why do they not count?

Many writers abuse their responsibility by answering this question in the dreariest possible way: "Because you are going to grow up." C. S. Lewis's Narnia books are probably the best-known examples of this abuse. In them, Peter and Susan, the two elder children, are unable to enter the magic land of Narnia once they get old enough to entertain thoughts of sex; and of the four adults who enter, two are outright villains and the other two are ignorant working people. Nobody else gets to Narnia until they are dead. Now Narnia, although it has Christian overtones, is preeminently the vivid land of the imagination and, to judge from Lewis's other writings, I do not think he meant to imply that only criminals, young children, and the uneducated working class can be allowed to exercise their imaginations. It was more as if he was here obeying what he thought were the rules of the genre. But the fact is that the implication is there, a glaring flaw in some seminally wonderful books, and has caused writers to believe that this is the rule for children's books even to this day. When I first started writing for children, everyone was certain it was the rule. Publishers and agents were alarmed that I allowed adults not only to notice that magical events were going on but actually to take part in them; and they also got very concerned that I did not give the ages of the children involved—being worried, I suppose, that these children might be past puberty and thus disqualified from figuring in imaginative fiction.

I have made this sound absurd deliberately. Everyone (including children, who can't wait to do so) knows that children grow up and become qualified to play a different role in the world. But it seems strange that so many people believe that they must at this stage cease to use their imagination. Let us look at imagination for a moment. Few people would disagree that it is the growing point of the mind. This means it has to be the point where a mind can expand beyond accepted ideas, examine and then envisage new shapes for the future. Quite often these new shapes will be put in the form of fantasy simply because they do not exist yet. To take a few concrete examples, airplanes have been envisaged ever since the story of Daedalus; a thermos flask figures in several Celtic tales as one of the Treasures of Britain[1]; the steam-engine grew from someone's pipe dream while the kettle boiled; and the microchip was thought up by several twentieth-century science fiction writers. There are also thousands of more nebulous examples that have brought about changes in morals, politics, architecture, and most other fields, and this will continue to happen provided a sufficient number of adults go on using their imagination. This is why it is so foolish to propagate to children the notion that their minds have to stop growing as soon as their bodies do.

This abuse of responsibility arises, I suspect, from romantic thoughtlessness. Recently, however, while I was reading for the children's book section of the Whitbread Awards,[2] I came across no less than five books that abused their responsibility in a way that was positively pernicious. Each of them depicted a child in some kind of melancholy situation—unhappy at school, trouble with parents, the wrong color, and so forth—and then had that child vividly imagine some kind of better or more exciting life. The child is then shown, as a result of this imagining, to be unable to tell which bit of life is physically real and which is only in his or her mind. In other words, imagining things has made this child mad.

Now this is an appallingly irresponsible threat to hold over children. Such writers, who are usually teachers annoyed at finding their pupils addicted to Dungeons and Dragons or folk who equate fantasy with drug abuse, may not be wholly aware of what they are doing; but the fact is that by making this threat—imagination drives you mad—they are closing off for their impressionable readers the main route to sanity. Their grounds for doing this seem to be that what a person has in his or her head does not exist in everyday life.

What a person has in their head is of course rather more than nine-tenths of life. Everything comes to the brain to be sorted out: sensory input, adding and multiplying figures, how to write that memo, and the need to do something about Smith's behavior. All these things pile in at once, together with the crisis on the news, so that it might truly be said that most persons have most of the world in their heads anyway. In order to deal with all these things coming in, the mind has to have the capacity to say, "What if I do so-and-so? Would that solve this problem?" Luckily it has. It has survival value. At a fairly low level it will say, "What if I turn this wretched tap *this* way? Will that make water run?" And this capacity, running right through to the very highest levels of speculation, is imagination. But you can see that from the point of view of survival value it would help enormously if this capacity is exercised with a lot of pleasure and in great hope. This way, the "what ifs" proceed with verve and look forward to a happy solution of the problem. Luckily this is true too. There is—or should be—always a strong element of play connected with the use of the imagination. People "play with ideas" in order to get them sorted out, and when the solution comes, it is often accompanied with wonder and delight. *Eureka!*

The irresponsibility of those writers who claim that imagination drives you mad is twofold. First, they wish to cut off the "what if" process at around the level of turning on taps; and, second they are concerned to make it almost wholly joyless—this regardless of the fact that children are above all people who play, particularly with ideas. And I invite you to think of the kind of person who goes in terror of speculation, and then add to that a horror of delight and excitement. At the best it is a hideously limited person; at the worst, since the capacity is in us all and has to go somewhere, it is someone who gets excitement from "What if I rape this woman? Kill this child? Trundle this whole race to the gas chambers?"

A good children's book, written by someone aware of the responsibilities, tries to follow the pattern of the mind when it is working properly. Very early on it will say "what if?" and proceed with enjoyment and wonder to run through the possibilities resulting from that. It may go to surprising lengths here, and there will be things half heard and only hinted at, possibly, as people's minds have the built-in tendency to respond with excitement to mystery. The "what if" often (though not invariably) entails fantasy, and it is over the element of fantasy that many writers, not only those who say imagination drives you mad, get the wrong idea. They assume that because a thing is "made up" it is unreal or untrue (disregarding the fact that any kind of story except the most factual biography is always "made up"). They see a child reading a fairy story, or constructing his or her own fantasy, and they at once conclude that the child is retreating into make-believe simply to get comfort in a melancholy situation.

Fantasy certainly does provide comfort—and who is not entitled to a little comfort if they can get it? For those who need that, it is the mind's perfect safety valve. But a child reading, say, a fairy story is doing a great deal more. Most fairy stories are practically perfect examples of narratives that fit the pattern of the mind at work. They state a problem as a "what if" from the outset. "What if there were this wicked uncle? That evil stepmother who is a witch? This loathsome monster?" Stated in this way, the problem (parent? bully?) is posed for the widest possible number of people, but posed in a way that enables the reader to walk all round it and see the rights and wrongs of it. This uncle, witch, or monster is a vile being behaving vilely. As these beings will invariably match with an actual person: parent, sibling, schoolfellow, what a child gains thereby is a sort of blueprint of society. Reading the story, he or she is constructing a mental map—in bold colors or stark black-and-white—of right and wrong and life as it *should be*. Turning to the actual parent or schoolfellow, where right and wrong are apt to be very blurred, this child will now have the mental map for guidance.

An important part of this mental map is that the story should usually have a happy ending—or at least an ending where justice is seen to be done to villains and heroes alike. This is again part of life as it *should be*. The mind, as I have said, is programmed to tackle problems, joyfully, with a view to solving them. An ending that suggests—because the writer believes it to be "realistic"—that all you can attain is some lugubrious half measure, means that all children will set out to achieve will *be* that half measure. And, since you rarely achieve all you aim for, what these children will actually get is an even drearier quarter measure, or less. So it is important that the blueprint instructs them to aim as high as possible.

If you bear in mind these responsibilities as you write, you need have no fear that any child will mistake the blueprint for the actual world. Children recognize the proper workings of the imagination when they are allowed to see it and may quite well remember your story, joyfully and gratefully, for the rest of their lives.

The Heroic Ideal: A Personal Odyssey

Children's Literature New England, which was founded in 1987 "to promote awareness of the significance of literature in the lives of children," sponsors annual Summer Institutes on topics of interest to teachers, librarians, critics, and authors. The topic for 1988, presented at the Massachusetts Institute of Technology, was "The Heroic Ideal in Children's Books: Legacy and Promise," for which Diana Wynne Jones was invited to discuss her own work in relation to the theme of "The Heroic Ideal." The following talk was then first published in the journal The Lion and the Unicorn, *Volume 13, Number 1, June 1989 (Johns Hopkins University Press).*

Good evening. It is very kind of you to want me here. I feel very honored to be asked. I am also very lucky to *be* here. I have this travel jinx, you see. Something always goes wrong. This time it manifested early, when the ticket I had booked was mysteriously canceled. . . .

I have subtitled this talk "A Personal Odyssey." Hackneyed though this is, I think you will find before the end that it is relevant in more than one way. My first reason for calling it this is that I have never been able to think of heroes or the heroic without taking them to some extent personally—particularly when I was asked to talk about these topics in relation to my book *Fire and Hemlock.*

Obviously we have to start with some basic definition of the hero and the heroic ideal. Having done that, I'd like to touch briefly on the way I found it to apply to children's books in general, and then go on to *Fire and Hemlock* in particular.

As a child, I was an expert in heroes. The eccentricity of my parents meant that there were almost no books in the house except learned ones, or books they used for teaching—and I was an avid reader. So before I was ten I had read innumerable collections of Greek myths, including Hawthorne's *Tanglewood Tales*, and the unabridged version of the *Morte d'Arthur*, in double columns and tiny print, from which, besides being very puzzled about just what Lancelot was doing in Guinevere's room, I made a mental league table of the Knights of the Round Table: Galahad went even below Kay, as a prig— my favorite was Sir Gawain. I also read *Pilgrim's Progress* and folktales innumerable from all over the world, including all of the Grimm—and also a certain amount of Hans Andersen, but as Andersen reputedly made his stories *up* my parents only admitted him to their house in limited quantities. I then went on to the *Odyssey*, which I preferred to the *Iliad*.

I was saddened to find that, as an eldest child and a *girl*, I was barred from heroism entirely—or was I? I puzzled long over the story of Hero and Leander.[1] Hero did nothing but let her lover do all that swimming. Obviously the girl was a wimp. But she had that *name*. When I was nine, much pleading wrung a frivolous book from my parents—*The Arabian Nights*, bowdlerized. Scheherazade, I was delighted to find, was an elder sister. So even though she did nothing but tell stories (literally for dear life), maybe there was some hope. I found it later in that book, in a tale in which the sultan's jealous sisters tell the sultan that his wife had given birth to a puppy, a kitten, and a log of wood. The log of wood was a girl, and she most heroically set things to rights. Good. It was possible for a girl to be a hero, then.

By this stage, I had acquired a firm mental grasp of what a hero is. A hero, first, is the one you identify with in the story. (Although this is not quite intrinsic to heroism, it *is* a fact that keeps flowing back into the definition and influencing it in all sorts of way. When I later read *Paradise Lost*, I saw at once that Milton had made the mistake of ignoring this.) Otherwise, heroes are brave, physically strong, never mean or vicious, and possess a code of honor that requires them to come to the aid of the weak or incompetent and the oppressed when nobody else will. In addition, most heroes are either related to, or advised by, the gods or other supernatural characters. The gods (even if they only appear in the form of fate) are important for heroism for two reasons. First, they supply a huge extra set of dimensions that put the hero in touch with the rest of the universe and render his actions significant for the whole of humanity. Second, the fact that the god, or gods, are watching over him serves to keep the hero up to his code. If he does chance to behave in a mean or vicious way—or break any of the other rules, for that matter, which are part of the world of that particular story—then he is at once punished and corrected.

But above all, heroes go into action when the odds are against them. They do this knowingly, often knowing they are going to get killed, and for this reason they impinge on a hostile world in a way others don't. When they die, their deaths are glorious and pathetic beyond the average.

Now this probably sums up Hector of Troy, and Hercules, and certainly applies to King Arthur—who has a double supernatural dimension, since he is guided both by Merlin and the Christian God—but I was aware that it did not quite apply to people like Jason; or to Theseus, who coolly abandoned Ariadne on an island; or to the heroes of innumerable folktales who, like the Brave Little Tailor, start their heroic careers with a gross deception; nor, particularly, did it apply to Odysseus. Odysseus, while being billed as every inch a hero, nevertheless conned and tricked and sweet-talked his way all round the Adriatic. This used to worry me acutely. I was quite aware, of course, that Odysseus belonged to the second type of hero—the foxy, tricksy hero, the hero with a brain—but this being the case, was it proper to regard him as a hero at all? For a long time I felt I only had Homer's word for it—that he was only a "hero" in the sense of being the person you identified with in the story. Then it dawned on me that the most heroic thing Odysseus does was never properly explained in my translation of the *Odyssey* (maybe Homer doesn't explain it anyway). This was to have himself tied to the mast with his ears open, while his sailors plugged their ears and rowed past the sirens. My translation represented this simply as a sort of musical curiosity on Odysseus's part: he wanted to hear whatever it was the sirens did. But if you look at this episode from the point of view of the rules of magic, you see at once that it is a calculated attempt to break the sirens' spell. Obviously, if a man could hear their irresistible song and yet resist them, this would destroy the power of the sirens for good. As soon as I saw this, I realized that Odysseus was a real hero.

Around this time, my grandmother gave me a book she had won at the age of six as a Sunday school prize (which she confessed she had chosen for its grand and incomprehensible title). It was called *Epics and Romances of the Middle Ages*. It contained almost every heroic legend from northern Europe that was not part of the Arthurian cycle: the Charlemagne cycle, the stories connected with Dietrich of Berne, the entire Nibelung cycle, including the bits that Wagner did not use, the story of Beowulf and of Wayland Smith, and many more, all illustrated with wonderful woodcuts but otherwise in no way adapted for children. I read it until it fell to pieces. Many of the stories were unutterably sad, particularly those in which the gods took a hand—so much so that, when I later heard the saying "Those whom the gods love die young," I thought that, though thoroughly unfair, it was probably a profound truth.

Out of all this reading I had by now the basic hero story well plotted. Your average hero starts out with some accident of birth, parentage, or person which sets him apart from the rest and often, indeed, causes him to be held in contempt. Even if he seems normal, he has at some point to contend with his own physical nature (as when Beowulf fights the dragon as an old man, or when Odysseus listens to the sirens). Nevertheless, he sets out to do a deed which no one else dares to or at which others have horribly failed. The story often does not state the heroic code that demands this. That only manifests when, along the way, the hero's honor, courage, or plain niceness causes him to befriend some being who will later come powerfully to his aid. (This is one of the places where being a hero overlaps with "being the person in the story with whom we identify," because your hero is after all also your goodie.) After this, he may well make some appalling mistake: as Christian strays from the straight and narrow path, or Siegfried forgets Brunhilde—and this lands him deep in trouble. He can then end tragically. Or he can call in the debt from the powerful being he befriended earlier and, with difficulty, prevail.

So much for the male heroes. But it seemed to me that the women were a mess. All over the world they were either goaded into taking vengeance, like Medea, or Brunhilde in my grandmother's book, or they are passive, like Hero or Andromeda or Christiana. A medievalist I consulted about this opined that Christianity had substantially affected the heroic ideal, especially where women were concerned, by introducing ideas of patience and endurance and the solitary personal struggle against one's own fleshly instincts. But you have only to look at the stories I have cited already to see that all these things are there in pre-Christian heroic stories. There seems to have been an overwhelming acceptance that meekness was the lot of a good woman, until she was goaded into turning evil. In the *Odyssey*, Penelope can only stay good by tricksy passive resistance which doesn't do much to get rid of her suitors. But at least she was using her mind—like her husband.

By this time I was adding the rest of an education to this childhood reading. This involved reading Chaucer's *Canterbury Tales*. And here I found a man writing who was more subtle than Odysseus, *playing* with the kind of narratives I had previously enjoyed, telling them in different styles, delicately deflating the typical hero, altering the balance of the tale with sophisticated touches (not least of which was making some tales almost too appropriate to their tellers, as in "The

Clerk's Tale," where he has the ultimate female wimp). And most ironical and sophisticated of all, he tells the most truly and obviously heroic story—"Sir Thopas"—pretending it is from his own mouth, and makes it an utter joke, a complete send-up. It was as if a super-Odysseus had passed that way, listening with a delicate and caustic ear to the siren song of my childhood stories and breaking their spell entirely. I didn't quite see this at the time, but I *was* left with an uneasy sense that the heroic ideal was awfully banal and naive and straightforward.

When I got to Oxford as a student I came to see that this was how these stories seemed now to *everyone* once Chaucer had done with them. No respectable writer dared for centuries to write a straightforward heroic narrative. If you wanted to, you had to show that your narrative had a purpose that was not heroic; either to strip the illusions from a naïve hero like Candide or Tom Jones (*Tom Jones*, interestingly enough, was based on the *Odyssey*), or to make a moral and social point aside from the story as, say, Dickens does. And the bad things to be conquered had to be reduced to credible everyday targets, like the government. Not surprisingly, by the twentieth century, tricksy Odysseus-like heroes came to be preferred (Raymond Chandler's Marlowe is typical) if you still stubbornly wanted any element of heroism or naive storytelling. And the whole thing reached an apotheosis in a non-heroic non-story by James Joyce, called, appropriately enough, *Ulysses*. In the midst of all this I was very grateful to come across a writer called Edmund Spenser who had managed to retrieve at least six genuine heroes from this mess and put them in a narrative called *The Faerie Queene*. This is an allegory. Even in Tudor times you couldn't do it straight and be thought serious (I may remind everyone that Shakespeare didn't consider his plays serious: his serious stuff was *Venus and Adonis*, where the decoration almost hides the story).

To my joy, one of Spenser's heroes was a woman. Britomart. Now, I haven't space to go into everything I learned from Spenser—things such as how to organize a complex narrative, or how to implant the far-off supernatural into the here and now—but I must pause a bit on what a discovery Britomart was to me. A woman who was a proper hero (this may be a commonplace now, but it certainly was not in the fifties). True, she was also an allegory of Chastity and dressed in armor like a man, but the significant thing to me was that she had a vision of her future lover and set out to do something about it as a hero should. The vision of the future lover is of course a common folktale element. But in *The Faerie Queene* the vision serves as the high ideal, the thing to strive toward, and it is also, in plain human terms, love. And here I began to see just what Christianity had really added to the heroic tradition. It had reinforced the high ideal—for God is love—but heroes have always had that, even if they do not know it when they begin; but, more importantly, Christianity had modified the tradition that a hero is guided by a god or gods. For God watches over everyone. Thanks to Britomart and Spenser, I now knew that every ordinary man or woman *could* be a hero.

But the heroic ideal, I thought, had gone sour. It was not until I had children of my own and through them came to read the children's books I had never had as a child, that I realized that here was the only place where the ideal still existed. It flourished alongside the *story*, since children will not read much without a narrative, in a way that leads me to suspect the two things are closely connected. (Both ideal and story have since begun to flourish again in adult fantasy, but this hardly existed at the time I'm talking of: Tolkien had published only part of *The Lord of the Rings*.)

I think the reason that the heroic ideal had, as it were, retreated to children's books is that children do, by nature, status, and instinct, live more in the heroic mode than the rest of humanity. They naturally have the right naive, straightforward approach. And in every playground there are actual giants to be overcome and the moral issues are usually clearer than they are, say, in politics. I shall never forget the occasion when I was visiting a school as a writer and the whole place suddenly fell into an uproar because the school tomboy—a most splendid Britomart of a girl—had beaten up the school bully. Everything stopped in the staff room while the teachers debated what to do. They wanted to give the tomboy a prize, but decided reluctantly that they had better punish her and the bully too. They knew that if, as a child, you do pluck up courage to hit the bully, it is an act of true heroism—as great as that of Beowulf in his old age. I remember passing the tomboy, sitting in her special place of punishment opposite the bully. She was blazing with her deed, as if she had actually been touched by a god. And I thought that this confirmed all my theories: a child in her position is open to any heroic myth I care to use; she is inward with folktales; she would feel the force of any magical or divine intervention.

On the other hand, it is clear to me that children don't actually *demand* magical events in their reading. They differ as other people do. But it is a fact that all children's books that *endure* are fantasies of some kind. These seem to strike the deepest note.

Anyway, you must picture me in the seventies all set to write according to these discoveries. But there was a snag. In 1970, no boy would be seen dead reading a book whose hero was a girl. Children were then—and still are to some extent—rather *too* inward with the heroic tradition that heroes are male and females are either wimps or bad. Girls will read male-hero stories and (wistfully) identify, but not vice versa, not in 1970 anyway. I took this up rather as a challenge: I love a challenge. For instance, I made David in *Eight Days of Luke* a boy, but I put him in a situation with his relations that both sexes could identify with. In *Power of Three*, I provided Gair with a sister with apparently greater gifts, and the same in *Cart and Cwidder*, and I sneaked a female hero past in *Dogsbody* by telling the story from the dog's point of view. But a desire was growing in me to have a real female hero, one with whom all girls could identify and through that, all persons—a sort of Everywoman, if you like. This is the reason for the name Polly, when I eventually came to write *Fire and Hemlock*. The Greek *poly* means "more than one; many or much," and this, as we shall see, has more than one significance for the book. Another thing I had also long wanted to do was to show children how close to the old heroic ideal they so often are. I'd had a stab at it in *Eight Days of Luke*, by using the days of the week and the Norse gods they were named after to indicate that the big things, the stirring events—the heroic ideal—were as much part of modern everyday life as Tuesday, Wednesday, and Thursday are. But I knew that what I wanted to do *really* was to write a book in which modern life and heroic mythical events approached one another so closely that they were nearly impossible to separate. I also longed to base something on the ballad "Tam Lin,"[2] because that had one of the few Britomart-like heroes in folklore.

Meanwhile, feminism had become a force and was slowly changing the climate of opinion. I looked one day at a picture I own called *Fire and Hemlock*. It is a very peculiar picture, because sometimes there seem to be people in it and sometimes not. And I realized I was about to write the book. If anything sparked it off, it was probably the saying "Those whom the gods love die young." (I often find my books are founded on a saying or proverb. The maddest is *Archer's Goon*, which is founded on a dire pun: "urban gorilla.")[3] But there was another consideration. Janet, the hero of "Tam Lin," behaves throughout like a woman and not like a pseudo man. I wanted a narrative structure which did not simply put a female in a male's place—and, oddly enough, the structure I came up with was no other than that great favorite, the *Odyssey*. I think that at least part of the reason for this is Penelope, who, as I said before, is in her way as tricksy as her husband: she clearly has a *mind*. And Odysseus is a thinking hero. I knew my story was going to be a journey of the *mind* to some extent, both for Polly and for Tom.

Now you must understand that I came to writing *Fire and Hemlock* not only with the *Odyssey* in mind. My head was awash with myths and legends, hundreds of them, and they *all* contribute, but there are three which underlie it principally. The most obvious, of course, are the ballads of "Tam Lin" and "Thomas the Rhymer," seen as parts of a whole. This gives the emotive aspect of the story: that of a foray into the supernatural world of the imagination to rescue the one you love (and this love is seen in the same way as Britomart's:

as being the same as the heroic ideal). As to the second and third underlay, you must bear with me if I hold the third up almost to the end, but the second is the *Odyssey*, of course. The *Odyssey* accounts for the *shape* of the story, and the way it largely had to be told in flashback. For Homer's *Odyssey* starts in what we have to call present-day Ithaca, and when Odysseus himself finally appears, at least half of *his* story is in flashbacks. We find him disentangling himself from Calypso, a possessive nymph, then telling his story to the next people he meets: Nausicaa and her family. This gave me several elements. By association with Scheherazade, it made me see that Polly would be telling the story. It gave me Tom's recent divorce from Laurel. In addition, the witch Circe, when she lets Odysseus go, tells him he has to visit Hades first. This could be her way of saying "I'll see you in hell first!" but, since she is semidivine, it becomes literal truth and means "You'll have to pass through death first." This ties in so wonderfully with the "tithe to hell" that the fairy folk have to pay in "Tam Lin" and gave me the ending of the book. It also gave me an important fact about Laurel: this way she has of bending the truth to her own ends. Put this together with the gift of true speaking the Queen gives Thomas the Rhymer, and you have Laurel's gift to Tom: that everything he imagines will come true. It is not only a hellish gift from a supernatural female; it is the mark of a particularly terrible type of woman—I'm sure we all know at least one such person—a woman who confuses fact and fiction impartially for her own ends. For Laurel is Circe as well.

At the opening of the book, Polly, as well as Tom, is in thrall to this woman. She had to perform a strenuous and truthful act of memory to break that thralldom. This in itself is intended to be an act of heroism akin to Odysseus confronting the sirens. But as a girl, one would expect Polly to be in the role of Penelope—and she is, by and large, in that Tom ranges the world, while Polly stays at home—but there is another hero in the *Odyssey*, Odysseus's son, the young, naive Telemachus. Polly takes the role of Telemachus on herself when she first meets Tom, by naming herself Hero; and this begins a long series of heroic roles that both she and Tom adopt. Polly does this semiknowingly at age ten, because she knows instinctively that her only contact with him that Laurel cannot break is that of the imagination. At ten, children are good at knowing such things. Polly first expresses this knowledge in the naive made-up story of Tan Coul and his friends, with herself as assistant hero. As she grows older and recognizes the complexity of life, the naive make-believe becomes more and more marginal, so that as she searches for her ideal in a new form, she takes on a whole series of heroic roles. She is Gerda in "The Snow Queen," Snow White, Britomart, St. George, Pierrot, Pandora, Andromeda, and Janet from "Tam Lin" and many more, in a sort of overlapping succession.

Tom appears to cling to the role of Odysseus, which he takes on himself with the letter about the giant in the supermarket. Anyone reading that section closely may have noticed that the giant has only one eye, like Polyphemus the Cyclops. But in fact Tom loses that role to Polly around the time he meets his alter ego in the hardware shop and becomes in turn Leander, Kay kidnapped by the Snow Queen, the Knight of the Moon, Artegal, Bellerophon, Prometheus/Epimetheus, Harlequin, Perseus, Orpheus, and of course Tam Lin. He and Polly are continually swapping active and passive roles and sharing the part of Odysseus between them.

Now the way I did this was something else I learned from Spenser. Spenser's allegory ranges from large, overt personifications (pride is a woman called Pride who lives in a palace with a filthy backyard) to relationships so subtle that it is sometimes hard to call them allegory. And at other times the allegorical role is shared about among many characters, each of whom is some aspect of it. I tried to do the same with the heroic personifications and actions of Polly and Tom to find some way, you see, to call on the magical or god-guided aspect of all heroic careers. So sometimes I made the action overtly supernatural and sometimes so close to mundane factualness as to be indistinguishable from everyone's ordinary acts. And sometimes halfway between the two.

In order to organize this, I found that the narrative moved in a sort of spiral, with each stage echoing and being supported by the ones that went before. I had to work very hard in the final draft to make sure that echoes were not repetitions, because at the same time I was establishing another set of resonances that had to be hidden in the same spiral. These were directly concerned with gods and the supernatural. All the female characters are arranged in threes, with Polly always at the center. There are Nina (who is silly), Polly (who is learning the whole time), and Fiona (who is sensible); there are Granny, Polly, and Ivy, old, young, and middle-aged respectively. The first threesome may not strike people as significant, but taken along with the second, I hope it begins to suggest the Three Formed Goddess, diva triforma. Toward the end of the book, Granny takes on the role of Fate and Wisdom quite overtly, shearing fish and explaining the riddle of the ballad of "Tam Lin." Laurel is of course an aspect of this goddess. Consequently, the most important threesome is Laurel, Polly, Ivy. Ivy is the mundane parasitical version of Laurel, very green and clinging—Laurel as the Lorelei in suburbia, if you like. And Polly, make no mistake, is intended to be an aspect of Laurel too—Laurel as Venus and the Fairy Queen—but she is the aspect that appears not in "Tam Lin" but in "Thomas the Rhymer," the good and beloved Queen that Thomas first mistakes for the Virgin Mary and then submits to. The adventures Polly and Tom have together fairly carefully echo this second ballad. I did this not out of perverseness but because of what I had learned from Spenser, through Britomart, of the Christian contribution to the heroic ideal: that the deity is for everyone. There is God *in* all of us as well as *with* us. It follows that the major part of a hero's quest is to locate that deity within and to live up to its standards. And if the hero is female, it also follows that the deity is likely to be female too.

(If anyone wonders about the male characters, yes, they are surreptitiously arranged in the same way.)

You will probably be thinking by now that I had a rich mix and a complex structure to control. This is true. You may also be wondering about the third underlying myth that I mentioned. Before I come to this myth, however, I have to mention another factor. I needed a conscious, organizing overlay to this narrative. As you can probably see by now, it could well have run out of control without one. And, unlike the mass of myths and folktales in the story which came surging into the narrative almost unbidden, this had to be in my conscious control. The organizing overlay I chose was T. S. Eliot's *Four Quartets*. This, on a purely technical level, gave me a story divided into four parts and featuring a string quartet. It also gave me the setting and atmosphere for the funeral Polly gatecrashes in Hunsdon House:

Footfalls echo in the memory
Down the passage which we did not take
Toward the door we never opened
Into the rose garden. [. . .]

Quick, said the bird, find them, find them,
Round the corner. Through the first gate,
Into our first world, shall we follow
The deception of the thrush? [. . .]

So we moved [. . .]
Along the empty alley, into the box circle,
To look down into the drained pool.
Dry the pool, dry concrete, brown edged,
And the pool was filled with water out of sunlight,
And the lotos rose, quietly, quietly [. . .][4]

Chapter 2 is full of echoes from "Burnt Norton." The vases come from here. I chose the poem because it combines static meditation with movement in an extraordinary way, to become a quest of the mind away from the Nothing of spiritual death (Hemlock in my book), toward the fire which is imagination and redemption—the Nowhere of my book. A heroic journey from Nothing to Nowhere is what Polly takes.

Though I was always aware of Eliot's poem as an overlay, I

only, as it were, turned the sound up on it from time to time. I kept it low until the Bristol section after this initial *forte*, where Polly—now in the role of Snow White, Eurydice, and Britomart— is turned out, lost and looking down into the River Avon.

[. . .] I think that the river
Is a strong brown god [. . .]
Trying to unweave, unwind, unravel
And piece together the past and the future,
Between midnight and dawn, when the past is all deception,
The future futureless, before the morning watch
When time stops and time is never ending [. . .]

Where is there an end of it, the soundless wailing [. . .] ?[5]

I turned the sound down on Eliot after that until Polly remembers what it was she did to lose Tom and put them both in Laurel's power. Now here I must remind you of my childhood discovery that all heroes are likely to make one horrible mistake. On the human level, Polly's mistake is to behave like her mother, with possessive curiosity, and spy on Tom. On the mythical level, it throws the story back to the tragedy and failure of Hero and Leander, with which the story started. This unjustified curiosity, which leads the hero to spy on his or her partner, is a motif in dozens of folktales—"East of the Sun and West of the Moon" being the one which is mentioned in the book. Here the young wife sees her husband in his true shape in the night, and loses him. This summary will no doubt remind you all of a much better-known story— the story which is, in fact, the third underlying myth in *Fire and Hemlock*—the story of Cupid and Psyche. Now from long before C. S. Lewis this was a myth of the human soul in search of a beloved ideal, which is what Tom has now become for Polly. Tom in fact has Cupid's attributes, although few people seem to notice. When my British publisher was unable to see this, I simply asked her, "Who is mostly blind and goes to work with a bow?" and she said, "Oh, I *see*!" But, to go back to human terms, and Polly's loss of Tom, people *do* lose sight of their ideals quite often in adolescence and young adulthood—they tend to see life as far too complex and come up with the idea that things are only real and valid if they are unpleasant or boring. The myth of Cupid and Psyche is certainly about this. Or, as Eliot says: "human kind/Cannot bear very much reality,"[6] and the defense is to deny the imagination any reality at all. But the story of Cupid and Psyche is not mentioned in the book on purpose, because Cupid and Psyche are both in their own ways gods, not heroes—and anyway it always seems to me that powerful stories like that one always pull their weight better for only being hinted at.

Once Polly knows she has lost Tom, her quest becomes more urgent. So the narrative moves back to the present time, just as it does in the *Odyssey*, and becomes traditionally heroic in that Polly finds that she can call for help on those she has helped in the past. This includes the one she nearly misses because it is too close to her: Fiona. This sort of thing may be a traditional motif, but it does also happen in real life—you can be very blind to people close to you, both for good or evil. Polly has accepted Seb in the same blind way. But at last, having called in her debts and made her heroic act of memory, Polly sets out to retrieve her mistake. Now here I found I had to leave the tradition represented by Janet in "Tam Lin," because it was precisely by hanging on to Tom and being overcurious that Polly had lost him. Anyway, she has already done her hanging on as a child. It was clear to me that the only redress she could make was the reverse of possessiveness—complete generosity—generosity so complete that it amounts to rejection. She has to love Tom enough to let him go—hurtfully. This is the only way she can harness Tom's innate strength of character, and only when hurting can he summon the full force of the fire—which is to some extent physical passion and to an even greater extent the true strength of the heroic world of the imagination Polly and Tom have built together. But Tom has to do it himself. He has depended on Polly too much.

This is where I turned the sound up again on the *Four Quartets*. Polly has to take the same road that T. S. Eliot describes in *his* quest:

> *In order to arrive there,*
> *To arrive where you are, to get from where you are not,*
> *You must go by a way wherein there is no ecstasy.*
> *In order to arrive at what you do not know*
> *You must go by a way which is the way of ignorance.*
>
> *In order to possess what you do not possess*
> *You must go by the way of dispossession.*
> *In order to arrive at what you are not*
> *You must go through the way in which you are not.*
> *And what you do not know is the only thing you know*
> *And what you own is what you do not own*
> *And where you are is where you are not.*[7]

But I was talking about everyday life as much as Eliot was. I was also following the *Odyssey*, where Odysseus does at last come home, to a partnership and a personal relationship. And I wanted to indicate, however briefly, that though a relationship was possible between Polly and Tom, such a relationship is only likely to be maintained through continuing repeated small acts of heroism from both. This is what I tried to do in the coda—where the structure of the *Odyssey* most remarkably echoes what Eliot has to say:

What we call the beginning is often the end
And to make an end is to make a beginning.
The end is where we start from.[8]

Thank you.

A Talk About Rules

Diana Wynne Jones was a popular speaker at science fiction and fantasy events. In 1995 she was invited to appear as the guest of honor at Boskone, the annual convention run by the New England Science Fiction Association (NESFA) in Boston, Massachusetts.

Diana's 1995 collection Everard's Ride *was published by NESFA Press as part of its program to honor special guests. The following is her guest of honor address at Boskone 1995.*

I am very glad to be here at Boskone. I really thought I wasn't going to make it. First I didn't seem to be able to stop having to go to hospital—there will be a book before long giving my frank opinion of most doctors, which is not high—and then there were the airline tickets. Reasonably enough, my ticket was in the name of Diana Wynne Jones and Chris Bell's called her Chris Bell.[1] The trouble was, both our passports were in our married names, which are not the same. But I had been there before. You have to go to the office and argue, I told Chris blithely. The airline won't let you travel on a ticket that isn't the same as your passport, so you get them to change the name on the ticket. So we took the morning off from working on the *Encyclopedia of Fantasy* for John Clute[2] and went to the office and asked them to change our names on the tickets. "Can't be done," they said. Nonsense, said we, and we argued. We persuaded. We talked for half an hour. And it still couldn't be done. The Rules forbade it on that kind of ticket. Half an hour later, it still couldn't be done and we gave up and came home. But Chris refused to be beaten and tried another way round. She rang the passport office and asked if they could change our passports instead. "Oh yes, easily," they said.

Well, it wasn't actually *easy*. We had to order new passports and fill in forms that didn't have a section for what we wanted to do, but it got done. And all along the absurdity of it was exasperating—that it was easier to change your passport than an airline ticket! Rules! The whole thing about Rules increasingly exasperated me. While I worked on the encyclopedia, I kept discovering Rules in fantasy that had no business being there. Camels going through the eyes of needles in all directions. Or failing to get through, or getting stuck halfway. So many things you weren't supposed to do. So out of this exasperation I have decided to talk a bit about the Rules people insist on in various forms of writing.

There are a lot of Rules and they keep changing. Nobody knows who does the changing—everyone blames somebody else: publishers, librarians, teachers, reviewers, writers themselves, readers. But it is a fact you have to live with if you write, particularly if you write fantasy of any sort. There are Rules, and people—some people somewhere—keep changing the Rules and moving the goalposts. And when the goalposts are moved to wherever people want them at that moment, they look as if nothing will ever move them again.

When I started writing (writing with a view to getting published, that is), back in the very late 1960s, the goalposts looked fixed. They seemed immovable. There were Rules for everything, most of which had been in place since my own childhood.

For a start, the Rules said fantasy was strictly for kids. The only known fantasy for adults was *The Lord of the Rings*—and you should just imagine the trouble reviewers who thought of themselves as sane and adult had handling that in the fifties! There was this man—he seemed to get stuck with reviewing Tolkien, when he had far rather review what the Rules said were mainstream books (these were about angry young men at newly founded universities). And this man had been very patient with Book I of *The Lord of the Rings*, very patient, and accepted the fact that Hobbits, Elves, and Dwarves might wish to set out on foot in winter in order to destroy a ring. He wasn't sure, but he thought it was an allegory, and that made him much happier: it wasn't really about Hobbits, see, but something else entirely, possibly angry young men at newly founded universities. Then he got Book II. And Ents. Walking trees—he just could not take walking trees! I never saw how he reviewed *The Return of the King*—possibly he didn't, possibly he gave up journalism. It was just too much to be asked to read something that was properly only for children.

Now, to be fair, this Rule that fantasy is only for kids represents a huge advance on the Rules in my mother's day. When my mother was a small girl, around 1908–9, she was addicted to fairy stories—any story that began "Once upon a time" and went on to talk about princes and princesses and magic. These, in those days, were so much despised that you could almost only get them as little booklets printed on cheap paper and sold for two coppers at the slush end of the news agent's. But she saved up her pennies and she bought one booklet a month—and read and reread them avidly. Until the day her father caught her reading them. He was furious. He punished her. Then he took all the booklets away and burned them. He said they were not about real facts and so they would destroy her mind, and he forbade her ever to read such things again. And she obeyed him. He died soon after, which kind of fixed it for her.

I never met my grandfather—for which I am rather glad. I don't think we'd have got on. And I have often thought that his attitude, and the attitude of my mother's generation that received and obeyed the prohibition of their parents—is not unconnected with the fact that these two generations were responsible for two world wars.

Be that as it may, things had loosened up a little by the time I was a child. Thanks largely to E. Nesbit, fantasy was established firmly as kids' business. My mother, of course, was carefully shielded from Nesbit, and she took care to shield me. I only read Nesbit when I was an adult. But the goalposts had moved all the same. My generation was allowed fantasy, even magic, provided it was simply improbable. This means talking animals in situations that were harmless and jolly. This meant Winnie-the-Pooh—but not the last chapter of *The House at Pooh Corner*, because that chapter began to impinge on serious things like love and memory and the value of fantasy, and everyone knew the Rule: fantasy is for children and therefore not serious. It must not affect the child who reads it in any way. I was forbidden to read that last chapter—or not only forbidden: told that it was—well—not quite nice, that it was boring, that I wouldn't understand it, that it was silly. This is the way that the Rules most often get themselves enforced. In the same way, I was allowed *The Wind in the Willows* but prohibited from reading the chapter titled "The Piper at the Gates of Dawn" or the chapter about the old Sea Rat. Those were about numen and mystery and poetry, for heaven's sake! And highly undesirable. Needless to say I sneaked and read these things, feeling both guilty and bewildered.

But I never got to read the Narnia books, which were coming out all the time I was in my early teens. They were withheld as not quite nice too because they were about something—and hush! The Something was God.

Actually I knew all about books that were About Something. Nine-tenths of such few books we had, my sisters and I, were about instructing you morally, thinly disguised as a story. We saw through that instantly, and heartily despised this practice. We had the longest shelf in our bookcase devoted to such books—it was labeled by me in large letters: GODDY BOOKS—and none of us read them more than once. I suppose I should be grateful that C. S. Lewis was withheld because he would certainly have gone straight into that shelf and there is rather more to him than that. But I am not grateful. Not in the least.

This illustrates another major Rule of that time: that fantasy was to be used only to instruct you morally. People really didn't think it was right that kids should just enjoy a book. It had to teach you something too. By the time I was ready to start writing (for publication, that is), folk were a bit leery of God. God was too heavy or something. Most books preached on about how to Do Good in Community, with a sideways glance at How to Be a Better Person. Or they were books about Growing Up. You know. Growing Up was putting away games and fun and above all anything that smacked of Let's Pretend, and was going out into the Real World a grimmer and a duller person.

You cannot imagine how my kids hated that kind of book— or perhaps you can. Nobody likes to feel got at. Very outspoken my kids were about it too, far worse than my sisters and I were. "Why can't books be funny?" they wanted to know. But there was a Rule around at that time that fantasy in particular was not funny. Funny books were very slender. They were labeled "Humor"—for humor, read "Whimsy." That was the only kind you were supposed to have.

These Rules—that you shouldn't enjoy fantasy and that it should give moral instruction—seem to me to have been made up to excuse the writing of fantasy by people who still felt guilty over the prohibitions of my grandfather's generation. They made it All Right, you see, these Rules. Then somebody (mysterious unknown somebody) came up with an even better Rule. This was that children's books were allowed only to deal with Problems. You took a social problem—parents divorcing, mother a nymphomaniac, father drunk or gay (or both), brother on drugs, child crippled or bullied, a moron in the family, epilepsy, poverty (but only if you were stuck for a problem; poverty was too easy)—and you wrote about this Problem in stark, distressing terms. Then—this is the Rule—you gave it to the child with that problem to read. The child was supposed to delight in the insight and to see his own parents (or brother or disability) as a joyful challenge.

This Rule is still in force today. People truly believe in it— and this is despite the obvious question that Jill Paton Walsh once asked: if you were divorcing, what would you think of the person who made you read *Anna Karenina*? But it didn't truly bother me at that time. I had been looking for ways to break all these Rules without appearing to break them. And this problem Rule gave me a way to slide in. I sat down and wrote *Eight Days of Luke* (which was actually written about a year before anything else I had published). In it the boy, David, had problems—not very acute ones by the standards of the Rule, but they would pass. And I knew the problems were real, because David's relations were real people I had had to live with one unending school term, and I couldn't wait for the chance to make them funny as well as horrible.

My newly acquired agent sent the book to the Oxford University Press. Who sent it straight back again on the grounds that children were not allowed to strike matches.[3]

Ouch. I had forgotten all the other minor Rules. These were:

1. That children in books were not allowed to do or think anything a nineteenth-century child was forbidden.

2. Adults in children's books could do no wrong, unless they were baddies, in which case a dutiful writer must get them killed off at the end of the book, even if they had only stolen the silver spoons.

3. That adults did not have characters—although you were allowed one comic adult per book on condition he/she spoke dialect and called the central child "Master" or "Miss." I hate dialect. It gets in the way. If there is a need for dialect, you can render it quite easily by reproducing the rhythm of that form of speech. Then you don't need to bother with silly spellings.

4. You did not raise the nasty matter of sex, however indirectly. The elderly dragon lady at OUP had spotted the shocking fact that Astrid has an affair with Thor and put my agent through the third degree about it, demanding to know if that meant David was gay. This Rule lasted surprisingly long.

In the late seventies, the writer of *Watership Down* offered in my hearing to take a man outside and punch his face in for daring to include the words "children's books" and "sex" in the same sentence.

5. Above all, you must not allow any magic in the book to become serious. It must not affect or change the life of the child protagonist. This last Rule, oddly enough, made *Eight Days of Luke* extremely hard to get published. When I did find a publisher, they postponed the book for two years because they were afraid it would be accused of Satanism. Then they gave it an extremely lurid cover because they thought it was so controversial.

This was in the late sixties, early seventies. Fortunately for me, around this time the place filled with people who were either breaking the Rules too, or at least making sure they got thoroughly stretched. Some of these had been going a while— Joan Aiken, Leon Garfield, Susan Cooper, Peter Dickinson, John Christopher. Others, like Robert Westall, Ann Lawrence, Penelope Farmer, Penelope Lively, Tanith Lee, got into print about the same time as I did. There were many others. The Rules couldn't seem to stand up against such numbers. For a while, they just went away.

Probably this was because the time was ripe, but I don't think that was the whole of it. There was fertilization from elsewhere. For a long while, another form of fantasy had been growing and flourishing outside the Rules, mostly in America. It was called science fiction. The science part was because it based its fantasy on proven scientific facts such as that Mars and Venus are habitable by humans, that galactic empires are possible, or that faster-than-light travel could happen any day now. I had been an avid reader of SF for years, and I can vouch for the degree of cross-fertilization in my case. Science fiction is full of ideas (not all of them proven and scientific)—fine new ideas—and moreover the best of it is consummately well written. I would take a bet that if we were to take a scientific time trip to the future and go where they are studying twentieth-century literature, we'd find the professors ignoring so-called mainstream fiction and concentrating on the wonders performed by science fiction. But, from my point of view, probably the main and most liberating fact about SF is that the Rules were quite different. In fact, in the early period— the 1940s—the Rules were changing once a week, to the extent that you could sometimes think they didn't exist.

It needed something like that to help set the goalposts way, way back—to justify long, inventive fantasies that adults could also enjoy without worrying that it was against the Rules. There were films and TV that helped the process (*Star Trek* and *Doctor Who*). And the result was that, in the general loosening of the Rules, adult fantasy suddenly took off too. This delighted me. I read that just as avidly. And I hope no one will close their minds to the enormous amount of cross-fertilization there has been. Children's fantasy has been called a ghetto, and it is in its way, but it's a ghetto where you can do anything you want—or you could in the early eighties. There were adults reading and writing across all the three kinds I have talked about, and taking in horror on the way. And there were kids growing up on the new children's books, and then taking to the adult kind in their teens, and ending up reading and writing themselves of whatever came along. Everyone was joyfully leapfrogging about.

From my point of view, there was suddenly no need to watch in case I did something terrible like having kids strike matches. I really could do anything. It was just lack of time that stopped me trying. Every book I wrote was a new kind of experiment and nobody minded. There were only a few principles I knew I had to keep to—principles, not Rules—and the first of these was and is: you have to be responsible. By that I don't mean not having kids strike matches. I mean that somewhere, somewhen, someone is going to read your book at a time when such things stick for life. And you have to make it the kind of book that is worth remembering that vividly for that long. You have to make it an experience in its own right. That's the first principle.

My second principle is that you have to make your book follow, as far as possible, the natural movement of the human brain, when that brain is working as it is meant to work. This is not easy. Books have a way of doing their own thing. But what it amounts to is that the human brain really truly revels in solving problems. And the brain uses and needs emotions as part of the problem solving. It likes to do the solving by saying "What if . . . ?" and (sort of) fantasizing about what would happen if such and such were the case. It needs to overcome difficulties on the way to the solution—the difficulties can be intellectual, or terrors, or sadness, or anything else—but the brain also needs to come up with an idea that says "Hey! This is the way to go!" That is not saying that a happy ending is necessary, but it does mean the brain wants to say, "Let's think laterally if possible. Let's be surprised!" I love surprises. I surprise myself quite often.

There are one or two smaller principles too. Such as, you

can be funny and serious at the same time, and should be. Your brain likes to laugh. Have you noticed how many jokes are pocket fantasies? What is yellow and dangerous? Shark-infested custard.

Then there is the language you use. My feeling is that you ought to be able to say anything in simple words. And as a rider to that, those words ought to reproduce the thing you are trying to convey without relying on the way everyone else had tried to say it previously.

Those are my principles. I have one or two others, such as a hatred of long descriptions that don't add to the narrative, but I won't go on about that. Think of me having a great time (except no day was long enough) writing and experimenting away.

And then the goalposts moved back in again.

There seems to be something about the human race that makes it crave Rules. Or maybe it's a quirk of the human brain that it gets frightened if it's allowed too much exercise. Anyway, people seem to get agoraphobia without the goalposts huddling on top of them. They don't know where they are unless they can point to the Rule for what they are doing. I met a fine example when I was giving a talk in a library once. This scholarly looking bearded man, healthy, upstanding, middle-aged, asked me politely how long my books were. "How long?" I said, a bit bewildered. "In pages," says he helpfully. "Oh," I say, "not very long. I find it hard to get above two hundred pages mostly." "In that case," he answered regretfully, "I can never read your books. My Rule is that I never read anything above one hundred and twenty pages long." Naturally enough, I asked him why. And he couldn't say. He just turned pale and shook a bit. It was as if the wide open spaces of those eighty pages beyond his personal goalposts made him truly unhappy.

They got unhappy in this kind of way in the mid-eighties. They made the goalposts out of Genre.

Genre has been around as a convenient idea for a long time. A friend of mine has written a scholarly book in which he makes of Genre a delicate and beauteous thing, with an ancestry that goes ever so far, far back. But I prefer to think of it as a notion mostly developed in the 1920s, whereby publishers and reviewers could point people at the kind of thing each person most liked to read. It was a useful system of tagging stuff. They sorted books into Detective, Thriller, Children's, Ghost, Horror, and so on. And naturally they went on to do the same with the newer things like SF and Fantasy. Everyone in, say, the seventies knew what Genre was. The Science Fiction Genre was fantasy where you traveled on a spaceship; Fantasy was SF where you traveled on a flying carpet; and Horror was both of those in the claws of a demon. And nobody gave it too much thought. Until the writers themselves began believing in Genre. And it became a Rule.

And the Rule states that each Genre has absolute boundaries which Must Not Be Crossed. And the Rules add that if you do cross these boundaries, what you have written will be called "Not Really Horror"—"or Science Fiction or whatsoever"— and nobody will want to know.

The result is—I hope only temporarily—a fair old disaster for all kinds of writing. Particularly a disaster for the kinds I have been talking about. Each has hunkered down inside what it believes to be its own boundaries, and inside those boundaries the Rules for Being Of That Genre have proliferated and hardened until almost no one can write anything original at all. But the Rules say that if you write the same book all the time, that's okay. That's fine. That's Genre.

Horror obviously comes out of it best, because its Rules have always been most obvious—be as horrifying as possible. Be fiendishly supernatural. But it is so grandly jealous of its Genre that it has demanded sole use of certain topics. While Chris and I were working on *The Encyclopedia of Fantasy*, there were depressingly frequent occasions when we said "Oh, that's a horror entry. We have to leave that for *The Encyclopedia of Horror.*" You are almost not allowed to include demons because they aren't fantasy any more. And after *Aunt Maria* was published, I got stick from reviewers for writing what should be horror topics—not because the book might frighten children of tender years or anything like that. No. I had Crossed the Boundaries of Genre. I had broken the Rules. Oh tut!

Children's fantasy is in a way better off, because it has contrived to maintain within itself all the various Genres. But you have to keep them rigidly separate when you write. Or else. But here again the outer boundaries are being jealously guarded and defined. You so easily acquire the stigma of being "Not Really." The Rules are growing in number and rigidity again to make sure of that. The Rule that You Must Instruct has been brushed off and refurbished and is now linked to the ecology. You are supposed to go on about trees and ozone and things. Worthy subjects no doubt, but you do think about Hansel and Gretel and their father who was a poor woodcutter busily destroying the rain forests? Are Hansel and Gretel now "Not Really"? Or does their father get excused on the grounds that he never made any money at it? Seriously, the ecology

Rule has so far overridden the earlier Rules about instruction and behavior that you could get a book about an otherwise admirable person who chanced to cut down a tree and he would be a baddie. He would have to be, well, not killed anymore—because that's "Not Really" either—but put in prison. Prison is becoming "Not Really" too, so I don't know what you do with the wretch. Anyway, you see the problems. And a further major Rule has recently been invented. This is that you must not tax the mind of any person under sixteen. It has been decided (by someone somewhere somehow for some reason) that people under sixteen can only attend to anything for slightly under five minutes—and less than that if more than one thing is going on at one time. So you can't have your baddie cut down more than one tree or the readers go on overload.

Here's an odd thing. Less than five years ago it was a truth generally acknowledged that anyone who could follow the plot of *Doctor Who* could follow anything. Maybe that was going a bit far the other way, but . . . anyway, most adults professed to like their books simpler than children did.

Well, now they get them that way. The Rules have made sure of that. SF—which used to be spiced with imagination, weird philosophy, fantasy, and horror—is now only supposed to deal with ideas that are scientifically probable. Facts, facts, facts, Mr. Gradgrind[4], and a minimal story to frame them. About the only not-quite-yet proven things the Rules permit are that people can live for at least four hundred years, and people will live with a great deal of gloom. There may be a Rule that gloom is scientific. To be sure, you can flirt with more fantastic notices, even cheerful ones, but then you are in a watertight sub-Genre called Space Opera. And the hatches are sealed between. If you want to do anything else on these general lines—and thank goodness there are some who do—you are "Not Really" and have to call yourself Speculative Fiction (and this shows signs of getting a Genre and Rules of its own too).

As for adult fantasy, the Rules have become so detailed and so firm that there really is the same book being written over and over again. The Rules here state that there are two kinds of fantasy only. Comic fantasy and high fantasy. Comic fantasy hasn't quite got its Rules in order yet, I'm glad to say, except the Rule that states you must not stray over into high. High. Well. Basically you have this large empty map. The Rules state that no fantasy is complete without a map. Your protagonist will then travel to every spot on this map—except, for some reason, most major cities marked—visiting as he/she goes such stock people as the marsh dwellers, the desert nomads, the Anglo-Saxon Cossacks, and so on, frequently collecting magical bric-a-brac on the way and putting in obligatory time as a slave somewhere. At the end of this tour, he/she will either return to the mundane world through a portal or be crowned a monarch, whichever is appropriate. This of course will take three books to happen in.

Again there are notable exceptions, but they are now "Not Really," naturally, and are showing signs of joining Speculative. Rules may well soon follow.

Now, I ask you, why is everyone doing this to themselves? I really would like to know. You can buy me a drink while you tell me. Some of you may want to tell me that this is not so. But I tell you that from where I stand the whole Rule system exists. It exists and is without reason. Worse—it is stultifying. There is less and less cross-fertilization. There is less and less possibility of anyone thinking of something new to write about. Imagination? Forget it. We have the Rules instead. We have Genre.

What, in conclusion, I should like to point out is that the whole thing is back to front. Rules and Genres are not the absolutes they have become. They are humanity's way of trying to make sense and order of what they see. What you start with is the somewhat confusing scene you see. Then you can (if you are insecure enough) discover or invent Rules that it seems to follow. But what you see is the first thing. And what you see should be a magnificent, whirling, imaginative mess of notions, ideas, wild hypotheses, new insights, strange action, and bizarre adventures. And the frame that holds this mess is the story. You really should only need the story as the Rules that govern this particular mess. The story is the important thing. But we are now back to front, because what people have found in previous stories are being used to govern what should be in future ones. And this is ridiculous.

I would like to leave you with Prometheus's statement from *The Homeward Bounders*, which still seems to me to be the truth of this matter. Jamie asks Prometheus what the Rules are, and Prometheus, chained to his rock, gets almost angry for the first time in their conversation. "There are no rules," he says. "There are no rules, only principles and natural laws."

Thank you.

Answers to Some Questions

Diana originally titled this piece "The Profession of Science Fiction." It was first published in Foundation: The International Review of Science Fiction, *No. 70, Summer 1997.* Foundation *is the journal of the UK-based Science Fiction Foundation.*

Anyone who writes fantasy tends to be asked why they do it. Anyone who does it for children is liable to be asked all sorts of other things in addition, everything in fact from how much money you earn to "When did you write your first book?" I thought I would use this opportunity to answer some of the questions I am most commonly asked and, I hope, in the course of it, the question I have never been asked and which strikes me as the really important one. This is: "What do you think you're trying to do?" That is a question I ask myself quite often and find very hard to answer.

The most frequent question of all is almost as hard to answer: "Where do you get your ideas?" It is almost unfailingly asked by unfortunate people of ten to thirteen years old whose teacher has made them do a project. My very favorite form of it was asked by a twelve-year-old: "Where do you get your ideas, or do you think of them for yourself?"

Very shrewdly put, because some part of an idea, if it is going to start a book developing, has to relate to something outside me, even if I don't exactly *get it* from this outside thing. It has to be a creative mix of interior and exterior notions. The best ideas conflate three or more things, rather in the way dreams do, or the minds of very small children. A very good example is a baroque muddle of my own when, at the age of five, I was evacuated to the Lake District early in the Second World War. I was told I was there because the Germans were about to invade. Almost in the same breath, I was warned not to drink the water from the washbasin because it came from the lake and was full of typhoid germs. I assumed that "germs" was short for "Germans." Looking warily at the washbasin, I saw it was considerately labeled "Twyford,"[1] clearly warning people against germ warfare. Night after night, I had a half-waking nightmare in which Germans (who had fair, floating hair and were clad in sort of cheesecloth Anglo-Saxon tunics) came racing across the surface of the lake to come up through the plug hole of this washbasin and give us all Twyford.

This has all the elements of something needed to start a book off, the magical prohibition, the supernatural villains, the beleaguered good people, and for good measure, the quite incommunicable fears children have. I prefer my ideas to have this last element if possible. All children have these inexpressible fears and believe also that they are the only one who does. It is very hard for any other medium but a book to handle these fears, but a book can do it easily, since it is by its nature a private matter, like the fears are. And I suppose it is my good fortune that the world suddenly went mad when I was five years old and imprinted the memory of this (and other) muddles on my mind. When I consider how the ideas for most of my books came to me, I see they came as versions of this kind of conflation. All this one lacked was for me, as writer, to go on and say "What if this were true?" and then try to compose the story that conquers the fears in their own terms—which is something you have to be an adult to do. As a child, I *knew* it was true but could do nothing about it.

Another common question which naturally follows on from here is "Do you plan your book out before you start it?" and my answer is always unequivocally, "No, that kills it dead." This always shocks teachers, who are accustomed to telling their pupils that you can't write that way. But I am afraid I do, because I have to, for the sake of the book itself. A book, for me, is ready to be written when all the conflated elements of the initial idea come together to produce three things. First, and most important, is the taste, quality, character—there are no words for it—nature of the book itself, a sort of flavor that has to start on the first page and will dictate the tone and style and the words used, as well as the sort of action to take place. This flavor, quality, is something I have painfully discovered you have to be utterly true to. Any attempt to coax it to be different, as planning in detail might, is a sort of taxidermy, when what you need is the living animal.

The second factor acts as counterweight or control. I know how the story begins and how it ends, and I also know, in great detail, at least two scenes from somewhere in the middle. When I say great detail, I probably mean precise, total detail. Colors, speech, actions, and exactly where the furniture or outdoor scenery are and what they look like, are all with me vividly and ineradicably. Often I am quite mystified as to how you get from the beginning to one of these scenes, or from one of them to the end. Part of the joy of writing is finding out. And I deliberately do not ask more when I start to write, so that the book has room to keep its flavor and pursue its own logic. In fact, I suspect that some of the *ideas* that people doing projects are asking about are things that have happened because the story is pursuing its own logic. I know I have many times been surprised—and frequently surprised into laughing out loud and, on one occasion, laughing so hard I fell off the sofa where I was writing.

The third factor is impossible to describe in any other way than that a book (often not the one I thought I was about to write) shouts to me that it is ready and needs to be written NOW. Then I have to find paper—and there are never any pens—and do it at once. I write longhand for the first draft, because I find that easiest to forget. I do not, at this stage, wish to be interrupted by self-conscious notions of myself writing a book.

The planning stage, in a *Looking-Glass* way, comes next. I do a very meticulous second draft that sometimes involves rearranging and recasting, in which I examine every word and its relation to other words, then every sentence and every paragraph, and then all of these in relation to the whole book. I want a clear and harmonious whole. And I want people reading it to be in no doubt of what is happening. It is probably most important to be clear if the things happening are funny.

If this gives the idea that I am an inspirational writer, that is true. But inspiration is only about half the story. For a start, it took me ten or more years to learn how to tap that inspirational level of mind. How to do this is certainly different for everyone. For me, it was when I began understanding that I had at least to start with a dreamlike conflation—like that of

Germans giving you Twyford—and that I could trust some level of my brain to do this. I have to spend a lot of time sitting waiting for it to happen. Often I have the makings of a book sitting in my head maturing for eight or more years, and when I am considering that collection of notions I am aware of exercising a great deal of conscious control, trying the parts of it round in different ways, attempting to crunch another whole set of notions in with it to see if that makes it work, and so on. But I do not feel in total control, doing this. It is more as if I am moving the pieces of idea around until they reach a configuration from which I, personally, can learn. Practically every book I have written has been an experiment of some kind from which I have learned. It does not seem to me that I have the right to foist a story on people, most of whom are children who should be learning all the time, unless I am learning from it too.

"But why do you write for children?" is the usual adult response to this—as if, finding I have gone to all this trouble, they think I go on to waste it on people who are immature. That is a question requiring several layers of answer. Some of them I am going to postpone to the end. For now I will say that I was not at first aiming to write only for children and have never considered what I write exclusively for them. Indeed, one of the reasons for my doing things the way I do was the spectacle of my husband falling asleep whenever he attempted to read aloud from almost any children's book available in the late sixties. It seemed to me that he and other adults deserved to have something to interest them if they were prepared to read a bedtime story, and that people of all ages were more likely to be interested in something I myself found vividly interesting. My eldest son was continually and wistfully asking for books that were funny. For myself, I was bored writing anything else but fantasy and, when I started to write in earnest, there were simply no other openings for fantasy except with a children's publisher. And there seemed to be something in the air, pushing people to write for children. When I was a student at Oxford, both C. S. Lewis and J. R. R. Tolkien were lecturing there, Lewis magnificently and Tolkien badly and inaudibly, and the climate of opinion was such that people explained Lewis's children's books by saying "It's his Christianity, you know," as if the books were the symptom of some disease, while of Tolkien they said he was wasting his time on Hobbits when he should have been writing learned articles. Neither of them ever lectured on their secret hobbies. And yet somehow not only I but numerous others such as Penelope Lively, Jill Paton Walsh, and Penelope Farmer, to name just a few—and none of us knew one another there—all went away and produced books for children. Strange of us, really.

"Then what made you want to be a writer?" is the next question and much easier to answer. It was not a case of wanting. In the middle of one afternoon, at the age of eight, I knew I was going to be a writer—as if the future had tapped me on the shoulder and pointed out quite calmly what I was going to be doing for the next fifty years. Since I was wildly dyslexic, my parents roared with laughter, and even I realized that I needed training. At the age of ten I remember sitting sadly, thinking that there was something wrong with my imagination. I just could not see the scenery and actions in the few books I had anything like as vividly as their writers obviously had. My mind's eye was all blurred. But despite this, I wrote my first book about two years later and discovered that if you were writing a thing, it came clear. It had to. In order to write about any event, you had to make the event clear to yourself.

I wrote this book because my sisters and I had barely any books. The obvious explanation was the war and the shortage of paper, but it was not the real reason. Mostly it was my father's intense meanness with money. He had been a schoolteacher, so he did admit that children ought to have books, and he salved his conscience by buying the entire works of Arthur Ransome, which he kept locked in a high cupboard and dispensed to us, one between the three of us, every Christmas. I was at university by the time we got *Great Northern?* The third reason was censorship by my mother. She had been trained as a child to believe that fantasy was bad for you and that you should only read a book if it was literature. Luckily for us, the Alice books, *Winnie-the-Pooh*, *The Wind in the Willows*, and *Puck of Pook's Hill* qualified, but nearly everything else did not (*Puck of Pook's Hill* saddened me, much as I enjoyed it. There seemed no point in the children in it learning all these wonderful things if they were made to forget once they had). In addition, I was allowed Greek myths, Malory's *Morte d'Arthur* in the original language and a massive book called *Epics and Romances of the Middle Ages* which my grandmother had won as a Sunday school prize. I also read most of Conrad, which I thought of as verbose adventure stories, and conceived a hearty dislike of the narrator Marlow—the prig would keep describing things instead of getting on with the story. My sisters, who did not like literature in this form so much, were much worse off. My first full-length book was written to read out to them in their book starvation. It was very bad, but they clamored so much for the next episode that I went on writing and thus found I could finish writing a whole ten-exercise-book-long narrative. I suppose I should be grateful to my parents both for causing me to get writing and for the fact that I came to most other children's classics as a delighted adult, when my own children read them, but obstinately, I am not. Not one whit.

"Do you put much of your childhood in your books?" No, very rarely, for two reasons. First because it would be what I always derisively call "a loving re-creation of childhood"— an adult exercise in nostalgia—where children are entirely forward looking. It does not interest most children in the least what their parents or grandparents did as children—most of them would be surprised to find that the adults they know ever *were* that young. They have no historical sense and can't wait to grow up. I think it is this futureward orientation that I find most congenial about children's minds; but a lot of substandard didactic writers do nevertheless insist on writing books about "growing up." When I meet these kind of books, or those of the "loving re-creation" school, I must confess that I reach for my gun. This is absolutely not the right approach.

The second reason I do not put my own childhood into things I write is that it was mostly too bizarre to use directly. In addition to the general madness of wartime and the eccentricity of my parents (my father's meanness, for instance, caused him at one point to obtain me three lessons in Greek in exchange for my sisters' much-loved doll's house), there was the village where I spent the years from nine to adulthood. *Everyone* there was peculiar in some way, singly and interactively. Some people behaved like witches, other people frankly admitted that they were. A man sat in the church porch who said he went mad at full moon. The vicar preached Communism from the pulpit and people came in hobnailed boots from Great Dunmow specially to walk out in the sermon. There were passionate folklorists, hand weavers, adherents of William Morris, persons who were hippies long before hippies existed, and the girls were always getting pregnant. Someone made life-size working models of elephants. Everyone danced in the streets. German prisoners of war mingled with Polish displaced persons and London evacuees to cause a profusion of eccentricity, shortly augmented by the American airbase nearby. Also nearby was a colony of painters, one of whom did antivivisection naive art, and there were strange folk in outlying farmhouses either getting into debt or keeping boa constrictors and dragon lizards in their attics. The as-it-were conference center which my parents ran added to the general peculiarity, both by importing mad musicians and insane actors and causing myself and my sisters to have to live, as one of the guests described it, "in the margins of a dirty postcard," and by employing a succession of local eccentrics. The gardener there had had a vision on the road to a nearby village, Sampford, in which an angel descended to him and told him always to go to chapel and never to join a trade union.

It was only as a student that I realized that these things were not normal. It has taken me all these years to realize that some of the episodes from this lunatic place make very good stories in their own right; but I shall write them primarily for adults, not for children.

But naturally a childhood like that has to be an influence somewhere. In a way, it lies behind everything I write, in that it has to expand your notions of what is credible and make you readier to believe that extremely odd things *can* happen. Enough of it was hilariously funny, too, to make me aware that humor is essential when things get wild. Oddly, the most insanely funny things were nearly always part of something intensely tragic (for instance, when my father lay dying to the sound of young men beating on our door shouting "We want women!")[2] and I came to the conclusion that the two states are, in fact, closely related and that fantasy—the times things go wild—is the connecting factor. For all this, the perpetual riot and mayhem in which we lived then was always like a brick wall cutting me off from anything truly imaginative. Life was too restless and pragmatic to give one a chance to think. I got glimpses of what was cut off from books. Among my few books was a volume of Arthur Mee's *The Children's Encyclopaedia* with a picture in it of a girl learning to play the piano. The piano was up against a brick wall, beyond which was a wonderful garden to which the girl had access only through strenuous endeavor. I actually cried when I first saw it, not only because my mother had forbidden music lessons on the grounds that I was not musical, but because it seemed exactly to describe my situation—and I could see no way to penetrate that wall.

The queer thing was that the conference center did in fact possess just such a garden. It was known as the Other Garden. The garden that everyone saw was pleasant enough, though somewhat boringly laid out around a large square of grass. The Other Garden was quite different. It was like that garden in folktales where the king has counted all the apples. It was across a road, walled away from everyone, a blaze of manicured lawn leading to a tunnel of roses ending in an inlaid wood summerhouse, where espalier apple trees of types that are no longer grown surrounded plots of fruit, flowers, and vegetables.

The bees had a plot of their own because they did not get on with the visionary gardener. Something about this garden caused him to build little shrinelike places in the wall niches and ornament them with posies and old Venetian glass.

My father would not let anyone go there. He kept the large, old key to it in his pocket and it often took several days of pleading to get him to release it to me, grudgingly, for an hour or so. When I got there I simply wandered, in utter bliss. I talked to the bees, who never once stung me, although they pursued the visionary gardener once a week, in clouds, and occasionally turned on my father too; I ate apples; I watched things grow; and I never once connected it with the garden in the piano-playing picture, though that was more or less what it was. I remember I *did* try to connect it with *The Secret Garden*. I dragged a copy of that past the censor, with my mother saying, "Oh very well then, read it if you must, but remember it's nothing but sentimental nonsense!" and tried, in a puzzled way, to lay it alongside the Other Garden. But the Other Garden had nothing to do with sentimental nonsense. I couldn't make it out.

I see now that the two gardens of the conference center came to represent to me the activities of the two sides of the human brain, the first concerned with day-to-day living and the second with all creative needs. But I put it to myself more in terms of enchantment as opposed to the mundane.

"Is this why you made use of myths and folktales so often?" people will now ask. Only up to a point. One thing the existence of the Other Garden made plain to me is certainly that there are times when everyday life echoes or embodies traditional stories. These are more frequent than most people think. Anyone who does not believe this ought to ask themselves how often they have felt like Cinderella. And it was with this in mind that I wrote *Eight Days of Luke* very early on, using the days of the week, which have the names of deities hidden in them and yet are presented to us on a daily basis, to try to express how the ancient and chthonic things are in fact nearly always present to everyone. But I do this kind of one-to-one correspondence fairly rarely. For one thing, the immense and meaningful *weight* of all myths and most folktales could drag a more fragile, modern story out of shape; for another, I do not find I *use* these things. They present themselves, either for inclusion or as underlay, when the need arises; so that you can have, at one end of the scale a book like *Wilkins' Tooth* where the solution is from "Puss in Boots" (or "Rhinegold"), or at the other end of the scale, one like *Fire and Hemlock*, where, once I had conceived the idea of founding the story on that of Tam Lin, about ninety other myths and folktales proceeded to manifest, in and out all the time, like fish in dark water. The beauty of such tales is that the weight they carry is only to be grasped intuitively. They cause readers to grasp far more than the surface meaning, but they combine with that surface meaning more easily and successfully than anything else, even for those who do not know the story in question. (*Fire and Hemlock* goes down rather well in Japan, where myths are not the same.)

The other wonderful thing about myth and folktale elements is that nearly every story is in segments, which can be taken apart and either recombined or included on their own. In this form they carry the same weight, but their meaning often alters. I first grasped this at the age of about eleven, when I was allowed to read a scholarly book when I was ill ("But don't you dare get it crumpled!"), which was mostly sixteen versions of the same Persian folktale—the one where the younger prince fetches the princess from the glass mountain—placed in such an order that, as the details of the story altered, you watched it changing from one sort of narrative (the trial of strength and valor) to another (the test of character), while the outline of the story itself never changed. This kind of thing fascinates me. When I was a student I imagine I caused Tolkien much grief by turning up to hear him lecture week after week, while he was trying to wrap his series up after a fortnight and get on with *The Lord of the Rings* (you could do that in those days, if you lacked an audience, and still get paid). I sat there obdurately despite all his mumbling and talking with his face pressed up to the blackboard, forcing him to go on expounding every week how you could start with a simple quest narrative and, by gradually twitching elements as it went along, arrive at the complex and entirely different story of Chaucer's "Pardoner's Tale"—a story that still contains the excitement of the quest narrative that seeded it. What little I heard of all this was wholly fascinating.

"How do you think of the characters in your books?" They come partly from life. A friend recently said that all the adult characters in my books struck her as completely mad, and I suppose this is because most of the adults I knew as a youngster behaved as if they were precisely that. Though I have never yet found a niche in a book for either Professor Tolkien or the visionary gardener, I have not despaired of finding one for both in the end. Those that I do draw from life, I use sparingly, one per book usually, to ensure that the other people, who come from my head, will behave as real people would. The majority are, you might say, made up, and these are of two kinds: those I have known for a long time and who have been kicking their heels in the corridors of my brain, waiting for the right narrative to go into, and the ones who suddenly present themselves, as entire people, because of the logic of the book. It is, I find, essential to know real and made-up both as well as you would know your own siblings. One reason for knowing them that well is that you then need not describe them in any detail: if you know them that well, they come over. But the main reason is that they are, after all, the flesh and blood of the story, the ones the things happen to, or who make things happen. So they have to be capable of being changed by what goes on, as people would change. You have to know their tricks of speech and the way they stand or walk, the way their hair grows, as well as you know the inward minds of them—or better, because I find they often surprise me by acting autonomously out of inward impulses I have not learned. The way different people behave in difficult conditions has always fascinated me. The second book I wrote (in twelve exercise books) was largely devoted to a group of people who got separated into smaller groups, and then to exploring these smaller groups, each of which surprised and fascinated me by developing a group dynamic I had not expected. The one I expected to make the decisions did not always do so. By the time I had written THE END in the twelfth exercise book, I knew all of them so well that I could draw pictures of them in characteristic attitudes.

Now we are nearer to answering the question I always get asked most irritably: "Why did you choose to write fantasy? Why magic?" Aside from the fact that much of my early life was *like* fantasy, I suppose the answer has to be that I learned its value from not having it, or at least not having it in books very much. There were glimmerings, just enough to set up a craving of the kind you have when you are seriously deficient in some vitamin and, oddly enough, nothing I wrote in those exercise books was fantasy. I did not think it was allowed. Fantasy was "sentimental nonsense." I was, for instance, forbidden to read the chapter in *The Wind in the Willows* called "The Piper at the Gates of Dawn," but of course guiltily did so and discovered in it something consonant with the Other Garden. They were both that extra thing, something beyond the usual. It took me years to understand that all the matters dealt with in fairy tales or myths (magic) and the deeper workings of the imagination are both functions of the right lobe of one's brain, and therefore are capable of overlaying and reinforcing one another. This seems to be true whether you are simply speculating about what happens if you stumble while wearing seven-league boots,[3] or conducting your protagonist on a journey of the spirit to the underworld. The magic leads to the exercise of the imagination and then the imagination supplies further meaning to the apparently magic events. At its simplest, magic can be considered as a metaphor, or as functioning in the same way as metaphor. In *Witch Week*, it begins as precisely that, with the burning of witches standing for the persecution of people who differ from the supposed norm, but I hope it then goes on to be more, because almost every character eventually turns out to be a witch. It should then become a way of saying "Think this through." This, it seems to me, is the best *intellectual* function of magic in fantasy. You start out by saying "What if this or that seemingly impossible thing were so . . ." and then following through the logic of it. The fact that it has been put in terms of magic (or impossibility) has distanced the problem (which may actually be one painfully near to most children, like secret fears or racial difference) so that it can be walked around, followed through, and if possible, solved in some way. To use magic by itself as a solution is merest cheating. The problem has to be restated in equivalent magical terms and then linked with the minds and actions of people in such a way that a solution can be worked out in human terms as well. Then, because magic is the matter of myths and folktales, the problem becomes exciting rather than painful or intractable and the imagination is available to come to grips with the problem.

The excitement generated by magic is incalculable and should never be underestimated. It is of the same order as creativity.

"But what value has fantasy? Don't you end up with people who do not know fantasy from reality?" The short answer to that second question is another question: Why do lie detectors work? The longer answer is twofold, part personal, part general. Recall my muddle over Germans giving us Twyford. I really did not know which part of this was fantasy and which reality. It was solved for me by an episode from *Mary Poppins Comes Back* (this book got past the censor by being a present from my godmother) in which Mary Poppins and her charges visit a circus that is the Milky Way, presided over by the Sun as Ringmaster, with Saturn as a melancholy clown (which puzzled me for the next five years until I learned of the rings of Saturn and saw that these were the ruff round the clown's neck) and the signs of the zodiac as performing animals. The episode was rescued from whimsy first by the cast uniting to assert they were all of the same substance—"child and serpent, star and stone"—and subsequently by the discovery that Mary Poppins had a sunburst burn on one cheek where the Sun had kissed her. None of Kipling's learning-and-forgetting here. I almost instantly recognized that my muddle was the same order of thing as this episode, truths presented in a shape they did not really have, personifications and similes acquiring the status of fact. The muddle dissolved, not only painlessly but in a gust of delight at the marvelous thing P. L. Travers had done. I am willing to bet that most good children's stories have inadvertently performed the same sort of cure for many children, many times. They show you the way your mind works. And, as I hoped to point out when I gave an account of my muddle in the first place, when your mind works in this way, it is closely allied to all sorts of creativity.

Fantasy is a very important part of the way your mind works. People trot out as a truism that man is a tool-making animal, but nobody pauses to think that before a caveman could make a stone ax or an obsidian arrowhead, he had to *imagine* it first. "What if I lashed this luckily shaped hunk of stone to this sturdy stick? Would it help me divide this tree into usable bits?" The caveman might actually laugh here at the idea of dividing a tree up at all. And the same sort of half-incredulous "What if?" applies to the most abstruse piece of engineering, except that here the laughter will be subsumed into a sort of keen enjoyment of the chase: "Nobody has done this before, but I'm going to do it all the same. What if I . . . ?" Man, before anything, is a problem solver. We have evolved practically requiring to enjoy solving problems, and foremost among our means of doing so is the half-joking "What if?" of fantasy. One of the mythical Treasures of Britain was a thermos flask, conceived long before it was possible to make one. And of course it is fun, solving something. Look at Archimedes, rushing outside dripping and shouting. Naturally we enjoy fantasy.

There is an extension of this fun-function. We also enjoy daydreaming—fantasizing, as they call it. In some daydreams, our problems are simply miraculously solved. Here, we recognized the problem and lowered the level of pain from it. Nobody solved anything while worried and hurting. That is one part of fantasizing. The other part is the actual practicing of situations in our heads. Reading a book constructed on these lines is only an augmented form of this. Both prepare you for a version of the situation in actuality. Without either, you really do not find it easy to distinguish the credible from the unbelievable, the obscene from the silly joke. I always think it is significant that the generation that trained my mother to despise all fantasizing produced Hitler and two world wars. People confronted with Hitler should have said, "He's just like that villain I imagined the other night," or "He's as mad as something out of *Batman*," but they couldn't, because it was not allowed.

"Why do I write for children?" There is one good reason. I would hope to encourage some part of one generation at least to use their minds as minds are supposed to be used. A book for children, like the myths and folktales that tend to slide into it, is really a blueprint for dealing with life. For that reason, it might have a happy ending, because nobody ever solved a problem while believing it was hopeless. It might put the aims and the solution unrealistically high—in the same way that folktales tend to be about kings and queens—but this is because it is better to aim for the moon and get halfway there than just to aim for the roof and get halfway upstairs. The blueprint should, I think, be an *experience* in all the meanings of that word, and the better to make it so, I would want it to draw on the deeper resonances we all ought to have in the other side of our minds. For me, those resonances will have something to do with the Other Garden, but I am willing to hope—or even to believe—that if I get the book right, I might actually provide these resonances for those who did not happen to have such a garden. I have anyway always hoped to write a truly memorable book, one that you go back to the beginning of and start rereading as soon as you get to the end, one that you think of in subsequent years as the one that really pointed you in the way you wish to go. I still don't think I have done it. That's life. Halfway to the moon. But on what I have done, I would not really like to set an age limit. I am always delighted when aunts and grandfathers write to me, saying their nephew/granddaughter has just introduced them to, say, *Howl's Moving Castle*, and they couldn't put it down.

Some Hints on Writing

Diana could address any audience, from a gathering of learned academics to keen schoolchildren. Here she provides advice to young would-be writers. This piece was written in 1999.

About Myself

I think I write the kind of books I do because, when I was five years old, the Second World War broke out and everything went mad. Perfectly sane neighbors began crawling about in the field by our house with bushes tied to their heads, training for the Home Guard. The time was dangerous as well as mad. Airplanes, barrage balloons, and searchlights filled the sky. People you knew died suddenly when a bomb hit the end of the street. Ordinary life became unsafe the whole time. *Anything* could happen.

Our family life became just as strange. I was sent with one of my sisters to Wales, where my grandfather was minister at a chapel in Pontardulais, but this didn't last long because—as far as I could tell—there was a massive family row and my mother went back to London with us. But London was very unsafe by then, and we were sent with a school to a big house in the Lake District. This was not safe, either. When the docks over the mountains were bombed, a German plane was shot down and the pilot bailed out and hid in the mountains for weeks. One night he raided the pantry of the house where we were and stole an enormous cheese. This was enough for the school people. They left, but we stayed on with my mother and the mothers of some of the other children.

This house was the home of the children in *Swallows and Amazons* by Arthur Ransome (they were real people), and Arthur Ransome himself lived in a houseboat on the lake nearby. He got annoyed by the noise some of the smaller children made playing on the lakeshore and stormed in to complain. This is how I learned that writers were real people (up till then, I had thought books were made by machines in the room at the back of Woolworth's). Beatrix Potter lived not too far away and she was real, too. She smacked my sister and her friend for swinging on her front gate. But the same house had also belonged to the secretary of the writer and artist John Ruskin—and John Ruskin was obviously real, too. The lofts were stacked with thick paper on which the man had drawn pictures of flowers, hundreds of them. Now, at this stage in the war everything was in short supply and there was no drawing paper. So one afternoon I climbed into the loft and fetched down a big pile of the drawings and started to rub them out so that I could use the paper to draw on myself. John Ruskin drawings fetch thousands of pounds these days. I must have rubbed out several hundred pounds' worth before I was caught and punished.

I started writing when I was married and had children of my own, and I think one of the things I wanted to tell people in my books was how to cope with the world when it goes crazy around you. It does that even without a war on, of course.

Hints about Writing a Story

Everyone is different, and that means that everyone is going to need to write a story in a different way. You have to discover how you need to do it. There is no easy way. You can only discover how to by doing it. These hints are to help you find your own way.

Planning It?

Most teachers will tell you that you need to make a careful plan of your story before you start. This is because most teachers do not write stories. Professional writers divide into four different ways:

1. Those who *do* make a careful plan. These are the rarest. Even writers who write detective stories often only have jotted notes about what order the clues come out in. You do a careful plan if it makes you feel safe. Otherwise, try one of the other ways.

2. Careful realistic writers. These writers have little cards written out with descriptions and past histories of all the people they might want in the story, and the same for all the places. This is quite a good way to work, because the story often falls into place in your head while you are discovering the things on the cards. But it takes a long time, though it can be fun. You will often find you have far more information on the cards than you will ever get into the story, and if this is so then DON'T try to get it all in. You will drown your story.

3. Back-to-front and inside-out writers. These writers start by writing chapter eleven and then chapter twenty. Sometimes they have no idea what the story is and have to put the chapters away until they see what the story is that they fit into. A writer

called Joyce Cary had a whole chest of drawers filled with chapters out of books that he never got round to finishing. When he did write a book, it always started this way, with a chapter from the middle. I sometimes work this way, but I warn you, it takes a very clear head to sort it out in the end. It is a good way to get started, however.

4. My way. If you're the kind of person who gets stuck writing a story, try this. When I start writing a book, I know the beginning and what probably happens in the end, plus a tiny but extremely bright picture of something going on in the middle. Often this tiny picture is so different from the beginning that I get really excited trying to think how they got from the start to there. This is the way to get a story moving, because I can't wait to find out. And by not planning it any more than that I leave space for the story to go in unexpected ways. Sometimes things happen that I never would have thought of, just because the story *wants* them to happen.

The important thing is that you should enjoy making up your story. If it bores you, stop and try something else.

Beginning It

To start, you have to have an idea. I can't help you there. Whatever idea you have, and everyone has ideas, it has to be something that really grabs you. Think of the thing that most excites you in a story and the kind of thing you most like to read, and take it from there. One part of it is going to make you much more excited than the rest. To get started, try to begin *as near* to the exciting bit as possible. That way, you will want to go on. You can do the rest as flashbacks, or change the middle to the beginning afterward. Above all, don't try to write something you think you *ought* to write.

Whatever you think of, DON'T make it too neat. Stories need loose ends to move. A girl wrote to me once that she could only get to chapter one of her book. She had two sets of identical twins who lived on two identical small islands and they had both just discovered buried treasure. It was not surprising she was stuck. It was just too neat.

Places In It

The places your story happens in are very important. For instance, if you want to write about a vampire, you might want him stalking someone in a narrow street by the docks. Or you might want him to attack at a picnic in the country. These would be quite different stories. A lot of people worry about having to describe places, but there is no need to worry at all. What you have to do is to *see* the place where this part of the story is happening, in your mind, as if you were there yourself. By the docks, you would see the shapes of the houses and sheds, and the stone or wood they were built of, and seagulls and boats and machines, and the paving you were walking on. At the picnic, you would see the grass and the insects and the shapes of the trees and the hills, *and* exactly where each person was sitting round the food. Then you simply write what happens. You don't need to describe. It will come over as you tell it. You could ask someone to do a drawing and they would draw it just as you had seen it. Promise.

People In It

People are even more important. They are the ones that make the story happen. You have to *see* them even more clearly than places. You have to know the shape of them and if their breath smells and how their hair grows. In fact, you have to know twice as much as you put in the story. Sit and think and *see* them before you start. And *hear* them too. Everyone has their own special way of talking. Make them talk like they should—and do remember that people don't talk in proper sentences and that they shout or they mumble, and try to get them doing this. If you have trouble, put a real person in your story. If you have an aunty May or an uncle Joe whom you don't much like, use them as the vampires and they will come out wonderfully real. You won't need to describe them, just do the way they talk and move. (You don't need to tell your aunty or your uncle either.)

Feelings and Actions

Some people get stiff and unhappy writing because they think they can't manage to write how it *feels* to have an adventure, or to be in the middle of very fast, exciting action. This is nonsense. Everyone knows. What you have to do, if you are stuck this way, is to stop thinking in *words* and then shut your eyes and think how it would be if *you* were the one having the adventure, falling down the cliff, or being attacked by a vampire, or whatever. You'll know at once. Then you simply put down what you know. It may come out queer, but queer is good where actions and feelings are concerned.

Finishing It

It is important to know you *can* finish a story, so you should if possible. Just bash on and do it. Endings are not easy. I find them the hardest part. You don't know whether to stop with everyone just at the end of the adventure, and not knowing what really happened to Aunty May or Uncle Joe, or to make sure that the right people are going to be happy and the wrong people not, or even whether to go on and tell what happens in the next twenty years. This is really up to you. If you want to know what happens in the rest of the lifetimes of your people, go ahead and find out and put it down. If you think you're done when you've got a stake driven through Uncle Joe's heart, then stop there. My feeling is that the best stories leave the reader trying to imagine what happened after the story stopped, but that is only one opinion.

Doing It All Over Again

If you want to make your story as good as you can get it, you have to go over it and *get it right*. Professional writers never write a book just once. They do a second or even a third rewriting. Even if you don't have the time for that, you must go over it for bits that have gone wrong (if you know you're going to do this, you can get on with the story the first time round and simply promise yourself that the bit that went wrong will get put right later). First, you must read your story *as if you had never seen it before*. Yes, this is difficult. You are going to read it and admire all the bits you like instead. But, while you admire, you will come across bits that make you sort of squiggle inside and say, "Oh, I suppose that will do." That is a sure sign that it *won't* do. So, secondly, think hard about these bits, what is wrong with them and how they ought to go to be right. If the wrong bit is supposed to be funny, think hardest of all. Funny bits have to have exactly the right words, or they are like jokes where someone has forgotten the punch line. But even serious bits can be like that, too, if you get them wrong. If you think hard enough, your story will be *much* better.

Giving It a Title

Sometimes this is harder than writing the ending. You have only a few words for a title; you don't want the same title as someone else; you want to say what the story is about, but not give it away; and you want to make people interested enough to read it. You probably want a snappy title. Difficult. If you are very lucky, you will have thought of the title before you wrote the story. Then you have to make sure it still fits when the story is finished. It sometimes takes me six weeks to find a title. I hope you have better luck.

Good luck. Enjoy yourself.

A Whirlwind Tour of Australia

In 1992, the recently published Black Maria *hit the bestsellers list in Australia. In association with the British Council, Diana's Australian publishers, Mandarin, arranged a whirlwind tour for her in Australia, fitting in three lectures about writing children's fiction, along with signings and interviews. (See "A Conversation with Diana Wynne Jones" for one incident on her Australian tour.).*

Lecture One: Heroes

Diana's first talk in Australia was at a conference in Perth organized by Magpies Magazine *on the topic of heroes. Diana considered that this lecture was a continuation of the themes she had begun in her 1988 talk in Boston. See "The Heroic Ideal: A Personal Odyssey."*

When I started thinking about what I should say here, I was just finishing the final draft of a *very* complicated book. It was so complicated that I had to break my usual rule and make a chapter-by-chapter plan of parts of it. It was a relief to find that the Wimbledon tennis tournament was on and that I could stagger away from time to time and watch a game and listen to the *phut-phut-phut* of the tennis balls. In fact, it wasn't a relief—it was a revelation. It dawned on me that tennis stars were perfect models of heroes—all kinds of heroes—folktale, myth, comic book, and above all, modern fantasy. And I found myself attending closely and thinking very hard indeed.

For a start, they all had that larger-than-life quality. They stood out among other people even if you didn't know that one was the star—and this is very like the way everyone follows the hero of a story, even if he or she is only designated the prince, or the youngest sister. And though they defeated the villain on the opposite side of the net, they didn't save the world, they simply won a tennis match. It is very unidiomatic to consider that a hero saves the world. What gives a hero his/her universality is the fact that the gods, or God, or the Fates, or some other supernatural agency is on their side. And tennis stars have that, too. If one of them is in trouble in a match, their ball is sure to start just flipping the net and rolling down the other side, or they get a lucky call—or it rains.

Of course some of these people don't have much brain, which qualifies them for the Hercules, Superman type of hero, who are mostly notable for deeds of strength. But those with brains do have enormous individuality and a larger-than-life personality—not always a very nice one. They sulk, they stamp, they throw racquets, and they insult the umpire and the linesmen. But then, very few heroes are like Sir Galahad. Achilles sulked worse than a tennis star—he was also vengeful and whined to his mother. Theseus made unscrupulous use of Ariadne (whom he left on an island, where Bacchus later found her—I always think that really meant she took to drink, poor girl), and Jason made similar use of Medea. Then there were those Irish heroes whose main heroic aim was to rustle cattle, the Welsh hero Gwydion who took *pride* in cheating people, and the Brave Little Tailor who started out, at least, as a complete fraud. I think my moment of revelation came when I saw this young man come on court in the most flamboyant clothes. He had a sweet smile and questionably blond hair and a generally chirpy glamour that in fact concealed huge skill. When he was interviewed he confessed to hating to get angry—and it was also said that he slithered out of winning when it came to the big matches. And I thought, My God! This Andre Agassi is the image of Howl in my book *Howl's Moving Castle*!

What I am saying here is not simply that heroes are usually flawed characters, which is true, nor that my books tend to come true on me—which is also a fact—but that the big, heroic things which we respond to are exactly the same nowadays as they always were. This was one of the things I was trying to say in *Eight Days of Luke*. The days of the week are named after the Norse gods and, just as Woden's Day and Thor's Day are part of our everyday lives, so are the big things for which these gods stand. And we respond to them as people always have done.

We respond to heroes, I think, not so much by identifying as by *following*, partly as disciples follow and partly by cheering on from the sidelines. Watching the crowd at Wimbledon, I concluded that people's response to heroes is a muddle of these two things, and it gets more muddled when we talk about a narrative rather than a tennis match. Perhaps this gets easier to see if you think about following the fortunes of a hero who is of the opposite sex from your own. You can never assume this hero is *you*, but you follow him/her just the same.

This fact has been very important to me. For a long time I couldn't write a story with a female hero. The identification was too close, and I kept getting caught up in the actual tactile sensations of being a girl—which meant you towered over boys the same age, were forced to wear your hair so that it got in the way, and that your chest flopped embarrassingly—and I knew that in order to *see* my hero as a real person, I had to be slightly more distant than that. There were other factors here, too. First, my own children were all boys, and I knew not only how they felt and behaved but what they needed in a book as well. Second, at that time—twenty years ago—neither my sons, nor any other boy, would be seen dead reading a book with a female hero. It really was absolute. They would not. But girls—partly out of necessity—didn't mind a male hero. But I think the third, hidden factor was the most important. According to the psychologist Carl Jung—and I think he is correct—every person has an open, fully acknowledged personality of the same sex as their own, and a submerged half which has all the characteristics of the opposite sex. Twenty years ago I was still learning how I wanted to do things, and what I wanted to do was to write fantasy that might resonate on all levels, from the deep hidden ones, to the most mundane and everyday. If I chose a male hero, I could go after my own submerged half and so get in touch with all the hidden, mythical, archetypal things that were lurking down there. Over the years I've grown to trust this primordial sludge at the bottom of my mind. I *know* it's there now, and I know I can get in touch with it as soon as I start writing hard enough to forget to eat or go to bed.

But to go back to those flawed heroes playing tennis. It was quite obvious that people in the crowd loved them for their faults. Some of it is, certainly, that the faults make the heroes human, and people can say, "Oh, he/she is not so unlike me." But when a hero swears at the umpire and the slow handclap starts, you see that the star is also a scapegoat, to be blamed for doing exactly what you would do yourself with that same prig of an umpire—the star carries your sins, in a larger-than-life, jazzed-up way, and you express your disapproval. The fact is, people can think of a hero in both ways simultaneously—that hero is me: that hero is not me, out there, being awful—and this is exactly the way in which people react to a narrative. Reading a story, you can have your cake and eat it too. For instance, while I was writing *The Ogre Downstairs*, I was certain that readers were going to *enjoy* Gwinny baking the gray cake in order to poison her stepfather, even while they utterly condemned it. And I think I got that right—you wouldn't believe how many adults have tiptoed up to me and confessed that when they were children they had baked just such a gray cake for an aunt or child minder or parent that they hated.

There was another kind of double thinking going on at the tennis too, at least among the commentators. If a male player hit the ball into the net when he didn't need to, they went, "Oh, what an appalling shot to play at this stage in the game!" But if a female player did it was, "Oh well, women are expected to make mistakes." I was pretty indignant about this, until I realized that the women players *didn't* actually make many unforced errors. The commentators' expectations were years out of date. The women's expectations about themselves had changed. It is one of those many fields in which feminism has made an enormous subtle difference. Exactly the same change has come about in children's books. About ten years ago, boys started being prepared to read books with a female hero. I found everything had gone much easier without, then, being able to say how or why. Females weren't expected to behave like wimps and you could make them the center of the story. By that time anyway, I found the tactile sense of being female stopped bothering me—which may have been part of the same revolution—and it was a real release. I wrote *The Spellcoats*, told by a girl, and *The Time of the Ghost*, from the point of view of a female ghost, and then—although this one has only just been published—*Black Maria*, which explores the traditional roles of the sexes. After that, with a feeling that this was the big one, *Fire and Hemlock*.

Fire and Hemlock follows a girl, Polly, from the age of ten to nineteen. Such was my sense of release at that time, that the book was written at white heat—I had absolutely no trouble in tapping the deepest, most resonating levels and relating them to normal present-day relationships. The heat of writing pulled in poetry, myth, and folktales by the handful. Polly kept flicking from role to role as hero of at least a score of folktales: "Cupid and Psyche" or its dark obverse, "The Wicked Wedding," "Tam Lin," "Snow White," "Thomas the Rhymer," "Bluebeard," "Cinderella," "Sleeping Beauty," "East of the Sun and West of the Moon," and many more. It was amazing to me as I wrote to find exactly how many well-known tales have a female protagonist.

Reviewers—who seem to perform the same function as commentators at tennis matches—did not like this. The chief review of *Fire and Hemlock* ran, "This is a girls' book and I don't see why I should try to understand it." End review. Last year *Black Maria* got much the same treatment. Things have not changed *that* much.

But back to the tennis commentators. Another thing that made me very indignant was their way of talking as if a tennis star was playing on his/her own. If the unfortunate opponent was not a star, then from the way they talked you'd think the hero was playing against a wall! In fact, on reflection, I saw the commentators had got this one right. Heroes are like that. Heroes of stories strive, fight, suffer, and maybe conquer. But whom they conquer or the reason for the fight is never so important. You remember the story *for* the hero, as if he or she carries the events of his/her heroism sort of in a cloud round them, like a nimbus. I think this is why there is always such a demand for another story about the same person—look at how many Robin Hood stories there are. These days it's expected you will do more—at least write a trilogy—and this is something I find very hard to do. Except where Chrestomanci is concerned, I usually find that the end of the book is the end of the important things I have to say about the central character. Being that particular sort of person, they require that particular story and no other—that story is their own special nimbus, if you like. As an example of my difficulties, let me tell you that for the last ten years, I have been supposed to be writing the fourth book about Dalemark. And I couldn't do it. That was because my then-publisher insisted that the next book should be about Brid and Moril—particularly Brid—and I knew that *Cart and Cwidder* had said most of what I wanted to say about Brid. It was not until I had changed publisher and been nagged by my agent that I began to think, well, maybe not Brid, but there are people in *The Spellcoats* and *Drowned*

Ammet who have only half of their rightful story there. But how do you put into one narrative the other halves of stories that happened several thousand years apart? I had to leave that there for a while—I had other heroes queuing up inside my head for the stories that fitted them—and it was only last year that things clicked around and I did write that fourth book.

I do find, myself, that the hero, the protagonist, *is* the story. This is not to say that the other people in it are of no importance. Before I can write about anyone, I have to consider them as my close personal friends, even the baddies. I often feel acute sympathy for baddies—for instance, for Gwendolen in *Charmed Life*, who never had a chance to be anything else— but then, I'm peculiar that way. There was a time in my life when I had to hurry out of French farces in floods of tears because I was so sorry for the deceived husband.

But of course I feel much more sympathy for the hero, and so does everyone else. The hero has glamour, warts and all, and carries the story *alone*—rather like the tennis star apparently playing against a brick wall. Yes, the opposition *is* there, but at least half the struggle is with the hero's own inner self. A tennis match makes a near-perfect paradigm here. You see the star stepping out confidently at first, sweeping away the other player. Then the other fights back and the star starts to lose. The hero's confidence vanishes. You see the star fighting with himself, muttering, swearing, stamping about, and his face is contorted with agony at his own incompetence. The crowd loves him for this agony. He has to fight his own feelings in order to get into a frame of mind in which he can win. And he does. Somehow he scrapes up, if not confidence, courage, calms himself with a huge, visible effort, and raises his game.

Slowly he claws back the advantage, gets on top, and then by the end the other player doesn't know what has hit him.

Watching this agony of tennis stars in action, I recalled an interesting fact. The word "agony" also makes part of the word "protagonist." And it is the same word in origin as "action."[1] It is as if the facts about heroes are built into our language—if you take action of any kind, you are going to suffer. But the whole complex of meanings round these words entails a great deal more than simply "You can't make an omelette without breaking eggs." "Agony," which means, in origin, a death struggle, is a word for both external pain and internal strife (as in "an agony of indecision"). "Action," derived from the verb "to act," *can* mean decisive doings of a physical kind, but it is usually partly in the world of ideas, as when a government *acts* to prevent inflation by raising interest rates, which is a seminotional thing to do, even if it does have physical consequences. And the other main meaning of "act" is, of course, to take part in a stage play—where the actor often enacts the agony of a hero. Interestingly, the actor is said to *play* a part in this *play*. If you think around the implications of this cluster of meanings, you can see that what an audience, or a readership, expects from a hero is a very serious form of a game, in which the hero is expected to struggle on two fronts, externally with an actual evil, and internally with his/her own doubts and shortcomings. The hero, out there as scapegoat, has to do the suffering for everyone.

Another thing that makes a hero is, of course, a miraculous origin. I was intrigued to find that the media do in fact treat tennis stars as heroes even in this. Large numbers of them are said to have extremely ambitious parents, so ambitious that they dedicated their child to tennis from the earliest possible age. Some are said never to have gone to school so that they could concentrate on the career their parents had chosen for them. This makes me think of that passage in H. G. Wells's *First Men in the Moon*, where the narrator discovers a society of large, intelligent lunar ants and, in the course of a tour of the anthill, comes upon numbers of juvenile ants who are obviously in acute discomfort with portions of their anatomies squeezed into strange-shaped jars. These juniors, he is told, are being shaped into the forms required of various specialist workers.

I suppose the most obvious version of this origin is the dedication of Samuel to the temple. Real life or not, tennis children are pure folklore. But those players who were not dedicated are treated as mythical too, as if they sprang forth fully formed, like Minerva from Jove's head, or simply lay about doing nothing—which equates with the folklore motif of the Bear's Son, who did nothing but lie by the hearth until heroic deeds were required. Or there are players who started poor as church mice and raised themselves to fame and wealth by tennis—which is a hundred stories from "Puss in Boots" on. These days you don't get the princess and half the kingdom, but you do get a great deal of money and attention, which is probably equivalent.

All these notions and expectations about heroes were in my mind when I wrote *The Lives of Christopher Chant*. Christopher, the future enchanter Chrestomanci, has tennis parents. In a big way. Both his mother and his father wish to shape him into a different kind of star, but they are each so concerned with their separate ambitions for him that they entirely neglect the welfare of Christopher himself. This much comes from real life: Christopher was based on the son of ambitious parents I know, a poor boy who eventually committed suicide, being unable to stand the pressure they put on him. Christopher's version of suicide is to scramble about in the spirit void of the Place Between and keep on losing lives—luckily he has nine. But he is also the other kind of hero, the Bear's Son, in that he seems totally incapable of working magic and therefore incapable of fulfilling his parents' ambitions for him. Significantly, it is Christopher's father who had caused this incapacity. I made the lifting of this inhibition by Dr. Pawson as funny as I could. There seemed no better way to express the sheer joy of release.

But before this, Christopher has fallen under the sway of his dreadful uncle and become a deeply flawed hero. It is not just that he has been conned into criminal activity. The uncle, and the governess who is his accomplice, have dug their way into Christopher's private worlds where he travels in spirit—in other words, they have got at the center of his personality, where Christopher's own imagination had been freely at work—and perverted this for their own ends. In a way, this uncle and governess stand for Christopher's actual parents and what *they* have done. The governess, in addition, makes sure Christopher has no confidence in himself. For a while, Christopher holds to his central being because he has met the Goddess, who is a child and, like himself, dedicated—in this case to be the personification of the Goddess in an actual temple. Christopher strongly identifies with her, rightly: not only is she an even more extreme case of tennis child than he is, she is also standing for the powerful, submerged female part of himself. But there comes a point when even the Goddess lets him down. This happens when a person is rendered so unhappy that they lose touch with their inner self. This, I suspect, is the point where the boy Christopher was based on killed himself. But Christopher is a hero. At this point he has to raise his game or lose—so he raises his game and, in doing so, realizes that his confidence has been undermined. Now he is ready to fight and win.

He has to do this twice. Once he knows he has to, he can defeat his uncle quite easily in physical terms, but before that he has to cope with what has been done to him internally, by uncle and governess and parents. So he has to set out into the hidden worlds again, to the world he has been unable to enter before, and there, with help from his other half, the Goddess, to face down the fearsome Dright. Here he at least comes off best. He does not kill the Dright—he loses another life to him, in fact, for the kind of damage the Dright stands for lasts for the rest of your life. But Christopher does defeat him and gains a little understanding. Then he can come back into his own world and defeat his uncle.

I mentioned earlier that my book *Black Maria* was not published when it was written. It was written rather before *The Lives of Christopher Chant* and concerns itself with the same complex of ideas, except that it has a female hero, Mig, and the part that is played by the Goddess as Christopher's hidden half is here played by Mig's brother, Chris. Because it was written fairly early on, at the time I was finding a new freedom to write from a female point of view, it concerns itself with the way the traditional female role affects a female hero.

But it was not my publishers who decided to leave this book

till later—though they often do. For instance, *Dogsbody* was written a year after *Power of Three* and my publishers insisted on reversing them, and the same happened with *Fire and Hemlock* and *Archer's Goon*, which were in fact written almost side by side. No. *I* suppressed *Black Maria*. I felt it was too frightening. A friend of mine who writes horror comics agreed. There was nothing, he said, that inspired him with more fear and horror than a polite tea party given by a dear old lady—an ordinary old lady, not a witch. And Aunt Maria is a powerful and unscrupulous witch, tea parties and all. She takes the place of the ambitious parents in *The Lives of Christopher Chant*, for she is secretly grooming Mig to follow her as the sorcerous queen of a small seaside community. Aunt Maria embodies a certain type of female, dominating by pretending to be an invalid and by barefaced manipulation, dividing things into men's business and women's business, and pretending to worry. In her world, it's a woman's place to seem to worry. This is where I got frightened. In a nightmare way, strength becomes weakness and, vice versa, right becomes wrong, and most other values are skewed too.

But Aunt Maria was based on a real person—in fact, there seem to be rather a lot of her; my editor met five women exactly like Aunt Maria on her way down the street after finishing the book—and I thought, People have to cope with her every day. Let's show them a hero coping with her.

Mig has to grope her way through Auntie's moral miasma. At first, like Christopher Chant, she succumbs—at least to the propaganda about her role, and can do nothing but write her real opinions in her journal. She leaves the active male role to her brother, Chris. Chris is forced by the same propaganda into a near-parody of an aggressive adolescent boy—and some of the things he says made me scream with laughter while I wrote them—until Aunt Maria, having driven him too far, blandly turns him into a wolf. This leaves Mig in the position of the lonely folktale princess who *has* to turn her brothers back into human form. Mig has to overcome real terror *and* the sort of intellectual sloth induced by the role Aunt Maria has thrust upon her. But she does it, and raises her game. Here she, like Christopher Chant, finds that she has to call on something buried and hidden, in this case a man. A man called Antony Green has been buried alive, on Aunt Maria's orders, twenty years before. He is even more than the sleeping, buried part of Mig herself: he is the buried part of the whole community, their life of the imagination, without which no one's intelligence can work well enough to see through Aunt Maria's moral miasma. Mig, in raising her game, has sensed that there is something *other* and better, and this is what she has to go for.

This sense of something other and better is what heroes give us a glimpse of when they raise their game. And this is why we need heroes. Younger children seem to understand this fairly readily, I think, because when you are nine or ten your life is lived at a high emotional pitch that is itself only a step from the heroic mode. Take a look at any school playground and you'll see what I mean.

My youngest goddaughter, at the age of eight, was always very fierce when she came across injustice. On one occasion, she saw a large bully in the playground beating up a younger, and disabled, child. She suddenly became a knight errant and, although much younger and slighter than the bully, she launched herself at him with such ferocity that she took him by surprise and knocked him down. Then she hammered his head on the playground. The bully naturally told the teachers that he had been attacked without provocation, and my goddaughter was punished. She was undaunted. She told me afterward that she had been quite right to attack. "It was so *unfair!*" she proclaimed. "It made me angry." She was terribly unhappy, but she was glowing with her deed too. She was in touch with the other and better, all right—she was Boadicea, Brunhilde, Britomart, you name it.

When this girl reached puberty, she lost touch a little with her heroic sense. As a teenager or young adult, your emotions may be at an even higher pitch, but the onset of the additional emotions to do with sex sort of scramble the other feelings and you become a rather frantic muddle for a while. This is when people need a hero to follow. Everyone that age has a fierce pride and doesn't want to be a *failure*, and a hero gives you this sense of something other and better, so that you can keep your head above the frantic muddle. What you look for is a sort of blueprint of how to manage.

Then, with the aid of whatever blueprint they choose, people school themselves out of the emotion—and often out of the pride that went with it. They become ashamed of the whole lot, including heroes. I think this is a pity. But I take comfort from the way people of *all* ages will follow a tennis match breathlessly—even if they're not actually interested in the game. We all need an ideal. And we all have times when we need to raise our game. Heroes make us know that this is possible.

Lecture Two: Negatives and Positives in Children's Literature

In her second talk in Australia, Diana develops her ideas on fantasy and the imagination. This talk was later published in issue 25 of Focus, *the writers' magazine of the British Science Fiction Society, in December 1993/January 1994.*

There is one bizarre and creepy fact about my books which never gets onto the backs of jackets or into reviews—that is that they come true. This usually happens after I have written them. For instance, I now live in the house in *The Ogre Downstairs*. When I wrote the book, I was living in Oxford in a house that was the reverse of that one in every way—for instance, it had a flat roof that was soluble in water—and I had no thoughts of moving to Bristol, where I now live. Sometimes, however, the book comes true while I am actually writing it, and this can be quite upsetting. *Fire and Hemlock* was one of those. One of the many things that happened while I was writing it was that an eccentric bachelor friend from Sussex University, who stayed with us while he was lecturing in Bristol, insisted on my driving him to some stone circles in our neighborhood. There, he began having mystic experiences, while I kept getting hung up astride the electric fences that crisscrossed the site. My outcries, he said, were disturbing the vibes, so he sent me to the local pub to wait for him. As soon as I got there, the landlady and the other customers began talking about these same stone circles and related the local story about their origins. This story is called "The Wicked Wedding": the bride, who is an evil woman, chooses a young man to marry, but at the wedding, the devil comes, kills the young bridegroom, and marries the lady himself. This is the story behind *Fire and Hemlock* and, believe it or not, I had never heard it before—I thought I'd made it up. Well, after various other strange experiences, my eccentric friend went back to Sussex and I finished the book. I then started, immediately, to write *Archer's Goon*. Just picked up a fresh block of paper and began. Now those of you who have read this book will know that it hinges on a man called Quentin Sykes discovering a newborn baby in the snow. I had just started the second draft of this book when my eccentric Sussex friend went for a walk in the middle of a winter's night and discovered a baby. He found it a very moving experience—but I felt acutely responsible. It is all very well my books coming true on me—it is a risk I take—but when this starts rubbing off on other people it is no joke. The trouble is, a book demands that certain incidents are present in it, and to deny this is to spoil the book. So I thought deeply about the matter. And though I realized I could do nothing about parts of my books coming true—that really is beyond my control— there are things very much in my control over which I feel a very strong sense of responsibility indeed. It is this sense of *responsibility* that I want to talk about.

Soon after *Archer's Goon* was published, I was invited to a fantasy convention in London. Here I was approached by a prolific and original writer of adult fantasy—a Canadian— who told me that he would not be writing the books he did had he not read my books when he was an adolescent. I was stunned—he has the most stunning blue eyes!—not only by the eyes but simply by that fact. It was hard to handle. Something I wrote had got so deeply into someone else's imagination as to become part of his adult personality and to influence his career. I wasn't actually able to look at this matter calmly until last year, when my American publishers sent me his latest book as a gift. This book had a postscript in which he declared that this particular book would not have been written had he not chanced to read, as a child, that chapter of *The Wind in the Willows* called "The Piper at the Gates of Dawn."

Now that I could handle. I knew what he meant because I could say exactly the same about almost everything I had written. When I was about seven, my mother read me *The Wind in the Willows* at bedtime. I wasn't sure I liked it because Toad kept being the wrong size. But when she came to that particular chapter, she turned it over in a hunk and went on to the one after that. "Why are you missing that one out?" I asked. "Because it's very silly and pointless—and you wouldn't understand it anyway," she said, and went on reading about Toad. I was consumed with a feeling that she had missed out a very important piece of the story. I peeped at the title—"The Piper at the Gates of Dawn" seemed suggestive of magic beyond my experience and totally haunting. After a week or so, I was so convinced this chapter was important that I sneaked the book when my mother was busy and, with tremendous guilt but quite compulsively, read the chapter. You couldn't say it was part of the main story, but it was important because what was in that chapter matched its title—numinous and strange and sad and urgent and very dangerous and utterly beautiful and *safe* all at the same time; so much so, that it has remained with me all these years as an ideal of what fantasy should do. Everything I have written is in some way a feeble echo of that chapter.

But the fact that another writer felt the same really brought it home to me—that people were liable to read what I wrote at the most impressionable times of their lives, and that this might actually determine the kind of people they grew up to be. To my relief, I realized that I *had* known this all along, deep down, but not really *believed* it before. And it was even more of a relief to me to see that from the moment I first started to write for children and young adults, I had proceeded as if I *did* know it. But at this earlier stage, it was mostly as if I knew that this position of extreme responsibility was enormously open to abuse—if you're going to influence someone that much, you have to be enormously *careful*—and so I mostly put it to myself in terms of what I *shouldn't* do.

One thing I realized at the outset was that this was a branch of writing entirely dominated by adults. It must be the only branch in which a writer *cannot* address his/her audience directly. In order to say something to readers of fifteen and under, I (who am an adult) must first speak to an agent (who is an adult), then a publisher (who is another adult), a reviewer (who is an adult whose brain hurts), a bookseller (again an adult), and if I make it through this barrage, then the book is usually bought by teachers, parents, and librarians, all of whom are adults too. All these people have preconceptions about what should be in this book—preconceptions brought about by their own early reading and their upbringing—and they are going to, quite inevitably, exercise an unprecedented degree of censorship over this book. Now there is a strong plus side to this: this phalanx of adults is going to insist on high quality. They are not going to let me, or any writer, get away with shoddy, unclear language, or a story that does not make sense, nor the whimsical changes of size that so worried me about Toad. Rather more importantly on the plus side, is that what I write, just *because* it has to speak to adults too, is going to be written on two levels at least—maybe more. This is something I shall come back to. For the moment, I want to look at the minus side.

The minus side is that many adults are going to make all sorts of insanely wrong assumptions about what should go into a good book for young readers. When I first started writing, many of these assumptions were elevated into rules—nay, *laws*!—which you broke at your peril. I broke most of them very deliberately, because they were truly absurd. For instance, all adults in your story had to be godlike and above reproach. This applied particularly to parents. The ideal was Daddy in Arthur Ransome's books, who is offstage mostly but occasionally sends godlike telegrams: "Don't be duffers." The only adults allowed to have faults were baddies, and they had to be killed at the end of the book even if all they had done was purloin the family silver. Now the absurdity here is that, just as children's books are adult dominated, so are children themselves. On my rough reckoning, most children spend two-thirds of their waking hours dealing with parents at home and teachers at school—and only spend the remaining third of their time in that ideal world of the old-type children's book, entirely composed of other children. And as everyone knows, adults are by no means flawless—especially if they happen to be divorcing—and children have to deal with a lot of that. So I put adults in my books who behaved like real people do (and *didn't* get killed for it). This worried publishers. Even worse, I also allowed these adults in the story to perceive that

strange things were happening to the children and—worse!—
to become involved in the strange things too. You wouldn't
believe how many publishers turned down *The Ogre Downstairs*
for that reason. I admit this is an extreme case, since the Ogre
does nearly get murdered, twice, by magical means. But what
really bothered the publishers was not that. It was that the Ogre
got *involved*. Adults were supposed to be sacrosanct.

This ties in with the next unwritten law from those days.
I had a number of books turned down at that time because
I didn't say what ages the children in them were. This was
another deliberate flouting of rules. You were supposed to *say*.
My most obvious reason for not saying was that you feel a
fool, if you are a mature twelve, if you discover you have been
eagerly identifying with a character who turns out to be five
years old. But there is a more important, hidden reason which
comes out if you consider the situation in C. S. Lewis's Narnia
books. Lewis doesn't say what ages his children are either, but
there comes a point where Peter and Susan, the two elder ones,
are unable to enter Narnia because they are too old. Susan is
specifically stated to have begun—horrors!—wearing make-
up and thinking of boys. But, oddly enough, four adults *are*
able to enter Narnia. These are two outright villains and two
industrious working people. Nobody else gets to Narnia unless
they are dead. Now, I know Lewis was certainly thinking in
religious terms—no one shall enter the kingdom of heaven
unless they become as a little child—but the land of Narnia
is, in spite of being an allegory of heaven, to most readers
preeminently the vivid land of the imagination. So what Lewis
has ended up implying is that only young children, criminals,
and the uneducated working class can be allowed to exercise

their imaginations. I think this has come about because, as well as thinking of Narnia as heaven, Lewis supposed himself to be keeping the rule that adults are not to be involved in children's books. But because he was gifted with penetrating intuition, he has in fact uncovered the basis for both the first rule and the second, which is that no one past puberty should have anything to do with fantasy.

In other words, after the age of fourteen at the most, you have to close down one very large area of your brain.

Put like this, the notion seems absurd, but it is still very much alive, unfortunately. I think everything I write is basically devoted to saying it is nonsense to believe you have to close yourself down like this, but there are quite a large number of adults who believe you have to, and earnestly devote a lot of effort into preparing children for what they regard as this inevitable shutdown.

To take an early example: around the time I wrote *The Ogre Downstairs*, my eldest son was given John Masefield's *The Box of Delights*. He read it at a sitting and then said that it would have been his all-time marvelous book—to him it had all the things I found in "The Piper at the Gates of Dawn"—except that at the end everything turned out to have been only a dream. He was utterly disgusted. He said it was cheating—and still says so more than twenty years later. And he is quite right. Masefield gives you a feast of the imagination with one hand and takes it away with the other. He says, "Now, as an adult I have to make sure you know none of this stuff is *real*. Ordinary life is what you're in for, my child, and that is *dull*. Prepare to close down that part of you that enjoyed this story."

This base trick is now out of date, I'm glad to say, but it has been superseded by another which is worse. This trick is played by the school of thought that identifies a child's problem—this child is of the wrong race, has a physical disability, has violent parents, or is the victim of poverty, and so on—and then writes a book in the most detailed and factual terms about a child with this problem. And *then gives it to the child with this problem to read*. I call this the white-of-egg approach: if it's nasty it has to be good for you (bearing in mind that most kids hate white of egg). There are two implications to this mistaken approach, both of them equally dreadful. The first implication is that only unhappiness is real. (Think about this—*can* this be true?) The second implication is that you should face up to this unhappiness like a man—facing problems is supposed to be an adult thing to do—and the problems will disappear. Well, of course they don't. I know this from personal experience. I had a miserable childhood—so miserable that I like to think that nowadays we'd be identified as the victims of abuse and put in care, though I doubt this because we were supposed to have come from what is called "a good home." Now I have an American friend who knows my background, and she is always giving me autobiographies of black ladies whose early lives, as far as I can bear to read of them, were as awful as mine. She thinks this will "help" me. But I can't bear to read the things. I start to shake and to weep, and lie awake many nights afterward reliving things I'm helpless to do anything about. This is the crux of the mistake. Children are *helpless*—helpless before problems that are superimposed on them either by birth or by society. It does not help anyone to be forced yet again into a situation in which they are impotent. And I know no sane adult who would force *themselves* into such a situation—but people do seem to think this is how to force children into adulthood.

What no one seems to notice is that children can't wait to grow up. The third dreadful mistake seems to stem from people not noticing this fact. This is the prepare-them-for-real-life-by-using-a-fantasy approach. There are lots of this kind of book. We used to call them Goddy Books when we were children. But books get used in schools too. When my youngest son was ten he had this teacher—I forget her name: she was always known as Fanny Cradock[2]—and she taught everything out of *The Wind in the Willows. Everything.* They did Toad sums and Mole stories and the Wild Wood for art—apparently she even contrived to teach history, geography, and social studies out of the book, but don't ask me how! The poor kids couldn't get away from *The Wind in the Willows*—significantly, however, they too never once got taught the chapter "The Piper at the Gates of Dawn." And after a whole year, they were sick of it. So I suggested that they have a party to relieve their feelings and offered to supply a large effigy of this Fanny. We roped the effigy to a chair and provided a large basket of windfall apples to throw at it. It was the most successful party I ever gave. Practically the whole class turned up, and they pelted that effigy, screaming abuse of Fanny. They went on until all the apples were pulp, and enjoyed it so much they almost forgot to eat the food. They broke the chair, but they didn't make much impression on the effigy.

This seems to me symbolic. You *don't* make much impression on people who are determined to *use* a book this way. I wish I could think of a way of avoiding it with my own books. Only last year I was proudly shown a passage of *Drowned Ammet* set in an examination paper. What saddens me about this, and about my youngest son's experience, is that none of these children are going to want to look at those books again. No one in my son's class is going to read that suppressed chapter, "The Piper at the Gates of Dawn."

Which brings me back to my mother's censorship of that chapter for me. Why did she do this? Well, a year or so after the Fanny party, my mother confessed to me that at the age of nine or so, she was addicted to fairy stories. You could buy little paper books of them for a penny, she said, and she bought a whole stack and buried herself in them avidly. And her father caught her reading them. He not only took them away. He burned them. Ceremonially, with disgust and loathing. They were not true, he said, not real, and were therefore harming her mind. And he forbade her ever to read such things again. So she didn't. For the rest of her life. Toad she could allow herself, because he was obvious whimsy and kept changing size, but not the chapter that takes you deep into the archetype of the imagination. She does read my books, but only because she knows I nearly always put actual, living people into them, and she likes to spot the ones she knows. And she's always asking me why I don't write Real Books.

This grandfather of mine died long before I was born, or I would have had a few things to say to him. Among the first things I would have said is that his belief (which I call the Don Quixote fallacy)—that reading things that are not true damages your mind—was held by far too many people in the first half of this century, and I do not think this is unconnected with the fact that we had two world wars during that time. Certainly my impression is that this burning of books has caused my mother to be one of the most unhappy and maladjusted people I know. And it does bring you hard up against the *responsibility* adults have, if only because it shows you what a truly lasting impression can be made on a child.

But this Don Quixote fallacy is not dead. It is alive and well and living in Britain. Recently I was reading for the Whitbread Prize, and I came upon no less than five books purveying this notion in an even more advanced form than my grandfather's. In the face of it they were "child with a problem" books. There was this young person who was the wrong color, or disabled, or with divorcing parents and so on, and each of these kids tried to offset their troubles by imagining some vivid, or better or more exciting life. This was usually a world in which they had splendid adventures. Then, halfway through the book, it became clear that the child who had invented this world was not able to tell which bit of life was physically real and which was only in his or her mind. In other words, imagining things had driven this young person mad.

This struck me as such an appalling, irresponsible threat to hold over impressionable people that I tried to find out who these writers were. Two of them seemed to be teachers who were annoyed that their pupils were addicted to computer games, and the rest were social workers who seemed to be equating fantasy with drug abuse. Possibly none of them were quite aware of what they were saying. But the fact is that by making this threat—imagination drives you mad—they were closing off for their impressionable readers their most important route to sanity. The source of their threat seems to lie in a grand combination of all the mistakes I have mentioned so far: the beliefs that the only reality is dull and unpleasant, that young people must be prepared to confront this and this only, and that the way to do this is to close down the imagination. To these, they have added a further error: that what a person has in his or her head does not exist in everyday life.

Now let's turn to positives in children's literature.

For a start, the only way we can *have* everyday life is inside our heads. We do quite a good job of convincing ourselves there is us in there and the world out there, but the fact is we get the out-there by sensory input, which then comes to the brain to be processed. Along with everything else: figures that need adding or multiplying, how to write that important letter, what *was* the title of that book now? Who wrote that lovely song on the radio? Must phone Mother. How *do* I deal with Smith? My shoes are killing me—and just look at this crisis in the newspaper! And masses more. You could reasonably say that most of us have the whole world in our heads. In order to cope with this flood of stuff, we have to have the ability to think alongside it, on a sort of different waveband: Hey, these figures add up to my telephone number—hell—I'm overdrawn. What if I write the letter back to front, starting with the hard bit? That book title will come to me if I just forget it. The song sounded Scottish. What if I wait and let Mother phone me— no peace for a month if I do that. What if I tell Smith to go to hell? What if I take my shoes off under the table? What if the newspaper got its facts wrong?

You'll notice that this band of thoughts begins to fill with "What ifs." This "What if" is a sign that your imagination is working. At this level, your imagination is your ability to solve problems. It takes a situation with a missing bit and then goes "What if we try this?" until it supplies what is missing. It can do this in a small way: "Okay, I'll kick these darn shoes off."

Or it can run through to the very highest levels of speculation, where it can expand beyond accepted ideas and envisage completely new shapes for the future. Even at a fairly mundane level, the imagination is the growing point of the mind: "What if I shook off this stupid fear of Mother's nagging and simply told her I was busy?" If your mother is like mine, this might strike you as a fantasy. And yet this is just what all advances are in origin, fantasies until someone makes them into reality. Airplanes have existed in fantasy ever since the story of Daedalus; Arthur C. Clarke invented communication satellites as part of a fantasy; a thermos flask figures in several Celtic tales as one of the miraculous Treasures of Britain. And so on. The ability to fantasize is the most precious one we know. Because it solves problems, it has tremendous survival value. And—fortunately—it is built into us so that, unless mistaken adults inhibit us, we all have to do it.

One of the signs of a *necessary* built-in faculty is that you enjoy doing it. Like eating, or sex. We all play with ideas. Children, of course, do it all the time, but even the most adult of businessmen in the most boring meeting will say "Let's play with a few figures here" or "Let's play around with this idea for a bit"—and this is the right way to talk about it because it helps if your imagination is exercised with a lot of pleasure and in a great deal of hope. Then your "What ifs" go with a verve and you're really likely to get somewhere. When the missing bit is found, it is often accompanied with wonder and enormous delight. *Eureka!* I always see Archimedes bounding about punching the air like a soccer player who has just scored a goal, and dripping all over the street.

People probably thought Archimedes was insane, but actually

what this element of play and delight is doing is keeping you sane. To go back to the stream of consciousness for a second: you're smiling inside your head at Smith's expression if you were to tell him to go to hell, even while your imagination is also warning you this would be most unwise—you can envisage Smith bringing a lawsuit—but still, it's a lovely thought and it makes you feel much better. It's hard to tell if the lovely thought is a joke or a fantasy—and in fact jokes and fantasy are very closely connected. Both are ways of keeping your mind cool enough and clear enough to deal with a difficult situation.

When I write, I find that when I am dealing with a difficult situation—particularly the kind of difficulty I mentioned earlier that is imposed from an outside source and before which children are mostly helpless—I nearly always make it funny. By this I do not mean *unserious*. To take an example from *Black Maria*, my latest book, Aunt Maria, the lady in the title, is a monstrous old lady who uses her age and infirmity to manipulate everyone around her. Worse than this, she plays on people's guilt in order to force them into very narrow traditional roles according to sex—certain things are "women's work" or "men's business" only—and toward the end of the book she frankly admits to boring people on purpose, getting them so fazed with tedium that their minds are not able to work. In other words, Aunt Maria is in the business of closing down the imagination for her own ends. She eventually closes down the boy, Chris, into an animal—and there is a hilarious episode when Chris tries to get his revenge by invading a polite tea party in wolf form. I gave little whinnies of laughter while I was writing this, and I still find it funny, but it is serious all the same. Because Chris has been closed down, rendered a wild animal—you could say that Aunt Maria has made Chris into a delinquent by her treatment of him.

I venture to say that more important things can be conveyed like this, playfully, while people laugh, than by any other means. Even if you don't take it in on one level, you do on another.

I do want to *convey* something when I write. I don't want to teach or preach. But I want to convey, responsibly, the experience you have when your mind is working as it should, and this means working very hard usually, though you're too busy to notice it, opening up new ideas with wonder and pleasure. Of course it helps if I am, myself, working at the same sort of pitch. And generally I do. I sit there, in the best chair, scribbling away, forgetting to eat, being a nuisance to my family, and occasionally annoying them acutely by bellowing with laughter and falling out of my chair. Most of my books get written at such fever pitch that it puzzles me afterward to say how I thought of this or that idea. For instance, while I was writing this speech, my husband was reading a book called *Hexwood* which I have just finished, and he chuckled appreciatively at a remark one of the characters made. I looked up and said, "*He* said that, not me—*I'd* never have thought of saying that." It was almost as if the book had been writing itself.

That's probably as it should be, if I am to start to catch the way the mind works. In some ways, a fantasy should be like a dream, where the mind is working hard, but not in your *conscious* control. And I think this is partly the source of John Masefield's mistake in *The Box of Delights*. He had all the elements of a dream there, and forgot that it should, ultimately, be in his conscious control. A dream, after all, seldom has a plot like a story has, and in this kind of writing the *story* is all-important. No one—particularly a child—is going to forgive you if you don't tell a story, first and foremost. I love telling stories. Finding out what happens next. And the bit where it all starts to come together at the end is the most marvelous thing I know. The conscious control generally comes in at the next stage, the second draft, where I work long and hard at making sure the story hangs together logically on all its levels. Part of my responsibility, which is reinforced by the number of adults connected with writing for children, is not to turn out shoddy work.

But there is an odd fact: the logic of a story and the way its plot leads is not the same as the logic of a particular book. Each book has its own personality and its own drive—which often leads in surprising directions—and that personality has to develop in the first page or so. If it doesn't, then I am not ready to write that book, or that book is not ready to be written (it feels like both ways), and I put it away. When the personality does develop it actually dictates the style—the language—in which the book is written, and this is one of the things I am most at pains to get quite right in the second draft. It is something like trying to convey the exact atmosphere of a dream, if you get me. We've all had dreams in which the events don't add up to the feeling the dream gave us.

The really difficult thing is that the book has to *give* that feeling.

But the main way in which a fantasy resembles a dream is that it works on more than one level, just as the brain does. I've already talked about the way the humor is liable to operate on two levels, one laughable, one very serious. Now I want to add in everything from the deep-down semiconscious level, where your brain mostly talks in symbols, right up to the surface story level—and if possible everything else in between. This is where all the adults necessarily associated with children's books are a great help. They practically ensure that I write on more than one level, because it's only fair that I give something to interest them as I go along—and they are going to *know* a lot more than children, and I can count on that. This does children no harm at all. I agree here with T. H. White in *The Sword in the Stone* when he claims it is actually good for children to encounter matters that seem above their heads. It gives them something to aim for.

Something to *aim* for is really what all this is about. This is where the adults who make the mistakes I talked about earlier truly are in error. They know—or assume—that being adult is very dreary because the world never gives you half what you aim for. What they forget is that aiming for the moon and getting halfway there, gets you farther than if you just aim for the roof and only get halfway upstairs. People's achievements in life depend quite startlingly much on what they *expect* to achieve. Now all children know they can achieve adulthood. All they have to do is wait. They need something more than this to aim for.

I find this something more comes mostly from myths and folktales. When I write at fever pitch, I find my story usually pulls them in whether I intend them to be there or not. Well, they are the earliest forms of fantasy. The beauty of these tales is that they come to pieces like Lego, and each of the pieces has shape and meaning on its own, so you can have a fleeting glance at Hercules here, base this section on Puss in Boots there, or take Cinderella and put her bodily in the center of the story there. A further beauty is that in such stories you find all the troubles and problems of this modern age—any single one you care to name as long as it is archetypal—becoming timeless and distanced, so that you can walk round them and examine them without feeling helpless. This is where fantasy performs the same function as joking, but on a deeper level, and solves your problems while keeping you sane. It is no accident that the majority of folktales at least have a happy ending. Most of them are very deep-level blueprints of how to aim for the moon. The happy ending does not only give you gratification as you read it, but it also gives you hope that, just maybe, a fortunate outcome could be possible. Your brain likes that. It is built to *want* a solution.

I prefer to have happy endings when I write—though my books do not always allow me them—on the grounds that it *is* better to aim at the moon. I would like to think that some day I shall write the perfect fantasy that acts like a dream on many levels at once and conveys the experience of the brain working joyfully flat out—*and* is a sort of blueprint of how things should be. But you know how it is with aiming for the moon. I don't get there. Each time I think, Damn it! That's not it either! It's quite a good book but it doesn't do what I'd hoped. But then I think that quite possibly somebody is going to read it and get influenced for the rest of their life. And, as I said at the beginning, I feel a tremendous sense of responsibility, and I think to that person, "All right. Someday I'm going to get it right for you."

Lecture Three: Why Don't You Write Real Books?

In her third talk in Australia, Diana explores the nature of "Real Books." The talk was based on an article she wrote for a children's science fiction edition of Vector, *the critical journal of the British Science Fiction Association, issue number 140, published in October/November 1987. The talk took place at the State Library of New South Wales in Sydney.*

It's a real pleasure to start answering this question. People have been asking me, "Why don't you write Real Books?" ever since I had my first book published. Sometimes they ask it by implication, sometimes they ask it outright—but they never stop asking it.

The question first came from close relatives, who were ashamed to tell their neighbors what I did. My mother-in-law, indeed, clearly felt that the only excuse for my not being solely a wife and mother would have been that I wrote for adults—provided of course that I did not write what she called "popular fiction." Because I was unable to oblige her in either of these requirements, she preferred to pretend that I did nothing but bring up her grandchildren. This could be very awkward at times. There was one occasion when she was due for a visit—arriving at teatime, for which she always required a heaped plate of sandwiches and at least two different kinds of homemade cake. I was in the middle of trying to produce these items, when my dog came in soaking wet and managed to convey to me that he was freezing and uncomfortable and needed to be dried off *now*. We were not in our usual house, but he nevertheless led me to the towel cupboard and opened it to show me what he wanted. And I thought, "That was clever!

How does it feel to be that intelligent, but without hands or speech? *Wait* a moment!" And I had the idea for *Dogsbody*—and I had it so pressingly that I had to race away and get down at least the outline of the first chapter. The result was that when my mother-in-law arrived, there was no cake. I explained and apologized, naturally, and my mother-in-law, having made it clear to me that I had committed a major solecism, then said, "Poor Diana—the children keep you so busy that I don't blame you for going to sleep." It was then that I realized that my books were so unreal to her that they were assumed not to exist. The odd thing was that, whenever I had a new book out, she always insisted on having a copy, in order, as far as I could see, to put it on a special shelf in her spare bedroom, ostentatiously unread.

Well, you can live with this kind of thing. But the question also shortly came at me from every other quarter, often in insidious and indirect forms. It came in the embarrassed look from the hairdresser, if I said what I did. Or the same look from the wives of my husband's academic colleagues, who would then gush on about this charming little book about frogs they had just given their grandchildren ("Such *lovely* little pictures and almost *no* text!")—the implication being, I always suppose, that what I do *must* be about frogs, with pictures. Or I will get the question in another form from teachers, who suggest that I should write about "real" things like racism and unemployment. Sometimes the teachers claim that fantasy is too difficult, or "beyond the average child," but a lot of them complain that it doesn't give them opportunities for class discussion of important modern issues. Tough, isn't it? As time went on, I kept getting the same question in yet another form from adult fantasy fans. When I first started writing, there was no such thing as an adult fantasy fan; they appeared in numbers about ten years later. These are always male, with interesting things written on their T-shirts, and they come up to me at conventions and explain that they *would* read my books—probably—if only the jackets looked less juvenile. Oddly, their female counterparts don't seem to experience this problem. Most recently, I have had a whole crop of letters from guilt-ridden students. These are mostly in their first year at university and not altogether happy in it, and they are afraid that there is something wrong with them because they're still rereading and enjoying my books at the advanced age of eighteen or nineteen.

But the real heavy brigade, the hardest of all to answer, are roughly two-thirds of the head teachers of Great Britain. I get to recognize these the moment I enter a school on an author visit. The male head advances on me with an outstretched hand, prepared to spare me half a minute of his time—and I know now to hold my hand stiff, because he is going to scrunch my knuckles. He does, always. As his hand tightens like a vise, he always says, "I haven't read any of your books, *of course.*" Always *of course.* The female head doesn't approach. She stands chilly yards off and says coldly, "I only read biography myself, *of course.*" Note again the *of course.*

The proper response, I suppose, should be, "What are you people doing *not* reading books someone has specially written for the children in your charge?" But I never say it. I am too annoyingly polite. Besides, I am continually bemused by the way the question—particularly in this form—is on the same lines as "Have you stopped beating your wife yet?" And the other thing that bemuses me is the way the question takes so many forms. Even at its simplest—"Why don't you write Real Books?"—it is truly protean in its implications.

Before I start to answer it, I'd like to take a look at these implications.

The first implication—my mother-in-law's—is that writing fantasy for young people is not respectable in a woman, because a woman's function is solely to bring up children, but it is probably peculiar enough to keep a secret record of. This rather resembles Dr. Johnson's strictures of a woman preaching, which he likened to a dog standing on its hind legs. I think it is this aspect of the activity which so embarrasses the hairdresser. But my mother-in-law is also worried by the fact that anything written for children is necessarily going to have a wide appeal. It is, in its very nature, what she would call "popular fiction." My husband's colleague's wife widens this assumption, by concluding instantly that this means it is going to be largely without content though possibly quite pretty. And lurking under this is the assumption that none of it can be either worthwhile or any good. The teachers who feel thwarted of their class discussions pick up on this assumption: to their minds, the only real or worthwhile literature is concerned with current modern problems posed in a narrative that purports to be a slice of everyday life. There is a further implication here— that such problems are only *real* if they are acutely distressing to read about and maybe even insoluble into the bargain.

The fantasy fans bring in another aspect. What makes a book unreal for *them* is that it is not written for adults. I think the implication here is that no one under the age of, say, eighteen is a real person. This is a very common assumption, as anyone will agree who has stood in a shop and watched adults pushing aside any children waiting to be served. And the students, who have just attained the status of being real people, are worried about the fact that their chosen reading makes them unreal all over again. And they *enjoy* my books, which worries them on another account, because they think that at their advanced ages books are not to be enjoyed. (The teachers would back them up there.) Another thing that perplexes the students is that they are, at this late stage in their lives, getting new things out of the books, which they did not see as they read them as children—and they tend to find these new things supportive. Most of them write because they are feeling let down and disillusioned: university in your first year seldom seems anything like it was cracked up to be. The heartening thing here is that most of the students then conclude that they have made the wrong assumptions about what makes a Real Book. Even though some of them simply regard their first-year reading as regression, like thumb-sucking or a security toy, and grandly give it up in their second year, quite a few seriously revise their opinion and go on to write theses about children's literature.

I get to know about the theses because they write to me again in their third year for further information.

But there stand the heads of two-thirds of British schools, like monuments engraved with what a Real Book should be. Implicit in *their* attitudes is the thing that causes the question to be put to me in the first place. I am a woman. The male head would not crunch the knuckles of a male writer; the female head would stand closer to him. Both might phrase their remarks more apologetically—at least without the *of course*—and they might even have had the politeness to skim through one of his books before meeting him. But with me they have the backing of all the other posers of the question, from my mother-in-law on: females shouldn't really be doing this. This is particularly noticeable when, as quite often happens, one of my books is reviewed alongside a book by a male writer. He, being a man, is assumed to have powerful motives for writing fantasy for young people (for who otherwise would?) and the delicacy and power with which he conveys his message is most seriously gone into. The felicities of his language are remarked on and praised. Then the reviewer passes on to me: Jones always does this sort of thing—it's in her chromosomes, she can't help it, take no notice—but, really, as a woman, she should stop being *clever*. My brain hurts.

I think the hidden but constant assumption that, as a woman, I can't help writing for children because it is a byproduct of my natural function as a mother, and therefore as meaningless as a lullaby or a nonsense rhyme, is the one I probably resent most.

Actually my Pig of the Year Award went to the male reviewer of *Fire and Hemlock*. I quote it here in full: "This is a girl's book and I don't see why I should try to understand it." End review.

The same attitude is implicit in the teachers who want class discussion. They are prepared to notice that the fantasy element in the man's book might be a metaphor for something else. At least I am spared this. When I wrote *Witch Week*, I was afraid my metaphor for oppression might be too transparent, and that teachers might notice and use the book for class discussion. But so far as I know, not a single one has noticed. Women's books don't *mean* anything. And I have noticed that the male fans of fantasy never seem ashamed to be seen reading Terry Pratchett's *Truckers*, despite its juvenile jacket. As for the students, they write to me as a mother figure, trusting me to understand. The trouble is, I *do*. There seems nothing to do about the fact of my femininity except teach people to live with it.

Anyway, to get back to the Real Book as engraved in the minds of head teachers. It is written by a man. For adults. It contains only facts, or narrative purporting to be facts. It should appeal to few people. It should not be amusing. And it should contain a message, or at least a serious discussion of current problems, set out in such a way that this can be extracted for teaching purposes.

And there is a rider to this, or maybe it's another underlying and hidden assumption: that any exercise of the imagination on the part of writer or reader instantly renders a book unreal.

Probably we should be thankful that there are so few Real Books around.

Put tendentiously like this, no one will wonder why I fail to write Real Books, but this definition of the Real Book was one I only arrived at *after* I had already decided not to write them, and in response to people asking me why not in all these protean ways. The true answer lies, at least partly, way back in the past and is probably almost as protean as the question. What I want to do now is to try to give you some of the answers anyway.

Looking back on it, I can see now that the entire shape of my early life was pushing me toward writing the kind of books I write, right from the moment in the middle of one afternoon, at the age of eight, when I knew I was going to be a writer. I went downstairs and made a solemn announcement of this fact to my parents, who responded with jeering laughter. At the time, I thought this was because I was wildly dyslexic and had the utmost difficulty writing—two lines at the top of the page took me most of a day. I now realize that this was my parents' stock response to almost anything their children said.

I was the eldest of three girls, and my parents ran what would these days be called a conference center, in which they were occupied full-time, with no time for children. We were put to live in an unheated outhouse away across a yard, just the three of us, and largely forgotten. And I mean forgotten. Such clothes as we had, until I started being able to make clothes, were castoffs from the local orphanage, and the people in the main house were quite often too preoccupied to remember to feed us. Looking back on it, I often wonder how we didn't kill one another in our outhouse, since the only heating we had was a crude paraffin stove which we knocked over daily, when it was alight, in the course of various games. In fact, at one point, my youngest sister and I pretty nearly hanged our middle sister—with two skipping ropes—at this sister's own earnest request, I hasten to say; she wanted to know how it felt to be a pantomime fairy flying on ropes across the stage. This would have been a sad loss in every way, because this sister, under her married name of Isobel Armstrong, is now professor of English at Birkbeck College in London. But luckily we noticed she was beginning to die and cut her down in time.

Anyone who has read *The Time of the Ghost* will probably recognize this incident, and indeed quite a bit of the rest.

What you may not recognize are the various deeply ingrained lessons I learned from this life. For a start, it occurred to none of us then to question the fact that my father, as the son of a patriarchal Welsh preacher, had nothing but contempt for girls, or that my mother hated all females and regarded her daughters as rivals (to the extent of dressing us in rags). We speculate now, like anything. None of us can see why our parents went on and had three of us. We can only conclude they were trying for a boy. But at that time it was just part of normal life. So was all the rest of it. We just saw it as *normal*. I can't stress this too strongly, how *ordinary* this seemed. If anyone showed us a factual story at that time in which our particular problems were represented, we were bored and disregarded the story as just ordinary, or, by the time we had reached our teens and were dimly aware that our life was by no means ordinary, we responded with acute distress. From this I concluded, very early on, that it was both unproductive and unkind to write the kind of book that was a factual presentation of any social problem. Either it passed you by, or it upset you because there was nothing you could do about it. I think teachers who demand discussion of such things are wholly insensitive to how *helpless* a child is before problems imposed by parents or society.

But where we *did* respond was to the same situations represented as fairy stories, or legends, or myths. My sister Isobel, for instance, was addicted to "The Little Mermaid," which she read once a week and cried pints over regularly. This was because my mother had early on decreed that my sister should be a ballet dancer, on the grounds that she had the right face for it. And her face was probably perfect for it, but my mother disregarded her body, which rapidly grew too big and caused her to be turned down by all the major ballet schools. This was a huge tragedy to my sister: she was deprived of her one chance to earn her mother's approval. She had failed. So to read once a week of the little mermaid, who was not built to dance, but had been enabled to do so, albeit with acute pain, was exactly what she needed.

As surrogate mother to my sister, I had a lot of comforting to do, but I tended to take a bracing and contemptuous line about the dismalness of "The Little Mermaid." This was because I had, of course, my own troubles too. My favorite reading, and from which I derived the same sort of help, was a huge old volume called *Epics and Romances of the Middle Ages*, which my grandmother had won as a Sunday school prize at the age of six. This was a collection of almost every heroic legend from Northern Europe that you care to name, although minus the Arthurian cycle and the *Kalevala*. It did not matter to me that not all the stories ended happily—although I preferred them to do so, because I needed to hope—nor did it matter that all the heroes represented, apart from Brunhilde, were male. I read and reread them because what I was after was paradigms of valor. Not useless valor like Roland's, who blew his horn too late—I only read that one once—but real, effective, striving valor that killed you the dragon, like Siegfried. When you are a small girl in sole charge of two smaller girls, you are very much in need of valor.

We were girls and we were children, and as both we were regarded as non-people by our parents and by every other adult we knew. But of course we knew we were people too. As a consequence I grew up keeping it firmly in mind that children *are* real people. Not only that, but I learned early on that childhood is such an important and impressionable time of anyone's life that very careful, special provision should be made for it. Having said that, at this stage I still thought I was going to write books for adults.

The conference center was in a very beautiful house in an even more beautiful village. The village was so beautiful that

American tourists began to arrive in the place almost before the war was ended, and were always very put out to discover there was no public lavatory. Almost every aspect of the place was bizarre in some way. The house was haunted. I never saw the ghost myself, although I always ran through the grand front hall with my eyes shut if possible, and never, on any account, lingered there. And a few years later one of the girls who was working in the house as a cleaner turned and talked to the other girl cleaner in this same hall. After a bit she wondered why Aline didn't answer, and then realized she could see through her. Whereupon she ran off screaming and took a job at the bacon factory in Great Dunmow—on the grounds that buckets of blood were better than ghosts. In addition, the place was filled with folk who made pots and wove very ugly cloth and did folk dancing in the streets. One of them was the only man I know who could dance the polka amorously. I could go on for hours. *Everyone* was cuckoo in some way, including most of the people who came to the conference center. To take just one example, the county music adviser, who was an aging tenor, decided he would sing an aria from the roof of the house—which he did, and got so carried away that he did an encore, scattering what seemed to be confetti. It was later discovered that the confetti was in fact every scrap of toilet paper in the house. More had to be hastily procured.

You can see from this that I grew up assuming that ghosts and witches were a natural part of life, and that bizarre events and even more bizarre adults were the norm. We spent a lot of time dealing with these adults. Our parents frequently went off and left us alone, and we were expected to act as hostesses to whatever lunatic turned up in their absence. I think this is why my books are filled with dotty and exacting adults: I have a very strong sense of how much time children have to devote to coping with the adults in their lives. But far more than that, I gained an even stronger sense of the value of laughter. We spent a lot of time doubled up with laughter at these assorted lunacies, and though we were all very unhappy, the unhappiness became bearable because we laughed. In fact, from quite early on, I became aware that unhappiness and hilarity are very closely associated.

At that point I was in my first term at university. There, I found I couldn't talk about my bizarre background at all, because I had by then realized that it was not normal, and it was clear to me that no one would believe me. I still have trouble this way. I very seldom put anything in my books which is directly about my childhood, and when I do, I always feel I have to tone it down for credibility. For instance, in *The Time of the Ghost*, Fenella ties her hair in two knots to keep it out of her eyes, and this fact is not noticed for four days. My sister Ursula actually did this, but the truth is that the knots—one large lump on either side of her forehead—were not noticed for *six months*.

I mentioned earlier two things that my sisters and I habitually read. These two books were about a quarter of the books we possessed at that time. We suffered from a perpetual book famine. I suppose there is nothing better calculated to impress on you the importance of books than being without them, but I do not find I am grateful for it. My father was the meanest man I know—he could have Scrooged for Earth against Mars and won—and he could not bring himself to buy anything for us. He allowed us one penny a week pocket money for years—and you could not, even in those days, buy *anything* for a penny—until my sisters managed to persuade him we needed more, whereupon he allowed us one shilling a week on condition that we bought our own soap and toothpaste. To give you some idea of the inadequacy of this, I must explain that a tube of toothpaste then cost one shilling and ninepence. But he had been a schoolmaster and he knew that even girls should read books. He salved his conscience by buying the complete works of Arthur Ransome, which he locked in a high cupboard and dispensed, one between the three of us, every Christmas. I was literally about to enter university when the last book was given us. What other books we had we begged and scrounged, mostly from folk who would otherwise have thrown the books away. These were largely Victorian or Edwardian volumes, redolent of mildew, and all of them were very poor examples of the kind of book of which *What Katy Did* is rather a *good* representative—the story was always about a girl who starts out as unfeminine and naughty, but ends up in a wheelchair as a model of piety, a perfect angel, but good for nothing else. When we arranged our books on our bookshelf, these books all went into the longest shelf which was labeled GODDY BOOKS. Half the shortest shelf contained GOOD BOOKS, and these were either folktales or adventure stories.

From the age of twelve, I was making clothes for my sisters and doing their washing and so forth, and it seemed a natural extension of this that I should try to supply the lack of books by writing books myself. I had a stack of music manuscript books given to me by my grandmother, and in these I wrote two long novels which I read out to my sisters in installments. If you have ever tried to write on music paper, you will understand why ever after I have not been able to bear any kind of lined paper. But I finished two books before I was fifteen. It is quite important to any writer to know that she can orchestrate and then conclude a long narrative. But it is also interesting to look at what was in those books. The first was a picaresque story from the point of view of one lad. For the second book, I took off and handled a whole gang of boys, from multiple points of view. And I remember that one of my chief delights in writing this one was in discovering that my characters had minds of their own. Whenever a small group split off from the main gang, it was not always the boy I expected who took the lead. But why boys? Well, if your main reading for girls shows them ending up in wheelchairs, it is obvious that boys live much more exciting lives.

This was still the assumption when I first started writing in earnest, which was not actually until I was over thirty. At that time, no boy would dream of reading a book with a girl as the main character. My children were all boys, so I had ample evidence of this. But the reverse was not true. When *Eight Days of Luke* was published, I did a radio interview with some Oxford schoolchildren—four boys and a token girl—and the interviewer kept saying that this book was an exciting read for boys. And the token girl said each time, louder and louder, "*And* gurrls!" in a vehement Oxford Town accent. This was 1975. The impact of feminism came later than that, and very slowly. I experienced it mostly as a slow easement—a sort of growing feeling that I wouldn't automatically halve my readership if I had a female central character.

But to get back to my juvenilia in its dozens of music books. Neither narrative was a fantasy. I can see now there were two reasons for this. The first reason is a bizarre reversal of the usual situation. If you are living the life of Cinderella, in a village where there are witches and ghosts and someone who howls like a wolf in the church porch at full moon, you are not going to want these things in a book. In a sort of way my narratives *were* fantasy, except that they were fantasies about what I conceived to be normal life. The second reason is more important, and it has nothing to do with assumptions about Real Books or anything like that. It was that I knew proper fantasy was the really difficult thing to write and that I wasn't ready to try. I had one model for what this difficult thing was— that was a book by Elizabeth Goudge called *The Little White Horse*—and it was clear to me that it would be years before I could even try to do anything like that. I had no illusions about my narratives in music books. I knew they were no good, and I cheerfully abandoned them in another haunted house near Nottingham where we moved after my father died. My feeling was that, as narratives about normal life, they were as forgettable as yesterday's newspaper.

This feeling seemed to be borne out by my own children. When they were old enough, they responded fervently to any kind of fantasy. Mindful of my own deprivation, I bought them book upon book, and I had all the pleasure and astonishment of discovering almost a hundred excellent books for children, but as an adult. It was quite a bitter discovery that most of these hundred books had been available during my own childhood and that I could have read them then; but, looking back on it, I suspect it was a great advantage to read them with an adult and analytical mind for the first time, to discover how they were put together and to be able to watch three young children's response to these books. When they were older and about to leave school, I asked my sons to make a list (before they forgot) of all the most memorable books of their childhood. All three responded with a list of fantasies, except the middle one put in Rudyard Kipling's *Kim*, and, when asked about that, said he thought it was set in an alternative world. He had had no idea Kipling's India was real.

All the books on the lists were nearly as old as *Kim*. The huge resurgence of children's books that happened mostly in the 1970s was then only beginning, and it was a sad fact that most of the newer books were hardly worth reading then. My sons complained vociferously. I suppose it was quite natural for me to try to write something they might like better. It was something my childhood had trained me to do. I knew by then the kind of book I wanted to write, but it proved quite as difficult as I had supposed in my teens. I had been brought up, if you can call it brought up, reading and writing from the wrong model, you see, and I had really to think through *and* to practice doing it in what seemed to me the *right* way—no, worse, I had to *discover* the right way for me. It took years.

Meanwhile, as I said before, I assumed I would also write for adults. It seemed easier. The trouble was, what I started writing was what is now called adult fantasy, and there was no such thing in those days. The *only* adult fantasy was Tolkien's *The Lord of the Rings*, and that was not considered a Real Book at all. Whenever it was mentioned there was a chorus of people saying "Why can't he stick to what he's good at— being an Anglo-Saxon scholar?" And, besides, what I was writing was not at all like Tolkien. I have always been very determined to do my *own thing*. I wrote a long adult novel called *The Incubus*,[3] about a young wife and mother who was having the sort of terrible time women were *expected* to have in those days, who as a sort of defense created this fantasy that she had hired a devil from hell—by the usual means of selling her soul—to be her ideal lover. Or *was* it her fantasy? I remember when about a decade later I read Germaine Greer's *The Female Eunuch*, I was crying out at almost every page, "But this is just what I was saying in *The Incubus*!" And I really was, but, it seems, rather before the proper time. At any rate, I sent this novel to an agent, and it was very clear she thought I was deranged. She summoned me to London to have a look at me, and the moment I saw her expression, I remember thinking "She believes I'm mad!" and I remember trying very hard not to appear even neurotic—which was very difficult, because I was extremely nervous. I have no idea how well I succeeded, but she agreed to try and place the book. She was an odd woman with a way of proceeding which was extremely strange, although at that time I thought it was normal. She sent me a carefully escalated series of publishers' rejections. When I didn't seem to be discouraged by one, she sent me another that was nastier, and so on. (As my present agent does no such thing, I conclude this lady was unusual.) The letters were to the effect that "Women don't *do* this! This mixing of make-believe into real life is preposterous, and besides, it's rude to men! This is not a Real Book."

Eventually I did become extremely discouraged and withdrew the book, concluding that events were forcing me toward writing for children. Here at least, women were allowed to operate. It seemed the only thing I was allowed to do—and it had the advantage of being an infinitely open and versatile field, where, at that time, there was, as I said, a dearth of good books.

You can probably see by now what I meant when I said that the entire shape of my early life seemed to be pushing me toward writing unreal books. But I would not like to give the impression that my decision to write solely for children and young adults was either a gloomy one or a cynical one. I had started off by writing for my sisters, and I had always intended to write for people of this age *as well*, and events seemed to push me steadily that way. You will have noticed how the ingredients of my nonreal books simply seemed to gather as I went along. In order to show you how very uncynical the whole process was, I would like to add one more ingredient, again from my childhood.

The conference center had two gardens. The one beside the house was empty and formal, and this was the public one that everybody used. The Other Garden, as it was called, was beyond this, across a road. This garden was kept locked and no one from the house went there. The county council, which ran the conference center, employed a gardener, who would periodically emerge from this Other Garden, very grudgingly supplying the minimum of the vegetables and flowers from it. He attended to the public garden, but only briefly, and always retired back to the locked garden after he had had his morning cup of tea. Over this cup of tea he would tell anyone who cared to listen about the mistakes of his youth. As a young man, he said, he had been very worried about whether he would get to heaven when he died, so every Sunday he was accustomed to go first to church and then to chapel. Then one day he was cycling on the road to a village called Great

Sampford and an angel descended to him in a blaze of light and told him two things: that he should always go to chapel and not church, and that he should never, ever join a trade union. He was very matter-of-fact about this. I have noticed since that everybody who has had a vision always speaks about it in this matter-of-fact way.

Anyway, whenever things got difficult for me—and believe me they do if you are the least wanted of three unwanted children and the wrong sex into the bargain—I would go and beg the key of this Other Garden from my father. He would give his ritual response: "Don't bother me now, child." And I would persist. Eventually, if I didn't get hit, I got the key, and could go into this amazing, deserted, utterly beautiful garden, where most of the time I was completely alone and totally removed from the lunacies and the unhappiness in which I normally lived.

Someone is going to say that this was like Frances Hodgson Burnett's *The Secret Garden*, and I must say at once that it was not. Not at all. I got hold of that book when I was fourteen—begged a loan of it from someone, I think—and it never occurred to me *once* to identify that garden with the Other Garden. The Secret Garden was a wild garden. Overgrown, and moreover rather obviously symbolic. The Other Garden was lovingly cultivated, perfectly maintained. It was crowned with well-pruned standard roses and apple trees of every kind, and soft fruit and vegetables in rows behind espaliered pear trees. Every so often you came across strange little shrines made of broken pieces of Venetian glass that had been built by the gardener—oddly pagan things for such a God-fearing man. The gate opened on a half-circle of perfectly tended, shaven lawn, which was so unused that it was usually covered with dew, in which the only footprints were mine, and a further avenue of lawn led under rose arches right to the other end, where there was an ivy-covered, octagonal summerhouse. I usually went there when the gardener had gone, so I only once saw the marvelous sight—which I was told happened almost daily in summer—of the gardener racing down this central aisle in a crowd of angry bees, trying terribly hard not to swear (for, as I think I have made clear, he was a godly man). Those bees lived in hives by the summerhouse, and they were of a strain notorious throughout the county for their aggression. My father could only approach them wearing special clothes and waving a smoke maker. But the real marvel was that they never went for me. Ever. The hives stood in a wide patch of weeds, because the gardener had only to go near for them to attack him, but I used to be able to go right up to them and watch them landing and taking off. I had read that you should always tell the bees your news, so I told them things. They never seemed to mind.

This garden strikes me now, though it didn't at the time, as a perfect analogue of what a good book (as opposed to a Real Book) should be, though I must confess I'm not too clear as to how the gardener and the bees fit in. A good book should be another place, beyond ordinary life and quite different from it, made with care and containing marvels. But though it is beyond everyday life, it is by no means unconnected with it. You have to beg the key. And—maybe this is where the bees at least fit in—you can tell the bees things. The bees don't solve your problems. You have to do that. But the mere fact of having taken your mind to another place for a while, if that place is sufficiently wonderful, means that you come back with *experience*. I know I always came back from the Other Garden much more able to deal with what was sometimes truly frightful pressure.

My aim nowadays is to provide this kind of *experience*. I would like to provide it for adults too, but most of them don't seem to want it. But I can provide it at least for people on whom it may make a lasting impression. Taking someone *away* from the pressures under which they live is much more valuable than grinding their noses into the fact that they are, say, of the wrong race or that their parents are divorcing, or both; particularly if, while they are away, this person is given a chance to use their imagination. Imagination doesn't just mean making things up. It means thinking things through, solving them, or hoping to do so, and being just distant enough to be able to laugh at things that are normally painful. Head teachers would call this escapism, but they would be entirely wrong. I would call fantasy the most serious, and the most useful, branch of writing there is. And this is why I don't, and never would, write Real Books.

Inventing the Middle Ages

"Inventing the Middle Ages" was the title of a one-day conference organized by the University of Nottingham's Institute for Medieval Research on May 17, 1997. As Diana says in her preface, the organizer, the late Professor Christine Fell, hoped that Diana would have a fresh viewpoint on the topic. Diana wrote that her subsequent talk was about influences.

When I was asked to speak at this conference I wondered if there was anything I had to say at all. I was rather off the whole idea of the Middle Ages, since I had recently finished writing a thing called *The Tough Guide to Fantasyland* which pokes fun at large numbers of adult fantasies set in what the writers fondly believe to be a medieval landscape. That is to say, all towns have the houses leaning out over the pavements so that the occupants can empty chamberpots on those below and contain lots of winding alleys heaped with refuse. In the countryside there is subsistence farming, if that. As *The Tough Guide to Fantasyland* says:

FARMING obviously takes place, since produce appears in the markets, and the Tour will sometimes take you past cultivated fields. But most fields will have been trampled and burnt by armies, or else parched by magical drought. Dairy farming seems very rare. This probably accounts for the extreme dullness of most meals in Fantasyland.

Or, again in the countryside:

*HOVELS are small squalid dwellings, either in a village or occasionally up a mountain, and probably most resemble huts. The people who live in hovels are evidently rather lazy and not very good with their hands, since in no cases have any repairs been done to these buildings (*tumbledown, rotting thatch, *etc., are the official clichés) and there is no such thing as a clean hovel. Indoors, the inhabitants* eke out a wretched existence *(another official cliché), which you can see they would, given the drafts, smoke, and general lack of house-cleaning. This need not alarm you. The Tour will not allow you to enter a hovel that is inhabited. If you enter one at all, it will be* long deserted *(another official cliché) and there will be sanitary arrangements out the back.*

And merchants tend to be rushing about the place with nameless merchandise in bales. And when the story gets to a castle, you will always find the occupants chewing chicken drumsticks and then throwing the bones to the dogs.

My spleen was aroused about this kind of thing while I was helping a friend compile an encyclopedia of fantasy. We were going through the possible entries alphabetically, and it was at the point when we came to the entry of Nunnery and both chorused "Nunneries are for sacking," that I said, "You know, these books are all so much the same that I could write the guidebook for this country!" after which I thought, "Why not?" And did so. Here are the entries from *The Tough Guide* for "Nunneries" and "Monasteries":

NUNNERIES. The rule is that any nunnery you approach, particularly if you are in dire need of rest, healing, or provisions, will prove to have been recently sacked. You will find the place a smoking ruin littered with corpses. You will be shocked and wonder who could have done this thing. Your natural curiosity will shortly be satisfied, because there is a further rule that there will be one survivor, either a very young novice or a very old nun, who will give you a graphic account of the raping and burning and the names of the perpetrators. If old, she will then die, thus saving you from having to take her along and feed her from your dwindling provisions; if a novice, she will either die also, or else prove not to be as nunnish as you thought.

MONASTERIES *are thick stone buildings on a steep hill. They are full of passages, cloisters, and tiny cells, all with no heating, and inhabited by monks who are mostly elderly and austere, some rather addled in their wits. At the head of the monastery there will be an abbot, who is usually portly and sly. These establishments have three uses:*

i) For Scrolls. Any Scroll containing information vital to the quest is likely to be jealously guarded in a monastery. It is not advisable to say you have come to look at this Scroll. In cases where the monks are willing to let you see the Scroll, you will find that the Keeper of Scrolls has recently lost his reason and the Scroll with it. . . .

ii) For sanctuary and rest. In this case you will come pounding up to the monastery at dusk, with the forces of Dark hard on your heels. You will have to hammer on the huge oaken *(an official cliché) door, but they will let you in. Once inside, you are safe. . . . But the problem comes when you have to get out again. . . .*

iii) For sacking. Here you come pounding up to the building with the forces of Dark half a day behind, only to find it a heap of smoking stones. But there will be one survivor. . . .

It is all very historical, in that all the characters wear cloaks and go round waving swords, and the only transport is horses.

These effusions are mostly written by people in California, which probably accounts for the fact that all the inhabitants of the barbarian North go round in the snow wearing nothing but a fur loincloth, and the writers are quite frank about their attitude to historical knowledge. As *The Tough Guide* says:

HISTORY is generally patchy and unreliable. Any real information about events in the past is either lost or in a Scroll jealously guarded by a monastery or temple. All that can be ascertained with any certainty is:

i) That there was once an Empire that ruled the continent from coast to coast . . . but this shrank to one city a long time before the Tour, leaving only a few roads. . . .

ii) That there was once a wizards' war that occurred earlier still . . .

See LEGENDS, as more reliable sources of information.

After all, what does any of this matter when the main point of the book—or books: they are nearly always trilogies—is a quest to conquer the Dark Lord and Save the World?

You can see that this left me with a jaundiced view. These writers are inventing the Middle Ages, all right, I thought, but this is very much How Not to Do It. But then I thought, "Oh come on! There is a positive side to the matter or I wouldn't have got so irritated." What I, personally, think of as the Middle Ages has to have been an abiding influence on me—I know that, and it's not simply because I happen to be married to a medievalist. For instance, in the book I'm currently writing I called two of the characters—quite spontaneously—Kit and Callette. And it was only after a while I thought, "Those names are familiar from somewhere else," and recalled they were the names of Will's wife and daughter in *Piers Plowman*.

My two characters happen to be griffins, which rather hid the connection from me at first. But the influence is hard to pin down for one very good reason. I write mainly for children.

Children as a group have almost no sense of history at all. They are by their nature the most forward-looking section of the population. They are intent on growing up. Most of them can't wait to be adult. For this reason, they are not going to be very interested in books that are not about here and now and what is to come. When I first started writing for children, I made a conscious decision to write mostly about the present day (or a semblance of the present day set in an alternative world) and not to go out of my way to inculcate a sense of history that isn't there.

Now a lot of children's writers do write historical novels, and a lot more introduce people out of the past in the manner of Kipling's *Puck of Pook's Hill*. I don't find this easy to do. The one time I tried to write a historical novel—about tenth-century Iceland—I did quite a lot of research for it, until I came hard up against a fact I just couldn't get my mind round: there were no trees in Iceland at the time. I found I just could not conceive of a landscape wholly without trees. And I couldn't write the book, or any other with a proper historical setting. Those absent trees caused me to realize that there was always going to be *something* I couldn't get my mind round, whatever period I might choose. I do actually quite envy people who don't have this problem, but as far as I am concerned it is a complete block. Mostly it is that I suspect that my thoughts have been trained to run in certain grooves, according to the twentieth century, and the thoughts of people living at different times in the past would have been trained to run in quite other grooves. I wouldn't be able to get my mind round *their* minds, if you see what I mean.

I have two other powerful reasons for not writing historically. First, as a child I hated overt didacticism in books. We had a long shelf of books that tried to teach you something under the disguise of a story, and we labeled that shelf GODDY BOOKS. My own children felt just the same. Second, one of my sons at about the age of twelve developed a total passion for Kipling's *Kim*, which he read over and over again. I was under the impression that, to him, this book was a historical novel re-creating an empire and an India which had disappeared long before he was born. Not a bit of it. When he was fifteen, he confessed that he had thought *Kim* was a fantasy set in an alternative world and that Kipling had made all the India stuff up. So much, I thought, for inculcating a sense of history. It's possible that many children regard historical novels as this kind of fantasy. In which they are not exactly wrong.

All the same, I have a strong sense that everything I do write is quite deeply influenced by what I perceive as the Middle Ages. I am grateful for having been asked to speak here. It has made me dig about and find out just what the influence is. It starts with two things dragged from memory.

First, when I was eight, I started reading Malory in the edition my mother had used as an undergraduate. My parents did not really believe in books especially for children, so the language was a bit of a struggle—and the small print—but I read with enormous enthusiasm. Things like "How Sir Lancelot slew three Giants and set a Castle Free" really turned me on. I had got to the middle of "Tristram and Isolt," when my mother told me sternly that I must remember that knights didn't really wear armor in King Arthur's day. This totally bewildered me. "How did they *manage* then, when they were fighting?" I wondered, and pondered deeply. My ponderings led me to locate that sense that everyone acquires, that there is a "story time" which has nothing to do with history. Story time is when things bizarre or adventurous or enchanted can happen, as in the "Once upon a time" of fairy stories. So of course the knights could wear armor: they were in this story time and it didn't matter. (I was slightly irritated, as an adult, when I read T. H. White's *The Sword in the Stone* and found him painstakingly and patronizingly describing his "story time." It is something everyone knows about. I just happened to know it consciously rather early on.)

Second, about four years after that, my father suddenly took it into his head to give his daughters an educational trip to the National Gallery in London. He did this sort of thing at arbitrary intervals and usually managed to arrive so late that wherever it was had shut for the day. On this occasion, his timing was off and the National Gallery was actually still open, and we went round. One picture caught my fancy. It was of a little bishop in pink robes appearing over and over again in a rocky landscape. He was obviously being in several places at once, the way saints and other supernaturally gifted folk can be. I was fascinated, because it was so clearly a story time picture. My father, looking over my shoulder, explained that the bishop was wearing the wrong clothes. He was dressed as a medieval bishop would be at the time of the painter, whereas in his real lifetime he would be wearing a toga. My father then led me in front of a huge painting of the martyrdom of St. Sebastian and delivered a lecture on the meaning of the word "anachronism." I stared at the archer bending down in the foreground of the painting—who, my father stated, should really have been dressed as a Roman legionary—and I stared at the points stretching so tightly across his linen drawers between his hose and whatever held the hose up, and I couldn't help thinking how *uncomfortable* this particular medieval fashion must have been—he'd have been better off in a Roman tunic. But it was interesting. It was quite obvious that in the Middle Ages (whenever that far-off misty time was) people conceived of this story time as being contemporary with their own. That made me very wistful at the time because I couldn't imagine my favorite knight, Sir Gawain, in a suit or tweeds however hard I strained to see it.

This is actually a very important idea. If you are going to write for a non-historical, forward-looking audience, you ideally need the story time to be here and now. I took this idea up with enthusiasm. It is why most of what I write is set in this modern age whenever possible. For instance, writing an early book called *Eight Days of Luke*, in which the Norse gods appear as modern men and woman and Sleipnir—Woden's horse—as a large white car chauffeured by a Valkyrie, I was quite consciously imitating what I took to be a medieval treatment of story time.

Anyway, in due course I went up to Oxford and read English, where a large part of the course concerned itself with what was called Middle English—and it is a very odd thing that there were quite a few women who were there at the same time as me—none of whom I met—who all went on to write successfully for children afterward. I have never known what quite inspired them all, but with me I know it was suddenly being confronted with the way writers from the Middle Ages handled narratives. They were all so *different*, that was the amazing thing, and all so good at it.

Foremost, of course, was the highly sophisticated Geoffrey Chaucer. In *The Canterbury Tales* you could watch Chaucer show his sophistication by adjusting his style and manner according to who was telling what kind of story. He seems to *play* with narrative in a way that can be perfectly wicked at times (and I know I thought recently, "Well, if Chaucer can send up tail-rhyme romance in 'Sir Thopas,' no doubt out of the same sort of irritation I feel at Californian writers of fantasy, then I can do the same in *The Tough Guide*"). But with Chaucer, apart from "Sir Thopas," each of his stories is a serious exercise in a certain type of narrative; he sets boundaries and shows what can be done within them, and without realizing it at the time, I joyfully picked up on this notion. There are fairly severe boundaries set if you write for children—and I don't mean tedious things like political correctness, which varies from decade to decade, I mean things like not using language that is too complicated and not using those kind of situations in which two people of opposite sexes are sparring for openings or dominance, because most children find both these things puzzling. And you want to give your readers the benefit of your own knowledge of the world without being overtly didactic, as I said. So you see what you can do inside these limits, and usually also, sadly, within certain limits of political correctness—as Chaucer himself says, making a virtue of necessity. And of course you can do a very great deal. It's a challenge. Chaucer himself only seems to have scratched the surface of what might be done—he didn't finish the exercise of *The Canterbury Tales*. I think among what he did do, I admire most his ability to tell a story which is well known—as in "Troilus and Creseyde"—or a story in which it is quite clear what is coming—as in "The Reeve's Tale"—and still get you to respond as if you had no idea what was coming next. That is something I have tried to do too, and I know the difficulties. But Chaucer is such a deft and elastic writer, so experimental as well as serious, that I at least came away with the feeling that because he so obviously made narrative an exercise of skills, no one was ever quite comfortable telling a straight story again. It wasn't quite respectable to write a naive narrative like Malory did later. Malory wasn't respectable and probably didn't care; he just crashed ahead telling his story in *and-and-and* chunks, building brick by brick, telling the relevant and irrelevant things in almost exactly the same tone of voice, so that the overall shape was not apparent until he got to the end. But you feel everybody else found they couldn't do that; they had to make that kind of story at least an allegory, or put in a lot of philosophy. Or something more refined.

Now the beauty of this situation is that it frees up the straight story to be devoted to children. Unfortunately, it also frees it for writers from California to get to work with their quests and Dark Lords—there's a reverse side to everything. I know I did pounce on this freeing up: I can tell a story because no one else wants to! Oh good.

But then, by complete contrast, I came up against William Langland, who is doing something entirely different and wholly serious and not exactly straight narrative at all. Langland haunts me because he is such a strange mixture of deep thinking and jamming down what happens to be in his head and hoping, then thinking, thinking, taking in another swatch of ideas and thinking again. His work reminds me of the tide coming in: you know how one wave comes frilling up and erases a few footprints in the sand, and then goes back, and the next comes in over the top of it and gets a bit farther, until the sea is right up where the deep footprints and the ice-cream papers are. Langland seems to me quite as inexorable, and he covers pretty well everything in his way. And at the end of *Piers Plowman* the tide goes out again. Damn! Still haven't quite got to the seawall. Have to go out and look for Piers again. What has always impressed me here is what you can achieve if you get behind your narrative (or as-it-were narrative) and really push. The ideas start to run about over the top of it, interlaced like the foam on the top of waves. The first thing Langland taught me is that ideas are just as important as a story—I hadn't grasped that before then. The next thing was slightly more accidental, that is the way *what* you are saying and *how* you are saying it are very closely linked. I don't know if anyone here has ever tried to write Langland's kind of alliterative verse. I had a go once or twice. It's not easy. You find, unless you are violently inventive about it, that the form forces you to go back and repeat the latest half line at the beginning of the next line, only in different terms. Langland is good enough at it that he doesn't do this much, but the impulse is there and contributes to the overlapping, wave after wave, tide-coming-in nature of the narrative.

Learning a little from this, I discovered that I always had to let the book I was writing find its own style. Only in that way can you be sure that you are doing the right thing by your subject matter. It's a strange feeling, as if the book has a life of its own.

Of all the writers I discovered as a student, Langland gets under my skin most—witness the way I called my two griffins Kit and Callette. A long time ago, I wrote a novel that was based on *Piers Plowman*. Oh dear. Publishers to a man and woman sent it back to me on the grounds that the main character was not present at the most important parts of the action. Quite true. Probably only Langland could get away with something like that. Much later, I wrote another book called *Fire and Hemlock*, in which I tried not to make that mistake and in which I got behind the narrative and pushed, Langland fashion. Langland lies behind that particular book in a way I find it hard to define, even more than the ballad of "Tam Lin" or T. S. Eliot's *Four Quartets*, which are present in the foreground (possibly rather as the Bible and prayer book were to Langland—or so I hope). I think it is in the movement of the narrative that his influence lies, but I am not sure. It is orchestrated in a tidelike advance and retreat, full of partial repetitions, where some things acquire a new meaning at each advance. Or so I hope.

On the other hand, when I think about learning to orchestrate a narrative, particularly the more ordinary, clipping style of narrative, I realize that I learned that from the Gawain poet. He has it down absolutely in *Sir Gawain and the Green Knight*. He knows when to pass quickly over time, and when to dwell on episodes. That is, he knows when to just tell you things were so and when to make you feel them so in your gut, and he knows what action to dwell on, and what colors, noises, details to highlight (or show in close-up); when to give direct speech, when indirect; and, even more important, how to balance the mixture out, so that the story is never overweighted in the wrong place. This is all the organizational stuff that Jane

Austen had laboriously to teach herself when she rewrote *Pride and Prejudice* using an almanac. The Gawain poet has got it all. I think I use him as a sort of paradigm narrator all the time. Furthermore, he backs up my discovery in the National Gallery by having his story time in his own present time, really. His magical characters live in an up-to-date modern castle, with all the latest architectural features. I think my Chrestomanci books owe quite a lot to this.

I'll pass over Robert Henryson. I never got on with him. But there is one other work from within the time I think of as the Middle Ages, which almost did more than teach me—it came as a revelation—and that is "Sir Orfeo." This is a work that, alas, lies behind quite a lot of the Californian quest stories and any modern Pre-Raphaelitism (which is still alive too, and living in California, where writers make romantic stories about elves and mist and dim blowings and things) and it is, of course, a romantic poem. I never could work out whether the person or persons who wrote it knew what they were doing or not. At any rate, the reason I found it such a revelation was that it was the story of Orpheus and Eurydice, which is the kind of story you might call "hard myth" (on an analogy with "hard science fiction," meaning the crystal-clear, nitty-gritty, no-nonsense kind) which has been transmogrified into, as it were, "soft myth," as a story of fairyland and enchantment. Orpheus goes to Hades. Sir Orfeo has to negotiate with something hazier, possibly with wider powers than a mere god of the dead—something that can grab you at midday if you sleep under a certain kind of tree. Until I read this poem, I hadn't realized that this sort of translation from one type of story to another was possible. Once I did realize, I did some furious thinking, lasting for about ten years, and came up with the discovery that translating need not apply only to types of story. You can make other kinds of translation as well, all equally useful and all equally telling. The other kinds I began to use straightaway and almost habitually. Are there minorities persecuted for physical facts they can't help? Then translate those minorities into witches who develop at puberty powers they can't suppress and get burned for it. Or I wanted to write about children of divorced parents whose mother remarries. Translate the problems these children have into magical or alchemical misadventures. Or a boy struggling into adolescence in the face of an unkind family? Have the boy's feelings appear in the shape of the Norse gods. But in all these instances you must not cheat. You must have the magical occurrences strongly effective in their own terms. They must leave their mark on the everyday life of the characters in the story, just as "Sir Orfeo" hangs together consistently in terms of faerie rather than Hades.

Oddly enough, it took me a while to learn to translate an actual story. I suppose I began doing it with *Charmed Life*, which is really what they call a Gothic Romance reversed— young heroine defenseless in frowning Cornish castle ruled by a flinty-hearted macho lord—only in this case the young heroine is a sort of fifth column for an attack on the castle and most people are defenseless before her. By then I was up and running and did it again with *Howl's Moving Castle*— fairy-story heroine goes bravely to castle to rescue prince under enchantment—except that in this case they rescue one another, quarreling fiercely while they do. And in *Hexwood* I had real medievalizing fun translating chunks of Arthurian stories into a story about a super-computer.

Actually, I find I have abashed myself considerably by comparing the things I do with these masterpieces out of the past. What I am really trying to describe are the things I found in the Middle Ages and what they meant to me. I think the Middle Ages invented *me*, rather than the other way round. And I'd like to conclude with telling you about the lady in Australia. I was in Sydney giving a talk and the lady came up to me saying she was writing a study of a book of mine called *The Magicians of Caprona*. I enjoyed writing that particular book. I got the name Caprona from Dante (another borrowing from the Middle Ages), and like Chaucer and Shakespeare after him, I'd cheerfully borrowed the story of Romeo and Juliet and put it in there. What the lady said to me was, "Pardon me, is your intertextuality intentional?" I said, "Your *what*?" And she said, "Did you know that you've put the story of Romeo and Juliet into your book?" "Oh that," I said. "Yes, of course." It seemed extraordinary to me that anyone could think that one could write anything without being heavily indebted to things that had gone before—and not know it. What I want to say is, yes, I do know really where I'm getting it from, and it is intentional, and very grateful I am too.

Some Truths About Writing

This was a talk given at the Children's Books Ireland conference in May 2002. Children's Books Ireland aims to create a greater understanding of the importance of books for young people.

The reason I gave this talk the title I did is that I found myself wanting to do something I have never seen properly done before, and that is to try and tell at least some of the truth about the way one actually writes a book—to describe what people call "the creative process" in fact.

This is something writers are always being called upon to do, usually for radio interviews. And I never listen to one of these without thinking, "She's lying!" or "He's saying what he thinks they want to hear." Or just, "The same old guff!" For of course I have said the same kind of things myself—a sort of rash approximation to what the truth appears to be, along with a few spiky little insertions, usually to the effect that this particular thing really happened, or that thing was taken from real life, so that interviewer and listeners don't run away with the idea that fantasy has no connection with actual mundane existence. Most interviewers seem to me to have left both real life and fantasy so far behind that one is at a loss to know where they do stand. Some kind of media virtual place, perhaps. And, desperate to contact this person and to please them—and, above all, not to let oneself down in public—one produces something that sounds as if it might be true.

I had a bit of fun with this process in a story called "Carol Oneir's Hundredth Dream." Carol is a twelve-year-old professional dreamer who suddenly finds she is suffering from, as it were, dreamer's block. She goes to the enchanter Chrestomanci to get this sorted out. Having pried away Carol's pushy mama, Chrestomanci invites Carol to tell him exactly what she does when she makes a dream.

This was something Carol had done hundreds of times before. She smiled graciously and began, "I get a feeling in my head first, which means a dream is ready to happen. Dreams come when they will, you know, and there is no stopping or putting them off. So I tell Mama and she helps me get settled on the special couch . . . and I drop off to sleep to the sound of [the spindle] gently humming and whirling. Then the dream takes me. . . . It is like a voyage of discovery—"

"When is this?" Chrestomanci interrupted in an offhand sort of way. "Does this dreaming happen at night?"

"It can happen at any time," said Carol. "If a dream is ready, I can go to my couch and sleep during the day. . . . It is like a voyage of discovery, sometimes in caves underground, sometimes in palaces in the clouds—"

"Yes. And how long do you dream for? Six hours? Ten minutes?" Chrestomanci interrupted again.

"About half an hour," said Carol. "Sometimes in the clouds or maybe in the southern seas. I never know . . . whom I will meet on my journey—"

"Do you finish a whole dream in half an hour?" Chrestomanci interrupted yet again.

"Of course not. Some of my dreams last for more than three hours," Carol said. . . . "I can control my dreams. And I do my best work in

regular half-hour stints. I wish you wouldn't keep interrupting when I'm doing my best to tell you!"

Chrestomanci . . . seemed surprised. "My dear young lady, you are not doing your best to tell me. You are giving me precisely the same flannel as you gave The Times *and the* Croydon Gazette. . . . *You are telling me your dreams come unbidden—but you have one for half an hour every day—and that you never know where you'll go in them or what will happen—but you can control your dreams perfectly. That can't all be true, can it?'*

". . . This is the way dreams are," Carol said. "And I am only the Seeing Eye."

"As you told the Manchester Guardian," *Chrestomanci agreed, "if that was what they meant by 'Oosung Oyo.' I see that must have been a misprint now."*[1]

Poor Carol. She is in a situation very familiar to writers being interviewed, called upon to supply graceful facts that will interest her audiences and to say simple things about a matter that is both very complicated and very, very private. So she doesn't exactly lie. She temporizes by describing external physical details—in much the same way as writers will describe how they have a special hut for writing in, or how long they work at their computers (I even heard one writer claim that he actually was a computer)—and then she adds a puff for her dreams. And as Chrestomanci points out, none of it adds up. There must, he implies, be more to it than that.

And of course there is. And this is the part that never ceases to fascinate me—the private things that go on inside your head when a book is being planned and written. For, as I said, Carol does not lie. Everything she claims is true, whether of dreaming or writing, and the things Chrestomanci declares cannot all be true at once, are in fact, indeed, all true at once. The human brain can lay one contradiction upon another and make the two things match without any trouble at all, and be aware of strict logic at the same time. This is what I find so fascinating.

Led on by this fascination, I once, when asked by a conference in Boston to give a talk about my book *Fire and Hemlock*, did have a stab at describing what went on while I wrote it.[2] I teased out every layer of this book. Starting with what I felt about heroes and the heroic, I went on to describe my passion for cello music and how a rereading of T. S. Eliot's *Four Quartets* sparked the actual book and gave rise to the presence of a quartet of musicians in it. I charted the various myths and folktales which surfaced and sank in the course of it, and of course I expounded on the ballads of "Tam Lin" and "Thomas the Rhymer"—regarded as the negative and positive of the same story—which were the framework for the narrative. I gave the paper and the audience nodded wisely. This, they seemed to feel, was real stuff. I then went to New York, where my publishers had taken a great interest and had asked for a copy of the talk. I went in to see Libby,[3] one of the editors—a wonderful wise lady with a voice like a sack of gravel being shaken. She was just finishing the paper as I walked in. She looked up from it and shook gravel at me:

"Very nice, Diana, but writers don't work like that."

I wanted to shout, "Yes, I do! It's all true!" Instead I sort of gulped and answered, "No. You're absolutely right." As soon as I thought, I realized that the book had not been written in at all the analytical way I had tried to describe. The second draft might have been, when I was trying to make clear all the various elements that went into it—a process I always liken to pointing up or grouting the basic brickwork—but the first draft had been written at white heat, in a state where I was unable to put it down. I wrote it in any spare five minutes I could find. I even got up at six in the morning to go on with it. This was so unheard of that my family wondered if I was ill. And such was the passion with which I was going at it, that it seemed to pull in all sorts of queer but relevant things from daily life—I can't tell you half the weird things, but I do remember being followed around by a van labeled KING'S LYNN,[4] and going to a lecture where the speaker turned out to be the image of Mr. Leroy, with great black bags under his eyes, who proceeded to talk about both the *Four Quartets* and the ballad of "Tam Lin," in a lecture that I think was supposed to be about Shakespeare.

Yet the book got written with a shape and a coherent story. The various elements I so carefully dissected out in my Boston talk got fed in at the right places. And I know I was very careful throughout, even in the first draft, to keep the supernatural elements just a bare thread away from things that could have a normal explanation after all. This was one of the prime requirements from the book itself when it first came thundering into my head.

In other words, I was in *control*, just like Carol Oneir was in her dreams. So, in an odd way, Libby was right, but so was I. Two seemingly incompatible things had been going on at once.

So the first truth about the creative process is that one is doing two mutually incompatible things. Logical souls like Chrestomanci find this hard to accept.

Let's go back to Carol and Chrestomanci then. Chrestomanci finds a solution to Carol's problems with the aid of Tonino, whose gift is to enhance the magic of others, and has him enhance Carol's dream magic in order to force her to do three things. First, he makes her actually enter physically into her dream. This, though it is put in fantasy terms, is truly and exactly what one has to do if one is to write any work of fiction properly. One has to see, feel, smell, touch, and thoroughly experience what is going on as one writes. George Meredith talks of it (in *Diana of the Crossways*) as living a double life. And one does. I vividly remember, when I was writing *Dogsbody*, being a dog a lot of the time, wanting to scratch under my collar or raise a leg to deal with an itch behind my left ear—I've felt itchy ever since, really—and living through that lovely, multiple stretch that dogs do, tail and back legs first, then up the back through to the front legs. Or that rotating shake that gets mud on the ceiling. At the same time, although I didn't ever believe I was a dog, I did so thoroughly believe in the story that I was sure the sun—Sol—was an animate being. Every time I came to a passage with Sol in it, I used to lay that sheet of paper in the patch of sun on my desk, so that Sol could check it for accuracy. Honestly.

Of course, all this makes you inadequate for your own everyday existence. I get terribly absentminded and walk about in the street muttering to myself (these days I tell myself it's because I'm old, but it isn't—I've always done it). And when I was writing *Charmed Life* (another one I couldn't put down), I did one evening put my husband's shoes in the oven to cook for supper—luckily I noticed in time. This is the price one has to pay for living in a story and, more, believing in it. And it is a very important truth.

Chrestomanci also forces Carol to acknowledge a second and much more private truth: that she uses the same five characters again and again under different disguises. Now this does indeed happen, but I don't think I've ever heard a single writer admit it. Sometimes the fact is obvious, as in Dick Francis's books, whose protagonist is always pretty much the same, but mostly it is a lot less so. I don't know why it should be such a shameful thing to admit. Painters are allowed to portray the same haystack a hundred times, or the same lily pond, or whatever, but a writer is not allowed to put the same person in more than one book unless it is a sequel and that character has the same name. Some of this prohibition comes from readers and reviewers (who consider it cheating and uninventive), but I suspect the true reason is that writers themselves don't want to admit it. They squirm and wriggle and say anything, rather than that they use the same character more than once. Such repeated characters are always very near and dear to a writer's heart (as Melville who plays all the villains is to Carol), and it is a true invasion of privacy to have other people know that you have been carrying this person about, nestled in the soft spaces of your head. But the fact is, such characters have your emotions vested in them, and usually you have had them long enough that they have grown as many quirks and facets as a real live person. This actually makes them doubly valuable. You can be sure that, once introduced into any narrative, they are going to pull your feelings in there with them (and so those of any readers), and that they are going to behave like a real live person. You don't have to perform any grinding, mind-bending feats of imagination to get inside them—you know what they are like inside. You know how they speak and how they will react.

The third advantage of such characters is the one that makes you use them more than once. They have lived with you so long and have developed so many sides to them that you can use a piece of them here and a piece of them there—split them down the middle like a billet of wood, as it were—and still present them as rounded personalities for that particular narrative. My hope is that nobody has hitherto noticed when I do this. Does anyone know that Mr. Lynn in *Fire and Hemlock* and the Goon from *Archer's Goon* both derive from the same person, split like a billet of wood? (Those two books were written back to back, both at white heat, using the two halves of a person who had been in my head forever.) Or did anyone spot that Howl in *Howl's Moving Castle* and the Keeper of the Silver Casket in *A Tale of Time City* are similarly made out of another single person? Or Torquil in *Archer's Goon* and Tacroy from *The Lives of Christopher Chant*? The similarity of names might give that one away, I suppose.

Of course, you can use an actual live person in exactly this way too—split them up and introduce part of them as a whole in the right story. Living people always have sumptuously many sides to their personality, and so I have cheerfully pirated parts of live people too. I find I use real people quite a lot anyway— it is extraordinary how many acquaintances we all have who ought to be in a story—and being multifaceted the way living folk are, they split up really easily. For instance, Douglas and Caspar in *The Ogre Downstairs* are both portraits of my eldest son at different stages in his life; and Himself in *The Time of the Ghost* and the Sempitern in *A Tale of Time City* are portraits of my father—neither of them terribly flattering, I'm afraid. Similarly, Angus Flint in *Who Got Rid of Angus Flint*, the savage visitor who picks children up by their hair, and Al in *Drowned Ammet*, who is just as brutal—only with words and a gun—are in fact both derived from the one actual man.

But to get back to Carol Oneir and her dreamer's block—Carol has made two major mistakes where her characters are concerned: she has not only overworked her main characters, she has paid almost no attention to the rest. She dismisses everyone but her five main persons as her Cast of Thousands, people who cluster at the edges of things and only say "Rhubarb" and "Abracadabra." She is astounded and indignant when they turn out to have feelings and needs like she does herself. And this is a really monumental error—because it causes her to be basically bored by her entire dream works. Being bored is the surest way I know to halt any kind of creative process.

If there is one thing I have learned, it is that you must have at least some emotional connection with every soul who figures in a story. You may like them, love them, find them disgusting, or hate them, but you must react to them in some way. You must see them as real and treat them with the same respect you would accord someone you meet in the street. Only then can they take on any life of their own. And they do. I always love it when people I know I have invented start behaving unexpectedly, as real people do—being themselves, in fact.

Naturally, if your people are doing their own thing, this is going to have an effect on the way the story goes. It is going to take on unexpected quirks and twists. It may even go in quite a different direction from the way you are expecting. For this reason, I always leave the story vague enough in my head that I can allow the characters room to alter it. And after an early shock when I was writing *Wilkins' Tooth*, I always allow room for unexpected characters to appear too. I was quite shattered in this early book when my main protagonists knocked on a door. I was all set to see the door opened by the vague father of the two little girls they were trying to talk to. And instead the door was opened by the aunt, tall and covered with oil paint, with a cigarette wagging in her mouth.

Since then, this has happened quite often, and I always love it. For instance, although I suspect some people will find this hard to credit, I had no idea what Chrestomanci was going to be like until he first appeared in Mrs. Sharp's kitchen. This is in spite of the fact that *Charmed Life* was a book that came into my head almost whole and entire from the start. I only knew there was going to be a great enchanter in it—I had left a sort of hole in the story where Chrestomanci was going to be, and all I did was trust that someone would be along to fill that hole. And Chrestomanci filled it more than adequately. It added no end to the excitement of writing that book, because I was discovering what Chrestomanci was like—and about his dressing gowns—quite as eagerly as anyone else might.

Poor Carol Oneir has probably secretly been dying to let all her characters loose and see what happens. She has certainly become mightily sick of at least four of her lead characters. But she has become trapped in commercial success and by the pressure put on her (mostly by her mama) to go on and do the same thing again. This is a pressure I find one really has to avoid if at all possible—that way lie boredom and blocks. Likewise it truly is fatal to yield to persuasion to write another book on the same lines as the first—unless, of course, your imagination is skipping expectantly up and down like a computer cursor, wanting to do just that. If it isn't, you shouldn't. But poor Carol is only twelve and has got herself stuffed into a mold. When Chrestomanci helps her free herself, the whole dream world explodes into an extravaganza of absurdities, the cast of thousands runs riot, her stock old man tries to behave like Santa Claus, and most of her other lead characters get drunk and head for the nearest casino. And Carol will have learned a valuable lesson. For there *is* such a thing as a character or characters running away with a story, and if you keep them on too tight a rein, my experience is that they do just that.

There is also such a thing as a story running away with itself, which is equally serious—because all narratives, long or short, need a definite shape, a shape you can usually actually draw as a diagram, and when this is not present, you don't get a narrative, you get a mess. In my experience, this happens when the writer's own idea of how the story should go conflicts with the story's idea of how it wants to be. This is where, like Carol, one is doing two incompatible things at once—for a book, when one is writing it, can be as willful as any delinquent character. You have to let it have its head, just as if it were a person, and at the same time try to coax it in the direction you think it ought to go. Sometimes it just won't. I have long been reconciled to quite a few books I write turning out quite different from the grand Platonic ideal I had when I first conceived and started to write them.

This brings me on to the really interesting bit. You notice that at the start of the extract I read, Carol Oneir says, "I get a feeling in my head first, which means a dream is ready to happen. . . ." Chrestomanci tactfully ignores this. It is not part of his remit to deal with the actual process of dream creation, only what has gone wrong with it. But this statement of Carol's begs all the important questions. The statements that I and other writers make to the media likewise blur over this most central matter, which is, what goes on in your head to cause you to think you're about to write a book? What things actually need to be present before you can?

This is what most younger readers are fumbling after when they ask, "Where do you get your ideas?" The trouble is, this is a question that has always struck me like "Have you stopped beating your wife yet?" I can get any number of ideas, but ninety-nine percent simply never could grow into a book that I could possibly write. It takes a certain specific something, and a certain kind of idea, even to get me started, and even then more than half of these don't come to anything. I have cupboards and drawers full of barely begun writings.

I have been trying very hard for years to define what I do need to get started, ever since, in fact, I ran up against one of those holistic doctors—you know—"cure your body and your mind together." A fine idea, if you can get it right. But this doctor would have it that my back problems were due to the fact that I spent too much time harking back to my past. "Look to the future," he said, "and you'll get much better ideas for your books then." He made me so angry. As soon as he was out of sight, I yelled and threw cushions and jumped up and down, and swore, and threw more cushions. I wasn't sure then quite why I was so angry, but I think I have it worked out by now.

First, of course, you can't look to the future because it is a blank. It hasn't happened yet. Even someone who is wanting to write about the year 9000 has to have something from the present day to base the narrative on—they have to rely on the fact that human nature and economics and physics tend to be the same whatever year it is. In other words, you need hooks to hang your story on to. We all do. And my hooks happen to be my childhood.

It was a very vivid and often very distressing time for me. Just for starters, the Second World War broke out when I was five and the whole world went mad. Some of the time it was terrifying. The adults I knew were frightened, which is something that pulls the rug out from under any childhood sense of security, guns barked in the night, and searchlights crisscrossed looking for raiding bombers—to this day, a low-flying airplane makes me nervous—and nowhere seemed to be safe. Some of the time it was plain crazy, like the time I encountered one of my father's friends crawling about in the next-door field with a bush tied to his head. "Hallo, Mr. Cowey," I shrilled innocently. "What are you doing crawling about with that bush on your head?" He rose up, bush and all, and tried to shout at me in a whisper, bright red in the face. "Shut up and go away, child! You're spoiling the exercise!" He was in the Home Guard, you see. Dad's Army.

The war caused complete disruption in what promised to be a peaceful suburban childhood, though, knowing my parents, I doubt the "peaceful." My father, for instance, carried financial economy to a new and zany art form. My mother enjoyed quarreling. She did it with everyone all the time.

At the start of the war we were hurried away first to Wales and then—after my mother had quarreled with her in-laws—to the Lake District, where, coincidentally, we were lodged in the house that belonged to the Arthur Ransome children. One of the things that I gained from this, which I have only recently realized, was a very strong sense of the changing seasons of the year, and the effect the season has on the way you think and act. With the increasing urbanization of children's lives, I find this more important every year. Children need to be kept in touch with the cycle of the seasons. Every one of my books has its own season, or seasons. It is part of the feeling they bring with them when they are ready to be written—*Charmed Life* is an early autumn book, *Black Maria* takes place in the raw new weather of spring, *Fire and Hemlock* goes round the seasons several times—and this is as important to each book as the characters or the landscapes.

We were in the Lakes long enough to have a taste of each season, by which time my mother had quarreled with all the other mothers evacuated there. We moved to a nunnery in York, another strange interlude, and then, after a brief stay in London amid the bombs and gunfire, to a village in East Anglia. There my parents had the job of running a sort of conference center. Both of them found the fact that they had children an extreme nuisance and preferred to forget about us. We ran about on top of roofs and once nearly hanged my sister. My youngest sister tied her hair in knots to keep it out of her eyes, and this was not noticed for six months.

In my only attempt at semi-autobiography, *The Time of the Ghost*, I found I had to tone down both the hanging incident and the knots-in-the-hair episode. No one would have believed the reality. And this is true about the whole of this part of my life. I don't ever really write about it, but on the other hand I write about it all the time. What I do is a sort of translating. Every time I get a notion that might start a book going, I find I ask myself, "Will this idea translate my experience into something of value for people today?" For the experiences were much wider than mere neglect.

The first, outer layer of what I knew then was the global violence and insanity of the war and later the Cold War, which had a sort of icy saneness that was even more insane. I have never really lost this sense that the world is basically thoroughly unstable. I think this is why I tend to write about multiple parallel worlds—anything can happen and probably *is* doing somewhere. The next layer inward was the village itself. It was beautiful and full of eccentrics. At the more normal end of things I might cite the extremely refined and tweed-suited local nymphomaniac. You were liable to stumble over her in a ditch at any time, in her twin set and pearls, having it off with one of the bus drivers.

A wealth of material, you'd say. But I have never wanted to put this in a book directly. It just lies behind the slightly more normal things I *do* do. This sense that most people are crazy, if you look deep enough. Adults particularly, and children have to deal with them.

Encapsulated in this craziness, and crazy too in its own way, was the grand and beautiful old house that contained the conference center—it was haunted, by the way: one of the cleaners met the ghost and left in hysterics on the spot. But the fact about it that lives with me and truly does provide the basis for all I write is that this house had extensive grounds, divided into three sections. The first section was a huge graveled yard. It was where the nitty-gritty everyday things were, like our outhouse and the kitchen, and it had a lethal clothesline permanently and mostly invisibly in place halfway up, just at throat height. I have seen people felled there like oxen, and been felled myself. This yard was where all the cat or dog fights happened and was the site of all my mother's best quarrels. It was also where the gardener once cornered me and showed me a small, wicked yellow revolver, which he invited me to hold. It was heavy. As soon as I had hold of it I was seized with total horror. "This thing is Death," I thought. But I tried to seem brave. I looked at it and sort of tweaked at a little metal bit hooked on to one side. "What's this?" "No, no, no! Don't move that! That's the safety catch!" he snapped. "That'll go off, that's loaded, you know." I gave it back to him. But ever since then, I have thought of that yard as the place of ordinary life and death. The place where everything starts when I'm writing a book.

The next section was a brick-walled formal garden, consisting mostly of a large lawn sedately surrounded by shrubby borders. The part farthest from the house was raised and made a good stage. This was where the village and the conference people interacted, either to watch plays or operas put on by the house inmates, or to folk dance, and many a crazy thing went on there, including the time one of the county music advisers got carried away and sang a tenor aria from the top parapet while he rained confetti on the audience. It turned out he'd used all the toilet paper in the house. When this garden was not in use, we children tended to play the make-believe kind of game there, the kind where you walk about inventing it as you go on—the yard was where we mostly did the run-about-and-shout stuff. And this seems entirely fitting. With this garden you moved into the formal patterns of fantasy, the place where stories get made or adapted and most of the quieter fun or lunacy happened. I suspect this is the place where the central part of what I write gets made.

But there was another garden, across a road, which was always kept locked, where the conference people were never allowed to go. And this one was truly magical. It was like that garden in the story where the king has counted all the apples, because my father had hung labels on all the apple trees and he kept the key.

This garden always seems to me the seat of the mystery and the beauty that should be, if possible, at the heart of every story. It stands to me for the old tales and the life-enhancing magics that ought to be there too. And no idea for a book ever seems to me good enough if it doesn't have something of this at the heart of it. But it has to have the other two places in it as well. You can't exist or write purely on this strange and elevated plane.

So what have we got so far? I am living in a place where I am not actually living, leading a double life, while doing two incompatible things at once. I am controlling characters that behave like real people, a story that behaves like a self-programming entity, a landscape in which the seasons change as seasons should. Beneath this is an underpinning from my own experience containing the nitty-gritty of everyday life, formally patterned fantasy, a dose of lunacy, and the deep magic of myth. Almost enough to get a book moving, but not quite. Along with the season(s) the book is set in, you need also a quite indescribable taste in the head, a feeling about this particular narrative that no other has. If this doesn't come at once, or in the first few pages, I find you have to leave that effort and try again. But if you have that as-it-were taste, and with it a sufficiently dynamic idea, you are off.

It took me awhile to distinguish what is a dynamic idea. A lot of things seem to start stories, but not all of them go on. To find the right kind of motive idea, I found I had to go back once again to childhood, but this time to the sort of mistakes children make. The sort that make you very ashamed when you think of them, but are actually one of the ways children learn. Everyone must remember some of the dreamlike confusions of their childhood—they may make you squirm in the memory, but if you look closely, you usually find that this mistake moved you on. Here is one of mine, from an article[5] I wrote for *Foundation* in 1997:

A very good example is a baroque muddle of my own when, at the age of five, I was evacuated to the Lake District. . . . I was told I was there because the Germans were about to invade. Almost in the same breath, I was warned not to drink the water from the washbasin because it came from the lake and was full of typhoid germs. I assumed that "germs" was short for "Germans."

Looking warily at the washbasin, I saw it was considerately labeled "Twyford," clearly warning people against germ warfare. Night after night, I had a half-waking nightmare in which Germans (who had fair, floating hair and were clad in sort of cheesecloth Anglo-Saxon tunics) came racing across the surface of the lake to come up through the plug hole of this washbasin and give us all Twyford.

This has all the elements of something needed to start a book off, the magical prohibition, the supernatural villains, the beleaguered good people and, for good measure, the quite incommunicable fears that children have. . . .

And of course it was how I learned that germs were small and Germans were human size, simply from working out why I knew people would laugh at me if I told them my fears.

A mix-up of notions like that is nearly always dynamic. You've got it. You go. If it works, it is like a long fuse that has been lit in several places, so that it gives off at intervals sharp blotches of white magnesium light. Each white fluorescence illuminates—with luck—a ring of landscape or a room with people moving and speaking in it, scenes from the story that is making itself. Around it, along the rest of the fuse, the rest of the story occurs like a photographic negative of a foggy day—faint white objects against black. And what I do is rush from flaring point to flaring point along this fuse, often at top speed, like a fire myself. Except I am, of course, sitting down and doing it all with words. Word by word.

I don't think I can find any other way to describe the way it feels, unless it is to echo poor Carol Oneir. "It is like a voyage of discovery. . . ." And if I've got it right, it should be. It is also my way of moving out of the past into the untouched future. This can be very scary.

The Origins of *The Merlin Conspiracy*

As with so many of her books, Diana Wynne Jones "germinated" the seeds of The Merlin Conspiracy, *and released it only when the idea was in full flower. This piece is a longer version of an article that she wrote to promote the Japanese edition, produced by Tokuma Shoten Publishing Ltd.*

It is hard to know where the idea for a book starts. But I do know that *The Merlin Conspiracy* was building in my head for more than ten years. It came in pieces and the pieces, at first, did not seem to add up at all.

Around the time I finished *Hexwood*, I was thinking I needed to write about a lone and powerful magician who lived on an island made of parts of several universes. But I didn't know what this magician was like. The only thing I was sure about was that his island came apart if he got ill. I spent the next ten years in and out of hospital, and it was after I came round from the anesthetic the first time that I knew my magician was called Romanov and that he was thin and ferociously energetic.

But two years before that there was the elephant. I always knew there was an elephant in there somewhere. We took my two-year-old granddaughter to Bristol Zoo, where they happened to be exercising their elephant, Wendy. We were four adults looking after one tiny girl, but Frances all the same escaped and darted across the path just as Wendy came along it. The child ought to have been trampled; but Wendy did a wonderful, agile sort of polka step with her huge front feet and missed Frances completely. She waved her trunk genially at Frances and kept walking. Wendy, sadly, is dead now, but ever since then I have wanted to pay tribute to that kindly, agile elephant. I just wished I knew how she fitted in.

And before the elephant, I had a repeated dream of a line of bright islands, which were universes, hanging in dark blue nothing. If you wanted to get to another universe, you jumped from island to island—and they dipped and turned sickeningly. Terrifying. In one of these dreams I jumped to a city that was built up the sides of several canyons; houses stacked on houses in a most peculiar way. I knew that this city was connected to Romanov and the elephant in some way, but it didn't add up to a story. Maddening.

Then, more recently, I had a strange experience in Cornwall. Exactly like Roddy in the book, I met a woman out of prehistory who dumped all her magical knowledge in my head, neatly filed under the headings of different flowers. Unlike Roddy, I couldn't use these spells, but I could put them in a book for everyone to see. It was then I realized that I was going to be writing two intertwined stories about two people with different kinds of magic.

All these things suddenly added up to a proper book when I was doing a signing in Ross-on-Wye. A boy there told me—very firmly—that he wanted to know more about Nick Mallory from my book *Deep Secret*. And I realized that I did too, and that Nick was the person who met Romanov and the elephant. Roddy was to tell the other part of the story. My only problem then was: where did Roddy come from?

A chapter in a learned book gave me the answer. I'd only read it because it was written by one of my sons. In it, just in passing, he remarked on how difficult governing the country was in the Middle Ages, because the king always kept moving from place to place, taking with him—in a vast campsite—all his courtiers and officials. And I thought: Suppose the king did that these days? With cars and buses and lorries, and the civil servants and the media following along in coaches too. Then I knew what Roddy's life was like. I knew all about the conspiracy, and I started to write the double story at once.

Review of *Boy in Darkness*
by Mervyn Peake

Knowing that Diana admired Mervyn Peake's work, Books for Keeps *commissioned this review for issue number 102, January 1997, to mark the first publication of "Boy in Darkness" on its own as a children's book. Diana's review was published alongside an article by P. J. Lynch on the challenges of illustrating Peake's story.*

Books for Keeps *was a British bimonthly print magazine for thirty years and is now online. Its readership is primarily teachers, librarians, and children's book professionals.*

This is a frightening book. Having said this, I must add that a large number of readers, whatever their age, actively *enjoy* a frightening book and find that it speaks to them. Furthermore, *Boy in Darkness* is the work of a genius and, as such, should not be withheld from anyone, even if that genius is twisted and baroque. Mervyn Peake always seems to me to start where Lord Dunsany and James Branch Cabell leave off, and neither of these writers can be read with perfect composure. From the very first page, when we are told it is the Boy's (Titus Groan's) birthday, and he is therefore at the mercy of rituals which "lead him hither and thither through the mazes of his adumbrate home" eventually to receive gifts presented by "long lines of servants, knee-deep in water" (gifts which are promptly removed again), Mervyn Peake is working to discompose his readers.

Part of the discomposing is done with words. "Adumbrate" is only the first of many peculiar words, used peculiarly. Later there is an "oleaginous river." "osseous temples," "an ulna between his jaws," and many more, all used to strike you between the eyes, not only because you have to consider what the word means, but also how well it sounds and how intensely *accurate* it is in its context. This kind of thing is wonderfully good for children. Those who are brave enough not to give up should gain a spectacular insight into how wonderful words can be.

Insights are what all this discomposing is about. On the face of it, this story is an adventure in which the Boy, sick of the lonely, ceremonial life at home in the castle, runs away at night and finds himself in a region of pure damnation, from whence he barely escapes with his life. But from the moment of the "long lines of servants, knee-deep in water" (at which we are meant to ask "Why?" and to conclude that the Boy was quite right to escape from something so senseless), Mervyn Peake is leading the Boy beyond a mere adventure story, and into seeing and understanding. With an acute draftsman's eye, and in sentences which vary from stabbingly simple to complex and meticulously punctuated, he has the Boy pursued across the "oleaginous river" by hounds "cocksure of themselves" (that have eyes of "that kind of bright and acid yellow that allowed no other color alongside"), where the Boy encounters the odious Goat.

Here is the first major insight. The Goat walks like a man, only sideways, on hooflike shoes, and wears clothes, old and dusty and smelly, and the Boy *knows* there is something terribly wrong here. "But why? The gentleman had done nothing wrong." But he *will* do. The Boy is fatally polite, the way children can be (and this, in the normal world, can lead to another small corpse in a hidden ditch), purely on the grounds that the Goat *seems* civilized. After that it is too late. The Hyena arrives and the Boy is caught. The Hyena is a horrid masterpiece of perfectly described body language. "The shirt he wore was cut off very short in the sleeves so that his long, spotted arms could be readily appreciated." (For "spotty" read "tattooed" in the mundane world?) "His trousered legs were very narrow and very short, so that his back . . . was at a very steep incline." We all know men like this. The two insights here are that the look of a person is important, and body language even more so.

The nasty pair take the Boy down into the regions of true damnation to their master, the snow-white Lamb, who has no soul and whose hands were "folded about one another as though they loved one another"—more body language and a further insight, this time of perfect selfishness. The Lamb's hands are in fact very important. With them, he changes men into half beasts. All of them have died, though, except for the Goat and Hyena—even the Lion, whose demise is truly heartbreaking. And the Lamb wants more. He wants the Boy so much that his hands "were moving so fast about one another . . . that nothing could be seen but an opalescent blur of light." This puzzles the Lamb's henchmen. Pretending to explain this, Mervyn Peake produces the major insight to which the rest has been leading: the brain needs the body, and the body will sometimes do strange things in order to express what is in the brain. In other words, watch body language.

Then the Boy is prepared to meet the Lamb. By this time he knows what is in store for him and he has to do something. Here Mervyn Peake reverses what he has just told us. Up to now, Titus has been a mere helpless body. He has to tell himself that this body is connected to a brain, and to *think*, in order not to become another half animal. Brain can lead body, and save it. The Boy tries it. First he argues (something most boys are good at) and sows doubt in the minds of the Goat and Hyena; then he acts, with a trick, and distracts the Lamb long enough to be able to cut him in half. And the Lamb is only sudsy fleece. This could be allegory (in which case, I am afraid it is somewhat wishful thinking), or magic. Anyway, it makes a perfect ending. The combined insights expose something we see all the time and usually disregard: that the way people talk and move is part of the way they are. It may seem like nothing, the way the Lamb does at the end, but I myself would prefer every child to gain these insights from being frightened by this book, rather than the hard way, in a deserted field a hundred yards from home.

Freedom to Write

Using quotes from The Tough Guide to Fantasyland, *here Diana explores fashions in fantasy.*

The writing of fantasy is much in my mind just at present, because I am one of the judges for the World Fantasy Awards (these are really only "World" awards if you happen to speak English, and they are handed out each September in a different venue, Montreal this year). Now, these awards are largely concerned with fantasy written for adults, but not entirely. Philip Pullman's *The Amber Spyglass* is one of the books up for consideration and we are trying to get hold of Robin McKinley's latest.[1] One of the judges even asked for my own book, *Year of the Griffin*, but I told him it was unethical, me being a judge.

Anyway, since mid-February enormous parcels have arrived for me almost daily, full of truly enormous books. The majority run from five hundred to nine hundred pages. It seems that books are long this year.

That makes them sound like skirts, doesn't it? With reason.

Writing is subject to fashions like most other things. It is one of the constraints you feel when you sit down with a pen (as I do) in front of a blank pad of paper. Oh, God, I may be about to do something dowdy and unfashionable! The lovely, crisp blankness of the paper ought to invite a huge sense of freedom. But it doesn't always. What it actually invites, in me anyway, is a challenge: How do I evade this particular fashion, or better still, turn it to advantage? How do I do this and give people something worth giving and not just what they were expecting?

What people *expect* is a very powerful element in their reading. A good half of readers, whether they are nine or ninety, are truly uncomfortable with anything that strikes them as new or different—this is why soaps are so popular—and some of these people get quite petulant if they get what they don't expect. Minor examples of this are two reviews I got recently of my book *Year of the Griffin*. One was quite short and said, more or less, "This isn't *Harry Potter* so I don't like it." The other was longer because the reviewer went through the book side by side with the latest *Harry Potter*, saying where they didn't match. The extraordinary thing is that he should have *expected* them to match.

Now, possibly because fantasy can be about almost anything really, people are more hidebound about what they expect of a fantasy than about any other kind of writing. About six years ago, I got so exasperated with the way that too many fantasy books deriving ultimately from Tolkien were so much the same that I wrote a book called *The Tough Guide to Fantasyland*. For those of you who haven't come across it, it pretends to be a tourist guide and starts with a map—like all the conventional fantasies do. Only in this case it is a map of Europe upside down—a brilliant notion of my goddaughter's and you wouldn't believe how hard it is to recognize!—on which my agent and I had enormous fun filling in idiotic place names. The bulk of the book is alphabetical, having entries on Astrology, Dark

Lord, Dragons, Galley Slave, Inn Signs ("Do not be surprised to find that every Inn Sign creaks loudly. This is a form of aural advertising"), Orcs, Magic, Stew, Temples, Wizards, and so on. The idea is that you take a selection of these and mix to taste, thus making a new book.

Of course, along with events and other features being so predictable, you get predictable language too. I had great fun picking out the most constant clichés and calling these Official Management Terms (OMTs): "reek of wrongness," "thick savory stew," "acrid smoke," and so on, and marking them as they occurred. And each section starts with a saying or piece of verse that has nothing whatsoever to do with the section. I believe Sir Walter Scott started this practice—he has a lot to answer for.

Bear with me while I read you a few entries. Color Coding first:

CLOTHING. *Although this varies from place to place, there are two absolute rules:*
i) Apart from Robes, no garment thicker than a shirt ever has sleeves.
ii) No one ever wears Socks.

Oh, sorry. I meant to read you Color Coding. As follows:

COLOR CODING, *section 3, Eyes.*
Black eyes are invariably evil; brown eyes mean boldness and humor, but not necessarily goodness; green eyes always entail Talent, usually for Magic but sometimes for Music. Hazel eyes are rare and seem generally to imply niceness. Gray eyes mean Power or healing abilities and will be reassuring unless they look silver: silver-eyed people are liable to enchant

or hypnotize you for their own ends. . . . White eyes, usually blind ones, are for wisdom: never ignore anything a white-eyed person says. Blue eyes are always Good, the bluer, the more Good present. And then there are violet eyes and golden eyes. People with violet eyes are often of Royal birth and, if not, always live uncomfortably interesting lives. People with golden eyes just live uncomfortably interesting lives and most of them are rather fey into the bargain. . . . Luckily, it seldom occurs to anyone with undesirable eye colors to disguise them . . . and they can generally be detected very readily. Red eyes can never be disguised. They are Evil, and surprisingly common.

Now Companions:

COMPANIONS are chosen for you by the Management. . . . They are picked from among the following (pretty well invariably): Bard, Female Mercenary, Gay Mage, Imperious Female, Large Man, Serious Soldier, Slender Youth, Small Man, Talented Girl, Teenage Boy, Unpleasant Stranger, and Wise Old Stranger . . .

Though a lot of these are Tolkien derived, many are cardboard figures from role-playing games, which have interacted with this type of fantasy for the last forty years.

As an example of Warrior, *The Tough Guide to Fantasyland* offers:

BARBARY VIKINGS wear horned helmets and fur cloaks, otherwise you could mistake them for Northern Barbarians. They swagger hugely, quarrel hugely, drink hugely, and boast hugely. The thing they like best is killing people, preferably lots at once . . . All of them are excellent seamen. And here is what the killing is done with:

SWORDS. You are advised to choose your sword with great care and, if possible, have it checked by a jobbing Magician. . . . Swords are dangerous. . . . Here are the hazards you should look out for:

i) Swords with runes on them. Runes are almost always a sign that your sword is:

> *a) Designed only to kill Dragons.*
>
> *b) Designed for some other specific victim, such as Goblins or the Undead.*

Both (a) and (b) are liable to let you down if you are attacked by ordinary humans. Others will be:

> *c) Designed for some other purpose entirely, so that when drawn it will proceed to raise a Storm or—gods protect you!—try to heal your assailant.*

Be wary of Runes. . . .

The entry goes on to list nine more preposterous swords, such as Swords with Souls, Swords with appetites—these tend to devour the wielder in various ways—Swords that signal the approach of enemies, Swords that are *not* Swords—being made of glass or something, Swords in Stones and so on . . .

Now you'd think that after six years readers might have noticed some of these absurdities, or that fashion would have moved on. But no. One of the fat fantasies I had to read—a mere five hundred pages—*Faith of the Fallen* (a Sword of Truth novel)[2] has: "He was too far away to see the green of her eyes, a color he'd never beheld on anyone else. . . ." One OMT of this kind of book is that people never just *see* a thing, they always *behold* it.

Another, calling itself Book II of the Chronicles of the Raven, *Noonshade*,[3] has at the start, on the page before the map—yes, they all still have maps—a list of companions on the journey:

Hirad Coldheart, barbarian warrior
The Unknown Warrior, a warrior
Thraun, warrior and shapechanger
Will Begman, thief [see the role-playing game archetypes]
Denser, dawnthief mage
Erienne, lore mage

I think one of these was female. The next tome I hefted out of the box was *all* about a warrior woman. At the court of King Arthur, too. Worrying.

Anyway, here they all are. The same things.

And the reason is that people *expect* them. Many readers of fantasy would be highly dismayed not to have them. If someone asked them to read about ordinary people with eyes of no particular color, they wouldn't do it, even if these people had magical adventures that were really interesting. The fashion for so-called heroic fantasy, derived ultimately from Tolkien, has been going so long that it has now set into a convention, and, it seems, is quite unalterable.

This unalterable convention is now getting incorporated into books for children and young adults. One of my less fat entries—only 382 pages—for the World Fantasy Award was a book pretty well straight out of *The Tough Guide*. In it, our heroine learns to consult a crystal. The *Tough Guide* entry for Crystal is:

CRYSTAL can be any color. It can be set in a ring, suspended on a chain as a pendant, or just be a lump on its own; it is Fantasyland's equivalent of the telephone, with attached vision. . . . The operator simply leans over the Crystal and concentrates. . . .

Crystal usually takes over where Mindspeech leaves off.

Our hero is a prince forced into slavery. We have entries for both in *The Tough Guide*:

MISSING HEIRS occur with great frequency. At any given time, half the countries in Fantasyland will have mislaid their Crown Prince or Princess. But the rule is that only one Missing Heir can join your tour. . . . They can be a right nuisance. All Missing Heirs shine with innocence (some of them quite dazzlingly) and most have very little brain, which means they will not pick up any hints as to their true status. . . . In addition, they all have a lot of inborn Royal Talents such as chivalry, extreme (and embarrassing) honesty, a tendency to give everything away to Beggars, and a natural desire for the best of everything for everyone. Heirs go missing for a variety of reasons. . . .

SLAVES, male, are used by bad Kings, Fanatic Caliphates, and some Wizards in large numbers as Guards, attendants, fan bearers, waiters and entertainment, and for Sex. Bad Kings and Fanatic Caliphates always have their male slaves in matching sets, as in the following official clichés: a litter borne by four gigantic ebony slaves, fanned by two beautiful young boys, a troupe of slender young athletes, and the door guarded by two seemingly identical Barbarian slaves, etc. *A Wizard tends to have his slaves more mismatched but rather attentive, unless he intends to rule the world, in which case he will try to be like a bad King.*

And there are OMTs all over the place: "Ah, my friend . . . There's said to be a mighty curse on anyone who lifts this sword for conquest." I'm afraid my first dismayed thought was, "Oh dear! It's spread here now!" As if it were foot and mouth disease—or I suppose sword and sorcery disease.

Of course there have been quite a lot of heroic fantasies for children and young adults, many of them original and good, but this is the first one I had met that was so conventional and full of sloppy writing, and yet deemed by its publishers worthy of an international award. Could this be an advance warning of a new fashion? One thing it certainly shows, and that is that it is suddenly acceptable now for this kind of crossover to happen. Adults are free to read and enjoy books primarily aimed at young adults or children and not feel ashamed of doing it. For a long time, this was not the case at all. Books for young people existed in an impenetrable enclave all by themselves.

I'll come back to any implications of this at the end. For now, I'd like to talk a bit about the way the various fashions and conventions have affected me as a writer.

Books for youngsters are unique in one respect—their supposed audience has almost no say in their nature and contents. The books are written by adults, edited and published by adults, sold by adults, and bought by adults—teachers, parents, librarians, aunts—and mostly reviewed by adults too. Generally this has to be so. Most children are unable to say what they want in a book and why. They have to take the adults' massed word for what is a good book, because they don't yet *know* enough not to.

In one way this makes this audience a delight to write for. So many of them will be meeting whatever is in the book for the first time. They won't necessarily know the myths behind my story of *Eight Days of Luke*, say, or they won't know that Philip

Pullman is plundering *Paradise Lost* in *The Amber Spyglass*—they will just see the remarkable things he does with it. That by itself does give you a joyous sense of freedom. On the other hand, they won't know a cliché from a felicitous turn of phrase. I vividly remember how *impressed* I was at age ten on coming across somewhere in a book where somebody knocks a table lamp, which then "swayed drunkenly." I thought that was so good! I had no idea this phrase had been used a thousand times before.

There is a good side and bad one to the freshness with which children come to things. And in the same way, there is a good side and a bad to the way the adults run it all. On the good side, there are enormously high standards. None of the editors I have worked with would have accepted much in the way of clichés. None of them have ever let me get away with any muddle in any plot, nor with any factual inaccuracy; and though some have queried things that struck them as peculiar, they have always been delighted by originality. This naturally has put me on my mettle. Knowing that everything I wrote was going to be subjected to extreme and shrewd scrutiny, I take pains to get the finished manuscript *right*, if I can. The bad side is of course that adults are a prey to fashion—and to fashion in its hardened-off form, as conventionality.

Yes, I know children are too. I can imagine the present fashion for mobile phones, despite government health warnings, turning into such a convention that teachers will say, as they say "Open your books at page nine," "Get out your mobile phones and call up the weather forecast." Perhaps they already do. But, unlike children, adults do have the last say in any matter to do with books.

For example, when I first started writing in earnest, it was perhaps lucky that I wanted to write fantasy for children, because anything whatsoever with magic in it was regarded with contempt as "only for children." The great outpourings of adult fantasy that I am currently trying to deal with had barely started then, and anyway they were not considered at all respectable. Even in the little enclave of juvenile writing, fantasy was looked at sideways and people tended to ask why I didn't write Real Books.

The convention then (it was more than fashion) was for these Real Books, in rigorously contemporary settings in which children were confronted with present-day problems—divorced or abusive parents, bullying, poverty, physical handicaps, all those things—and kids were supposed to be helped by reading them. Around that time I remember going to a talk given by Jill Paton Walsh who seemed to me to say the last word on this kind of book. "If you know two people who are divorcing," she said, "would you give them each a copy of *Anna Karenina*? Can you imagine a less helpful book? Yet people do this to children all the time."

I went away and thought about this deeply. And it seemed to me, and still does, that facing this kind of problem in your life is actually what most fairy stories do; and they do it much better than any realistic story because they can distance the trouble with magic, cool it off by setting it so often in a strange country, and make the reader able to walk round the bad stuff, pretend it isn't theirs, examine it, and then solve the problem along with the hero. And, what is more, have fun doing it.

This was the first time that I had seriously understood that around each fashion or conventional notion—each fixed idea held by those adults who managed books for children—there is what I came to think of as brain space. That there is a way to duck around these notions. You can show you know the convention is there, find a way to use it, and carry on. *Dogsbody* was, I think, my most successful swerve around the prevailing fashion for books about problems. It helped to take a dog's point of view. Dogs tend to think more about their next meal than the situation in Ireland. But I had a go with *Power of Three* and another with *The Ogre Downstairs*. The Ogre had a really bumpy ride around conventional thinking. One publisher insisted I send a synopsis, which read things like "Toffee bars come alive with animal spirits, commit suicide on radiators," upon which he concluded this wasn't about problems, it was just mad.

I was very lucky, however, that there was a huge interest among those who dealt with children's books. There were innumerable good writers and Kaye Webb to publish them all in Puffin Books. The stilted kind of book where the entire so-called adventurous plot took place in the school holidays had been forced aside by the Narnia books, and by the time I started writing it was completely outmoded. The plot could happen anywhere, at any time, and there was much more freedom. But the downside of all this interest was "caring." Caring meant you weren't supposed to set children a bad example, and this became a fashion and a fetish. I remember the huge and ridiculous outcry there was at the children swearing in Robert Westall's *The Machine Gunners*. My book *Eight Days of Luke* was turned down by a publisher on the grounds that children shouldn't strike matches, and then, when it did see print, it was accused of diabolism—but luckily not too seriously.

Along with the caring, there grew up an obsession with genres. No one had worried too much about genre up to the point where I started to write the Chrestomanci books— after all, they were all called children's books and the enclave was a little small to start splitting it up. But now the people concerned with children's books thought about genre. *Charmed Life* was one of my books that was impelled into being by this obsession, to some extent. At this point I was looking for brain space around the idea that the best thing was to *show* the reader that everyone has within themselves the power to achieve something—it is just a question of realizing this. But I was simultaneously annoyed by the way that things like alternate worlds were considered exclusively the property of science fiction. So I set the book in one. Later, I tried the same swerve into brain space with horror, and wrote *Black Maria* as a horror story that wasn't one, if you follow me. But before that I wrote *Witch Week*, in another alternate world.

Witch Week was my response to another fashionable obsession, that all witches were intrinsically evil. Are they? Even when almost everybody is a witch? And there had been a spate of racial bullying in schools just then too. Witches are an admirable example of people who are "different" but probably can't help it. But that fashion for deciding witches were intrinsically evil was one of those that came and went. It went out soon after I wrote that book and then came up again in the 1990s, when *Witch Week* was banned in libraries in the state of Massachusetts for having the word "witch" in the title. There's not much you can do about this sort of fashion except wait for it to go away.

Other notions come and go too. The passion for Real Books

modulated into a fancy that fantasy was bad for people because you ended up not knowing what was real. This was quite strong around the time I wrote *Fire and Hemlock*, and indeed it may have pushed that book into being. There was enormous brain space round that idea. I had long wanted to write something where the magic could be so close to seeming like an accident, or a child's not understanding some adult matter, that the child herself might end up doubting the magic. I have always been very pleased with that book because the magic did indeed end up like that, to the extent of motivating the plot.

But then there was political correctness. I have never been clear quite what this is or was, because the rules seemed to change every month. Under its influence, my search for brain space around it became like a rush down a slippery slope, dodging the latest manifestation in a sort of wild slalom. I think this particular set of fashions was what finally pushed me into writing for adults for a while instead.[4]

But now there is suddenly plenty of brain space again. Books are long, in this current fashion, which alone gives a sense of freedom—and I've always worried about length: the feeling I shan't be able to cram all the story into two hundred-odd pages. I shall be pleased about that—at least until someone sends my book back on the grounds that it's not long *enough*. And children's writing has, thanks to the Harry Potter phenomenon, burst out of the little enclave where it has been for so long and has become something the majority of adults are not ashamed to know about. Above all, writing that deals with magic, the supernatural, and other worlds has become almost respectable—even conventional. As you saw from the beginning of my talk, this brings all sorts of constraints with it, and I feel sure it will bring more—I do not, for instance, like the indications I have seen that this is bringing about an increase in sloppy practice and pushing the conventions of adult writing into writing for children. But there is much more freedom to write, and I am not grumbling. Or not really. Or not yet.

Our Hidden Gifts

This inspirational talk was given at the December 2008 Speech Day of Kendrick School in Reading. It was arranged by Diana's son Richard, a teacher at the school.[1]

I would like to say a few words about how gifted we all are. All of you sitting here have, among you, abilities that are practically countless. Some of you will be aware of *some* of the gifts you have, but you won't be aware of all of them, for the very good reason that the exact circumstances that will allow you to show these gifts have not been invented yet. Think of them as your *hidden* gifts.

To show you what I mean, think for a moment of the very earliest people to make it to Europe. They arrived at the end of the Ice Age, when it was, to say the least of it, very, very cold, and took up residence in some caves somewhere in the middle of France. According to the pundits who studied their remains, they were exactly like us. I mean *exactly* like us. They had the same physiques, the same brains, and probably looked a lot like us—give or take a certain amount of hair. There were no scissors in those days. Scissors were among the many things yet to be invented. No one had discovered iron or other metals. No one had even invented the wheel. They had fire, but that was it. It says a great deal about how gifted they were that they survived at all.

Now, since they were so very like us, it follows that they had the same abilities; but most of these must have been hidden because the way to *use* these abilities hadn't been invented yet. It was all right for the ones who had a gift for art: they could do cave paintings. But the real flowering of that gift actually had to wait thousands of years for the exact right time, in Renaissance Italy, for people like Michelangelo and Botticelli to come along. The ones who had all the abilities to make a lawyer were probably quite happy too, because they could settle disputes and stop fights—although there must have been times when the rest of the tribe rolled their eyes at the cave roof and said, "There she goes again! Hit her, someone."

But how did the people feel who were born with all the abilities to be a concert pianist, or a nuclear physicist, or banker, or—well—all the other things we can be nowadays?

The usual assumption is that they mucked in with the rest of the group, making the best of things. People say that if you've never heard of a thing, you don't miss it. But I think that is only half true. I'm willing to bet that large numbers of these cavemen had yearnings and forward-looking inklings flitting through their minds from time to time. Picture the young woman, tastefully dressed in tiger skin, with her hair greased into fashionable rats' tails, who goes into the cave and hits her head—for the hundredth time—on the bit where the roof is low. "Dammit!" she says. "Why can't I just press something and have a light here?" Or there is the man trudging for miles across the tundra, carrying a heavy dead animal. His feet are killing him, his arms are aching, and he is frozen to the bone. He would be thinking, "If only there was some way to get back to the cave without *walking*!"

My impression is that we all still have these inklings. My own is a strong desire to fly. I don't mean I want to boringly go on an airplane: I'm thinking of antigravity here, zooming on my own power above all sorts of interesting countrysides. I also dream of flicking to another, alternate world. I am quite sure I am adumbrating hidden gifts that some of my descendants are going to be able to use properly when the time is right.

When you have such inklings, don't dismiss them out of hand. Not having these sorts of notions is the way to stagnation. You can see this from the later history of our cave people ancestors. The climate warmed and living became easier. So what did these people do? They went and sat on the shores of seas or lakes and did nothing. They stagnated and ate seafood—at least, beside the lakes, it was mussels and minnows, but they still did nothing. There are piles of their rubbish where they sat, quite squalidly. This stasis is what comes with peace and plenty, unfortunately. I call the frame of mind that goes with it the "Oh no!" way of thinking. If someone wanted to use his/her gifts for something different, the rest of the tribe said, "Oh no!" If someone suggested building a boat or going inland, they said, "It's against the *rules*," or "It's not *traditional*!" or "The gods don't allow it" or, more hysterically, "He's a heretic" or "She's a witch." What they really meant, of course, is "We don't want anything to change." And this went on for thousands of years.

It was literally millennia before humanity pulled itself up by its bootstraps and started making use of people's hidden gifts, for taming horses, for instance, or cultivating crops, or domesticating cows and sheep. The static times must have been *maddening* for the ones with these ideas.

But they do come round, more than once, the times when humanity just sits there and says "Oh no!" to anything new. The "Oh no" party is always with us. You can hear them now in the people who refuse to admit that the climate might be changing. They say, "It's just a blip in the weather," or "The scientists are being alarmist," or simply and complacently, "God will provide. We're okay." And it really is important not to listen to them, just as it always was. Someone somewhere undoubtedly has the right hidden gift to cope with the coming conditions, but he/she has not recognized it yet. That person could be you. Or if it's not your hidden gifts that are needed this time, they might be just right for the next time. So please don't disregard any of the strange notions that come into your heads. They are certainly prompted by your hidden gifts. Just remember how incredibly gifted all human beings are. Thank you.

Characterization:
Advice for Young Writers

Always ready to give suggestions and advice, Diana wrote this piece to help aspiring young writers.

Your characters—the people in your story—are the most important part of what you write. They are the things that make the plot work. Things don't just happen. People *make* them happen. They do this by deciding to do one thing rather than another; by reacting to one another ("I like this person, I hate that one, this other person is a fool"); by having strong beliefs about life; by being vain or selfish; and sometimes by being feeble and not doing anything at all.

It follows that you have to find the right people for your story. It is no good, for instance, if the story you want to tell concerns someone getting to be king of the world, and you make that person feeble and timid—or, if you do, it would have to be a story about how this person got to be king by a set of accidents and misunderstandings. This would be very different from a story of a strong person forging on through all sorts of barriers, and getting to be king in the end. See what I mean? The kind of person the story happens to makes all the difference.

Some writers try to solve this matter in one of two ways: in the first, they have one main character who is a sort of stooge and observer, and have events and personalities happen in front of this person. The result is that the observer character becomes just a window for the reader to look through, with no discernible personality, and the plot is a set of disconnected episodes. What you get is a sort of variety show and not a story at all. A very *good* example of this is *Alice in Wonderland*, but it is not a method that anyone should imitate unless she/he is actually a genius.

The second way is worse: here the writer decides on a set of names (usually hard to remember) and has these names doing what the story wants them to do, without the *reason* for what they do being part of these named people at all. I think the hope here is that if you work them hard enough these cardboard figures will turn out to be real people in some way. In fact, it ends up with the reader puzzling about *why* Ertyulop ran off with the treasure, when in the last chapter he/she was trying to defend it. Or *why* Asdfgh suddenly decided to go on this quest when there was nothing in it for him/her. Or even why Oknmb abruptly starts to hate Ertyulop.

So how do you get it right?

You have to consider all the characters in your story to be *real people*. You have to get to know them, before you start, as if they were well-known friends. This applies to every single person in your story, not just those with leading roles. Look around you, at your friends, enemies, and most irritating aunts, and apply what you learn to whoever you put in your story. Each of these people will have a differently shaped body, for a start, which causes them to walk, sit, and gesture in a different way from the rest. Their hair will grow in an individual way—and hang over their eyes, or not, when they are excited. Some people's teeth will stick out, or be false ones. Some will make gestures all the time, others will remain still. Most important of all—because this is what chiefly appears in a written story—each of them will *talk* in a different way. Listen carefully, and you will find that every single person has her/his own special rhythm when they speak. Once you know the rhythm of your character's speech and can get it written into what they say, the chances are that this character will strike readers as a real person.

The other thing about real people is that they have jobs, hobbies, and a life outside the place where you usually meet them. This is another thing that you should be careful to know about your characters. Nothing is less convincing than a person who only seems to come alive at the moments when they take part in the story. Make sure you know what they are doing when you are not actually writing about them—what they have for breakfast, what their outside interests are, the kind of clothes they buy. Then, even if you don't actually mention much of this, the person will have proper depth.

Knowing what each person is like offstage, so to speak, is often a great help to writing the story. Let us say, for example, you are stuck in the writing because the plot demands that your main character finds out a vital fact, and you have no idea where she/he can get it. Then, fortunately, you remember that nervous old Mr. Buggins next door has a junk shop down by the market. Your main character can drop into the shop and— behold—the vital fact is there in the shop window. If you had not known this about Mr. Buggins, the story might be stuck indeed.

But take care: there is no need to go on about a character and put in all you know. This is another way to produce a cardboard effect. The fact is, *you* need to know, but the reader doesn't. Long descriptions of someone's appearance and lifestyle are a total turn-off. But if *you* know, it will come over without your having to tell it.

We come now to a thing you have to know best of all, and that is a character's inward life. Again, you do not have to go into it in detail (unless it is vital to the plot or particularly odd and interesting) but you do have to know what makes a person tick. If, for instance, you are writing about a mild and timid person, but the story requires that this person suddenly becomes fierce and bold, you have to know from the beginning that, somewhere in this person's psyche, there are the seeds of boldness. If you know that from the start, then hints of this will get dropped, and it will not seem wholly unlikely when this person suddenly rushes upon Uncle Bill and bites him in the neck. And this goes for the mind of every person you wish to portray. The kind of people they are inside gives you the *reasons* for what they do in the story.

There is a lovely bonus that comes with knowing your characters from the inside out. If you have got it right, there will come a moment when they start acting like real, independent people. They will do things and say things that even you do not expect. Let them. They will add immeasurably to the depth and excitement of your narrative.

All this applies particularly to the baddies in a story. You have to remember that villains are real people too. They have reasons for what they do, and motives for the way they behave, and they do not, as a rule, regard themselves as evil. They are acting for a cause, or out of deeply held convictions which have led them the wrong way. A lot of writers forget this. They make the baddie give evil laughs and rejoice in his/her wickedness—or worse, they wriggle out by making the villain mad. And they have the villain with no outside life except to torment the hero. The majority of bad people are not like this. It is much better to consider them as just like other people, but nasty.

And here is a tip, something I often do. Make your baddie someone you know and dislike. Use a real live person. Then there will be no trouble in making him/her convincing. You know them anyway. People are often shocked when I say this. But, since no bad person ever thinks of themselves as bad, these live people will always fail to recognize themselves and there is no harm done. Besides, they deserve it. So look around you. There must be someone bad that you know. Use them. And another bonus will be that the rest of your characters, because they are reacting to a real person, will start behaving more like real people too.

Something About the Author

This autobiography was provided for the Gale Autobiography Series Something About the Author, *Volume 7, published in 1988.*

I think I write the kind of books I do because the world suddenly went mad when I was five years old. In late August 1939, on a blistering hot day, my father loaded me and my three-year-old sister, Isobel, into a friend's car and drove to my grandparents' manse in Wales. "There's going to be a war," he explained. He went straight back to London, where my mother was expecting her third baby any day. We were left in the austere company of Mam and Dad (as we were told to call them). Dad, who was a moderator of the Welsh Nonconformist chapels, was a stately patriarch; Mam was a small, browbeaten lady who seemed to us to have no character at all. We were told that she was famous in her youth for her copper hair, her wit, and her beauty, but we saw no sign of any of this.

Wales could not have been more different from our new house in Hadley Wood on the outskirts of London. It was all gray or very green and the houses were close together and dun colored. The river ran black with coal—and probably

Diana's father, Aneurin Jones, 1952

always had, long before the mines: they told me the name of the place meant "bridge over the river with the black voice." Above all, everybody spoke a foreign language. Sometimes we were taken up the hill into suddenly primitive country to meet wild-looking, raw-faced old people who spoke no English, for whom our shy remarks had to be translated. Everyone spoke English to us, and would switch abruptly to Welsh when they wanted to say important things to one another. They were kind to us, but not loving. We were Aneurin's English daughters and not quite part of their culture.

Life in the manse revolved around the chapel next door. My aunt Muriel rushed in from her house down the road and energetically took us to a dressmaker to be fitted with Sunday clothes. On the way, she suggested that, to stop us feeling strange, we should call her "Mummy." Isobel obligingly did so, but I refused on the grounds that she was not our mother—besides, I was preoccupied with a confusion between dressmakers and hairdressers which even an hour of measuring and pinning did not resolve.

The clothes duly arrived: purple dresses with white polka dots and neat meat-colored coats. Isobel and I had never been dressed the same before and we rather liked it. We wore them to chapel thereafter, sitting sedately with our aunt and almost grown-up cousin Gwyn, through hours of solid Welsh and full-throated singing. Isobel sang too, the only Welsh she knew, which happened to be the name of the maid at the manse, Gwyneth. My mother had told me sternly that I was bad at singing and, not knowing the words, I couldn't join in anyway. Instead, I gazed wistfully at the shiny cherries on the hat of the lady in front, and one Sunday got into terrible trouble for

Diana brushing her sister Isobel's hair, 1937

daring to reach out and touch them.

Then my grandfather went into the pulpit. At home he was majestic enough: preaching, he was like the prophet Isaiah. He spread his arms and language rolled from him, sonorous, magnificent, and rhythmic. I had no idea then that he was a famous preacher, nor that people came from forty miles away to hear him because he had an almost bardic tendency to speak a kind of blank verse—*hwyl*, it is called, much valued in a preacher—but the splendor and the rigor of it nevertheless went into the core of my being. Though I never understood one word, I grasped the essence of a dour, exacting, and curiously magnificent religion. His voice shot me full of terrors. For years after that, I used to dream regularly that a piece of my bedroom wall slid aside, revealing my grandfather declaiming in Welsh, and I knew he was declaiming about my sins. I still sometimes dream in Welsh, without understanding a word. And at the bottom of my mind there is always a flow of spoken language that is not English, rolling in majestic paragraphs and resounding with splendid polysyllables. I listen to it like music when I write.

Weekdays I was sent to the local school, where everyone was taught in Welsh except me. I was the only one in the class who could read. When the school inspector paid a surprise visit, the teacher thrust a Welsh book at me and told me in a panicky whisper to read it aloud. I did so—Welsh, luckily, is spelled phonetically—and I still understood not a word. When girls came to play, they spoke English too, initiating me into mysterious rhymes: *Whistle while you work, Hitler made a shirt.* War had been declared, but I had never heard of Hitler till then. We usually played in the chapel graveyard where I thought of the graves as like magnificent double beds for dead people. I fell off the manse wall into such a grave as I declaimed, "Goebbels wore it, Goering tore it," and tore a ligament in one ankle.

After what seemed a long time, my mother arrived with our new sister, Ursula. She was outraged to find Isobel calling Aunt Muriel "Mummy." I remember trying to soothe her by explaining that Isobel was in no way deceived: she was just obliging our aunt. Unfortunately the voice I explained in had acquired a strong Welsh accent, which angered my mother further. We felt the strain of the resulting hidden rows as an added bleakness in the bleak manse. We were back in Hadley Wood by Christmas.

Looking back, I see that my relationship with my mother never recovered from this. When she arrived in Wales, she had seen me as something other, which she rather disliked. She said I would grow up just like my aunt, and accused me of taking my aunt's side. It did not help that, at that time, my hair was just passing from blond to a color my mother called mouse, and I looked very little like either side of the family. My parents were both short, black haired, and handsome, whereas I was tall and blue-eyed. When we got back to London, my mother resisted all my attempts to hug her on the grounds that I was too big.

Meanwhile, the threat of bombing and invasion grew. London was not safe. The small school Isobel and I were attending rented a house called Lane Head beside Coniston Water in distant Westmorland, and offered a room in it to my mother and her three children. We went there in the early summer of 1940. Here were real mountains, lakes, brooks racing through indescribable greenness. I was amazed—intoxicated—with the beauty of it.

We were told that Lane Head had belonged to John Ruskin's secretary and that this man's descendants (now safely in America) had been the John, Susan, Titty, and Roger of Arthur Ransome's books. Ruskin's own house, Brantwood, was just up the road. There was a lady in a cottage near it who could call red squirrels from the trees. This meant more to me at the time—this, and the wonder of living in a rambling old house smelling of lamp oil, with no electricity, where the lounge (where we were forbidden to play) was full of Oriental trophies, silk couches, and Pre-Raphaelite pictures. There was a loft (also forbidden) packed with Titty and Roger's old toys.

The entry to it was above our room and I used to sneak up into it. There were no new toys and no paper to draw on and I loved drawing. One rainy afternoon, poking about the loft, I came upon a stack of high-quality thick drawing paper. To my irritation, someone had drawn flowers on every sheet, very fine and black and accurate, and signed them with a monogram, JR. I took the monogram for a bad drawing of a mosquito and assumed the fine black pencil was ink. I carried a wad of them down to our room and knelt at the window seat industriously erasing the drawings with an ink rubber. Halfway through I was caught and punished. The loft was padlocked. Oddly enough, it was only many years later that I realized that I must have innocently rubbed out a good fifty of Ruskin's famous flower drawings.

The school and its pupils left the place toward the end of summer, but we stayed and were rapidly joined by numbers of mothers with small children. The world was madder than ever. I was told about the small boats going to Dunkirk and exasperated everyone by failing to understand why the Coniston steamer had not gone to France from the landlocked lake. (I was always asking questions.) Bombs were dropping and the Battle of Britain was escalating. My husband, who had, oddly enough, been sent to his grandparents barely fifteen miles from us, remembers the docks at Barrow-in-Furness being bombed. He saw the blaze across the bay. During that raid a German plane was shot down and its pilot was at large in the mountains for nearly two weeks. It is hard now to imagine the horror he inspired in all the mothers. When he broke into the Lane Head pantry one night and stole a large cheese, there was sheer panic the next morning. I suppose it was because that night the war had briefly climbed in through our window.

Being too young to understand this, I had trouble distinguishing Germans from germs, which seemed to inspire the mothers with equal horror. When a large Quaker family arrived to cram into the house too, bringing with them an eleven-year-old German-Jewish boy who told horrendous stories of what the police did—they took you away in the night, he said, to torture you—I had no idea he was talking about the Gestapo. I have been nervous of policemen ever since.

The Quaker family, all six of them, had a cold bath every morning. We were regularly woken at 6:06 a.m. by the screams of the youngest, who was only two. In their no-nonsense Quaker way, this family got out the old boat from the boathouse and went sailing. I can truthfully say that I sailed in both the *Swallow* and the *Amazon*, for though this boat was a dire old tub called *Mavis*, she was the original of both. I didn't like her. On a trip to Wild Cat Island[1] I caught my finger in her centerboard, and my father nearly drowned us in her trying to sail in a storm on one of his rare visits from teaching and fire watching in London.

The mothers gave the older children lessons. Girls were taught womanly accomplishments. Being left-handed, I had great trouble learning to knit until a transient Icelandic lady arrived with a baby and a large dog and began teaching me the continental method. She left before teaching me to purl or even to cast on stitches. I had to make those up. Another mother taught sewing. I remember wrestling for a whole morning to sew on a button, which became inexplicably enmeshed in my entire supply of thread. Finally I explained to this mother that I wasn't going to grow up to be a woman, and asked if I could do drawing with the boys. She told me not to be rude and became so angry that—with a queer feeling that it was in self-defense—I put my tongue out at her. She gave me a good shaking and ordered me to stand in the hall all the next morning.

The same day, other mothers had taken the younger children to the lake shore to play beyond the cottage of the lady who called squirrels. The noise the children made disturbed the occupant of the houseboat out in the bay. He came rowing angrily across and ordered them off, and, on finding where they lived, said that he wasn't going to be disturbed by a parcel of evacuees and announced that he would come next morning to complain. He hated children. There was huge dismay among the mothers. Next morning I stood in the hall, watching them rush about trying to find coffee and biscuits (which were nearly unobtainable by then) with which to soothe the great Arthur Ransome, and gathered I was about to set eyes on a real writer. I watched with great interest as a tubby man with a beard stamped past, obviously in a great fury, and almost immediately stormed away again on finding there was nobody exactly in charge to complain to. I was very impressed to find he was real. Up to then I had thought books were made by machines in the back room of Woolworth's.

My brush with the other writer in the area was even less direct but no more pleasant. We were at Near Sawrey, which was a long way for children to walk, but, if the mothers were to go anywhere, they had to walk and the children had to walk with them. No one had a car. Isobel and another four-year-old girl were so tired that, when they found a nice gate, they hooked their feet on it and had a restful swing. An old woman with a sack over her shoulders stormed out of the house and hit both of them for swinging on her gate. This was Beatrix Potter. She hated children, too. I remember the two of them running back to us, bawling with shock. Fate, I always think, seemed determined to thrust a very odd view of authorship on me.

The boy who kept talking of the Gestapo was only one of several disturbed children among us. The madness of those times got into the daughter of the sewing lady too. She began systematically pushing the younger children off high places. She told me and swore me to secrecy. I knew this was wrong. My grandfather haunted me in dreams and I kept telling myself that I was feeble not to tell someone—but I had sworn. Even so, when the girl pushed Isobel down a deep cellar I summoned my courage and told my mother. This caused a terrible row, as bad as the row in Wales, and I think that as a result of it my mother decided to leave Lane Head. She went to York to find a teaching job, leaving us in the charge of the other mothers. That night, the daughter of the sewing lady suggested it might be fun if I sneaked into her bedroom to eat aspirins with her. Feeling like an adventure, and also feeling bad at having betrayed this girl's trust, I did so. Aspirins were horrible. I swallowed mine with huge difficulty and asked her what she saw in them. Nothing, she said. It was just that you were forbidden to eat them. And she spat hers out on the carpet.

Here her mother irrupted into the room.

I remember that a Court of Justice was hastily convened. Three mothers. I stood accused of leaving my bed in order to spit aspirins all over another's carpet. I remember I was bemused to find that the other girl was not accused of anything. The sentence was that I and my bed were taken downstairs to a lumber room and I was to sleep there. I rebelled. I got up again and went into the forbidden lounge, where I did what I had always wanted to do and took down one of the heavy, slightly rusty Indian Army swords. I wondered whether to fall on it like a Roman. But since it was clear to me that this would hurt very much, I put it back and went out the open window. It was near sunset. The grass was thick with dew, but still quite warm to my bare feet. The sky was a miraculous clear auburn. I tried to summon courage to run away in my nightclothes. I wanted to. I also had a dim sense that it would be an effective move. But I could not make myself take another step. I went back to the lumber room knowing I was a coward.

In fact, when my mother came back late the next night, she thought I *had* run away—or been taken ill, since nobody had told her. I suspect that the punishment was aimed at her too. There were further rows before we left for York in September 1941.

Despite this, that time in the Lake District is still magical to me. The shape of the mountain across the lake has, like my grandfather, become part of my dreams. Since the mountain is called the Old Man of Coniston, they sometimes seem to be the same thing.

In York, we boarded in a nunnery. The blitz was on and the war was moving into its grimmest phase, which may have been why we never got enough to eat there. Granny—my Yorkshire grandmother—used to send us hoarded tins of baked beans which my mother heated in an old tin box over a gas ring in our bedroom.

Diana in Troutbeck Valley, the Lake District, 1985

My sister Ursula was now old enough to be a power. She was a white waif child with black, black hair and a commanding personality. While my mother was teaching, Ursula had various nannies, whom she ordered mercilessly about and did imitations of in the evenings. I had long known that Isobel was the best and most interesting of companions. It was marvelous to discover that Ursula, at two and a half, could make us fall about laughing. I knew I was lucky to have sisters.

My mother decided that Ursula was going to be an actress. Isobel, she told us, was beautiful but not otherwise gifted. As for me, she said, I was ugly, semidelinquent, but bright. She had the nuns put me in a class with nine-year-olds. This was the first time I knew that I was supposed to be clever. I did my best, but everything the class did was two years beyond me.

Religion was beyond me, too. The nuns, being an Anglican order, worshipped in York Minster and took us with them. This huge and beautiful cathedral must have been ten times the size of the chapel in Wales. I could not make head nor tail of the mysterious, reverent intonings in the far distance. I fidgeted and shamed my mother until one of the nuns took me instead to a smaller church from then on. There I sat, wrestling with the notions that Heaven Is Within You (not in me, I thought, or I'd know) and of Christ dying for our sins. I stared at the crucifix, thinking how *very* much being crucified must hurt, and was perturbed that, even with this special treatment, religion was not, somehow, taking on me. (I put it this way to myself because I had baptism and vaccination muddled, like germs and Germans.)

Weekdays, I joined a playground game run by the naughty son of another teacher. It was called the Soft Shoe Brigade, in which we all marched in step and pretended we were Nazis. I could not understand why the nuns put a stop to it.

My pleas to be put into a class of younger children were granted near the end of the time we spent there. After a few weeks' bliss, doing work I understood, we went back to Hadley Wood in 1942. By then, the bombing was beginning to seem like the weather, only more frightening. When the siren sounded at night, we went to the ground floor, where we sat and listened to the blunt bang and sharp yammer of gunfire and the bombs whistle as they fell, or watched searchlights rhythmically ruling lines in the sky. Recently I was talking to a woman my own age; we both confessed that any noise that resembles these, or the sound of a low-flying plane, still makes us expect to be dead the next moment.

The world was mad in daytime, too, not only with rationing, blackouts, brown paper stuck to bus windows, and notices saying CARELESS TALK COSTS LIVES. The radio talked daily of bridgeheads, pincer movements, and sorties, which one knew were terms for people killing people. My father was away most nights fire watching, and at weekends he exercised with the Home Guard.

One Sunday I almost fell over one of our neighbors, who was crawling about in the field behind our house with—inexplicably—a great bunch of greenery on his head.

"Oh, Mr. Cowey!" shouted I, in much surprise. "What are you doing crawling about with a bush on your head?"

He arose wrathfully, causing the greenery to fall into two horns. "Get out of it, you stupid child!" he snapped, the image of an angry nature god. "You've spoiled the whole bloody exercise!"

Considering this madness, it is not surprising that, at the latest of many private schools we went to that year, when the forbidding teacher announced, "All those children for elocution stand up and go into the hall," I mistook and thought the word was "execution." I trembled, and was astonished when they all came back unharmed. At that same school, Isobel's teacher used to punish her for writing left-handed. One day she was shut in a bedroom, being punished, when the air-raid siren went. The rest of us were marched into the moderate safety of the hall, but Isobel was forgotten. I wrestled with my cowardice and managed to make myself call out that Isobel was still in the bedroom. The teachers were, I suppose, scared to go up there during a raid. They told me fiercely to hold my tongue, and made me sit for the rest of the week behind the blackboard as a lesson for impudence. There was more disgrace than hardship to this. I used that time for reading.

I read avidly that year, things like *The Arabian Nights* and the whole of Malory's *Le Morte d'Arthur*. Soon after I was eight, I sat up from reading in the middle of one afternoon and knew that I was going to be a writer one day. It was not a decision, or even a revelation. It was more as if my future self had leaned back from the years ahead and quietly informed me what she was. In calm certainty, I went and told my parents.

"You haven't got it in you," my mother said. My father bellowed with laughter. He had a patriarch's view of girls: they were not really meant to *do* anything. Though he never said so, I think it was a disappointment to him to have three daughters. My mother, as always, was more outspoken. She said if it were not for the war, she would have more children—boys.

I think my mother was very discontented that year. She was,

after all, an Oxford graduate who had dragged herself up from a humble background in industrial Yorkshire by winning scholarships—and all she had for it was the life of a suburban mother. I know she encouraged my father to apply for the husband-and-wife job they took in 1943.

The job was in a village called Thaxted in rural Essex. My parents were to run what would nowadays be called a conference center for young adults, a place where teenagers who worked in factories in urban Essex could come for a week or weekend to experience a little culture. It was one of many schemes at that time which looked forward to the widening of horizons at the end of the war, and it had considerable propaganda value, since it was by no means clear then that the Allies were going to win the war. My father believed in it utterly, and it became his life for the next ten years.

I was already wrestling to make sense of the experience of the previous four years—particularly the religion. Now I had a whole new set, three or four new sets, in fact, all going on at once. Thaxted, to take that first, was straight out of a picture postcard, with houses that were either thatched and half-timbered or decoratively plastered, and a medieval guild hall straddled the main street. The church, at once stately and ethereal beside a majestic copper beech, stood at the top of the hill opposite Clarance House (the house my parents ran). Industry was represented by a little sweet factory at one end of the village and a man who made life-sized mechanical elephants at the other. The place was connected to the outside world by sporadic buses and by a branch railway that terminated a mile outside the village (but the train driver would grudgingly wait for anyone he saw panting up the hill to the station). On holidays, people did folk dancing in the streets. There was also much handweaving, pottery making, and madrigal singing.

This idyllic place had the highest illegitimate birth rate in the county. In numerous families, the younger apparent brothers or sisters turned out to be the offspring of the unmarried elder daughters—though there was one young woman who pretended her daughter was her sister without grandparents to help—and there was a fair deal of incest, too. Improbable characters abounded there, including two acknowledged witches and a man who went mad in the church porch at full moon. There was a prostitute not much older than me who was a most refined person, with a face like alabaster, a slight foreign accent, and tweeds. There was another who looked like an artist's impression of Neanderthal woman; she had a string of pale, thin children, each with huge famine-poster eyes.

I had assumed you had to be married before you had children, so all this was quite a shock. I began to suspect the world had always been mad. In self-defense, my sisters and I assumed our home life was normal, which it certainly was not.

Clarance House was as beautiful as the rest, built in the days of Queen Anne, with graceful wall panels indoors— although the interior was somewhat bare because the Essex Education Committee, which financed the place, could seldom spare much money. Here my father threw himself into life as an educator and entertainer, for he was as gifted in his way as my grandfather and could hold an audience like an actor, whether he was making intellectual conversation at table with my mother, introducing a lecture, or telling ghost stories to rapt teenagers. His main story was about Clarance House. There were the remains of an old stair in a cupboard where, my father claimed, you could hear disembodied feet, climbing, climbing. . . . We knew he was right to call the house haunted, but the really haunted part was the main entrance hall, which I always felt compelled to run through if I had to cross it, shaking with fear. Eventually one of the cleaners saw the ghost. She had been chatting to it while she polished the hall for some minutes, thinking it was the girl she worked with. Then she looked properly and found she could see through it. She had hysterics and left at once for a job in the bacon factory in Great Dunmow.

My mother organized the cleaners, the cooks, and the domestic side, and in her spare time went feverishly into local history and madrigal singing. Not a day passed without some fearful crisis, in which my mother raced about inveighing against the Committee, the war, or my father, while my father stormed through the house in a fury, forgetting to speak English in his rage. His life was wholly public: my mother's three-quarters so. Neither had time for us. For a short while the three of us children shared a room at the top of the house; but my parents were so dedicated to making a success of the center that they decided that room was needed for additional guests. We were put out into the Cottage. This was a lean-to, two-room shack across the yard from the main house. The mud floor of the lower room was hastily covered with concrete and our beds were crammed into the upper floor. And we were left to our own devices. Looking back on this, we all find it extraordinary; for damp climbed the walls, and almost as soon as we had arrived in Thaxted, I had contracted juvenile rheumatism, which seriously affected my heart, and Ursula also contracted it soon after.

Diana's mother, Marjorie, at a Clarance House reunion

The only heating was a paraffin stove—and how we failed to
set the Cottage on fire I shall never know. The stove was often
knocked over during games or fights, or encased in paper when
we dried paintings. There was nowhere to wash in the Cottage,
so we seldom bothered. Nor did we comb our hair. Ursula,
whose hair was long, wild, and curly, tied it in two knots on
her forehead to keep it out of her eyes. My mother did not
notice for six months. Then I got into trouble for allowing it.
But Ursula always did what she wanted. The following year
she refused to eat anything but three slices of bread and yeast
extract a day, whatever Isobel or I said, and my mother never
knew about that at all.

I was supposed to be in charge of my sisters and it weighed

on me. I did my best, but at ages nine and ten I was not very good at it. The worst thing happened just after Isobel had been to a pantomime with a school friend, where she had been entranced to find the fairies swooping over the stage in flying harnesses. She wanted to do it too. So Ursula and I obligingly tied skipping ropes together, slung them across a beam above the Cottage stairs, and hauled Isobel up there by a noose under her armpits. She dangled, rotating gently, looking worried. "Look more graceful," we advised her. She stuck out her arms—and her legs, too, like a starfish—and went on hanging. Absorbed in her experience and knowing that one had to suffer for art's sake, she failed to say she was suffocating. Luckily, Ursula and I became worried and cut her down with blunt nail scissors just in time.

Around this time, my mother decreed that Isobel should become a ballerina, because of her looks. My mother's main substitute for attending to us was to assert periodically that Isobel was beautiful and a born dancer, Ursula a potential actress, and me an ugly semidelinquent with a high IQ. Her other substitute for attention was to make our school uniforms herself. She would buy half the required garments, angrily protesting at their cost and the number of clothing coupons they took, and make the rest. Other children jeered, because our uniforms were always the wrong style and material, and it always mystified us that *their* parents could afford enough coupons for a complete uniform. Other clothing my mother got from the local orphanage. The matron, who was a friend of my parents, used to give us all the clothes donated which she did not think suitable for the orphans. We often looked very peculiar. When I protested, my mother would angrily describe her own childhood with a widowed mother in the First World War. "You're all extremely lucky," she would conclude. "You have advantages I never dreamed of." At which I felt acutely guilty.

Even so, I might protest that my mother had had proper clothes. I was prone to spot flaws in any argument, and I had an odd theory that you ought to be truthful about your feelings. This usually sent my mother into a vituperative fury. This was part of the reason why she called me semidelinquent. Another reason was that I had inherited my father's tendency to fly into towering rages. I also used to shout at my sisters because they seldom listened to mere speech. But I think the main reason was that I was always working at some more or less mad project: some of which were harmless—like dressing as a ghost and pretending to haunt the graveyard, inventing a loom, or directing a play, some of which were liable to cause trouble—like the time I tried to organize a garden fête without asking anyone; some of which were outright dangerous—like walking on the roof, or the time I could have attracted enemy airplanes by signaling Morse code by flashlights to friends outside the village. For some reason I believed it my duty to live a life of adventure, and I used to worry that, for a would-be writer, I had too little imagination.

Clarance House had two gardens, one ordinary one and a second, much bigger, across a lane at the back. This Other Garden was kept locked. I was always begging for the key. It was like paradise, or the extension of life into the imagination. Here were espalier apples, roses, lilies, vegetables, and a green path running under an arcade of creepers to an old octagonal summerhouse in the distance. Near the summerhouse my father kept bees. These were a notoriously fierce strain, and the gardener could often be seen racing down the green path pursued by an angry black cloud of them. But the bees never attacked us. I used to go and talk to them, because I had read that bees were part of your family and you should tell them all your news—although I never spoke to them when the gardener was by. He hated superstition. He was very religious. As a young man, he told people quite frankly, he had attended both church and chapel to be quite sure of heaven; but one day on the Sampford road he had had a vision in which an angel descended and told him always to go to chapel. And he was only one of a crowd of remarkable people who swarmed through the house. There were ham actors, gays, politicians, hirsute artists, hysterical sopranos, a musician who looked like Dr. Dolittle, another who believed in the transmigration of souls, an agriculturalist who looked like Hitler, a teddy girl, local vicars—one long, thin, and gloomy who grew tobacco, another stout and an expert on wine. . . .

The vicar of Thaxted was a communist and people used to come from Great Dunmow in hobnailed boots specially to walk out noisily during his sermons. Actually his politics derived more from William Morris than Marx. The church was hung with light drapery to enhance its considerable elegance, and he taught any child who wished to learn a musical instrument. "Not you," said my mother. "You're tone deaf." Or maybe just deaf, I used to think, on Thursdays when the bell ringers practiced. The Cottage was almost opposite the bell tower, and the sound was deafening. In fact, I had little to do with the church otherwise because I settled my religious muddles by deciding that I had better be an atheist.

School brought more strange experiences—with an uncomfortable tendency to pick up motifs from the past. Isobel and I were sent to the village school, where we came up against the English class system for the first time. As children of intellectuals, we ranked above village kids and below farmers or anybody rich, but sort of sideways. This meant we were fair game for all. The head teacher had only contempt for us. He said I was never likely to pass the exam to enter grammar school ("the scholarship," everyone called it), and almost refused to enter me. My mother had one of her rows over that (by this time I was dimly aware that my mother truly *enjoyed* a row). In school, we spent all but one afternoon a week knitting endless scarves and balaclavas for the forces, while one of the teachers told us about tortures, shivering with strange excitement while she spoke. I once nearly fainted at her account of the rack. The other afternoon, the boys were allowed to do drawing and the girls sewing. I protested about this. The head teacher threatened to cane me for impertinence. At which a berserker rage came over me. I seized a shoddy metal ruler and tied it in a knot. I was sent home, but not caned, to my surprise.

Being fair game for all meant that the school bullies chased you home. One winter day, in snow, a bully chased me, pelting me with ice. It cut. Terrified, I raced away down the alley between the blacksmith's and the barber's and shot into the glassy white road ahead. Too late, I saw a car driving past. I think I hurtled clean over its bonnet, getting knocked out on the way. I came to, facedown, looking back the way I had come. "Help!" I shouted to the blacksmith in his forge. "I've been run over!" Not accurate, but I *was* upset. The blacksmith's wife improved on this by racing into the barber's, where she knew my father was having a haircut, yelling, "Mr. Jones! Come quickly! Your daughter's under a car!" Even less accurate, because the car was down the hill, slewing about as it braked. My father dived out of the barber's with his hair short one side and long the other. The driver got there about the same time and his face was truly a light green, poor man. I was quite impressed at the effect I had had.

I passed "the scholarship" later that year. My parents' connection with the Essex Education Committee enabled them to discover that my marks were spectacularly good. I continued to get spectacular marks most of my school career. This is not a thing I can take much credit for. I just happened to have a near-photographic memory and an inborn instinct about how to do exams—which always struck me as cheating, because whenever I was in doubt about a fact, all I had to do was close my eyes and read the remembered page. But it was the one thing my parents cared about. My mother decided that I was to go to her old Oxford college, and added that to the ugly, semidelinquent, brainy list.

As a semidelinquent I was sent as a boarder to a school in Brentwood; but there was no room in the boardinghouse and I had to live for one endless term with the family I later put in *Eight Days of Luke*. Then a girl left the boardinghouse and I had her bed. This was an old, overused hospital bed and it broke under me; and the matron made public discovery that my ears were unwashed. As a punishment—and I am still not clear whether it was for the bed or the ears or both—I had to sleep on my own in an old lumber room. Just as before, in Coniston, I could not muster the courage to run away. Nor could I muster the courage to tell my parents; I was too ashamed. But I did tell them, because I enjoyed it so, how the matron marched us in line every Saturday to the cinema to see every film that happened to be showing. This philistine practice horrified them. I was removed and sent by bus to a Quaker school in Saffron Walden as a day pupil instead. I was there from 1946 to 1952. It was mainly a boarding school, which meant that I, and later my sisters, were as usual part of an oddball minority. Quakers do not believe in eccentricity or in academic success. They found me highly eccentric for getting good marks, and for most other things too.

As time went on, my parents had less and less time for us. We never went on holiday with them. When they took their yearly holiday, we were left with the gardener, the minister of the chapel, or the matron of the orphanage—or simply dumped on Granny. Granny was truly marvelous; five feet of Yorkshire common sense, love, and superstition. She was always saying wise things. I remember, among many sayings, when one time she had given me a particularly good present, she said, "No, it's not generous. Being generous is giving something that's hard to give." She was so superstitious that she kept a set of worthless china to break when she happened to break something good, on the grounds that breakages always came in threes and it was as well to get it over. I would have been lost without Granny, that I know.

That was a grim time in the world. The war, which had receded when we left London, came close again through rockets and pilotless planes. They were terrifying. Then there was the anxiety of D-Day, followed by the discovery of the concentration camps, which made me realize just how mad the world had been. This was followed by great shortages and the Cold War. Hiroshima horrified me; the Cold War made me expect a Hiroshima bomb in England any day.

Things were grim at home too. When a course was running at Clarance House—which was continuously during summer and two-thirds of the time during winter—we quite often came home from school to find that nobody had remembered to save us anything to eat. If we went into the kitchen to forage, the cook shrieked at us to get out. When no course was running, my father would sit slumped and silent in the only family room, which was also his office. He rarely spoke to any of us unless he was angry, and then he could not remember which one of us he was talking to and had to go through all our names before he got the right one. Almost every night during winter, my mother would shout at him—with some justice—that he kept all his charm for his job and none for her in private; whereupon he would fly into a towering Welsh rage and they would bawl at each other all evening. When it was over, my mother would rush into the kitchen, where we had retreated to do homework, and recount angrily all that had been said, while we waited with pens politely poised, knowing that any comment only made things worse. This routine was occasionally lightened by ludicrous incidents, such as the time the cat locked us all into that office by playing with the bolt on the outside of its door; or when our aged corgi suddenly upped and bit my father on the bottom while he was chasing Isobel to hit her.

My parents *did* remember birthdays and Christmas, but only at the last minute. That is how I remember that day peace was declared with Japan. It was the day before my eleventh birthday and all the shops were shut in celebration, so I got no presents that year. This left a void, for birthdays were the one occasion when my father could be persuaded to buy books. By begging very hard, I got *Puck of Pook's Hill* when I was ten and *Greenmantle* when I was twelve. But my father was inordinately mean about money. He solved the Christmas book giving by buying an entire set of Arthur Ransome books, which he kept locked in a high cupboard and dispensed one between the three of us each year. Clarance House had books, he said. True: it had been stocked mostly from auctions and, from this stock, before I was fourteen, I had read all of Conrad, Freud's *The Interpretation of Dreams*, Bertrand Russell on relativity, besides a job lot of history and historic novels—and all thirty books from the public library in the guild hall. Isobel and I suffered from perpetual book starvation. We begged, saved, and cycled for miles to borrow books, but there were still never enough. When I was thirteen, I began writing narratives in old exercise books to fill this gap, and read them aloud to my sisters at night. I finished two, both of epic length and quite terrible. But in case someone is tempted to say my father did me a favor, I must say this is not the case at all. I always would have been a writer. I still had this calm certainty. All these epics did for me was to prove that I could finish a story. My mother was always telling me that I was much too incompetent to finish anything. During her ugly, semidelinquent litanies she frequently said, "When you do the Oxford exams, you'll get a place, but you won't do better than that. You haven't got what it takes."

In his stinginess, my father allowed us one penny a week pocket money. Money for anything else you had to ask him for. Looking back, I see I accepted this, partly because I thought it was normal and knew I wasn't worth more, but also because asking for money at least meant he spoke to me while he was inquiring suspiciously into the use of every penny. He also allowed me to darn his socks for sixpence a pair (by this stage I was sewing clothes for myself and my sisters and doing the family wash in spare moments). My sisters, however, rebelled at their poverty and bearded my father in his office. Groaning with dismay, my father upped our allowance to a shilling a week when I was fifteen, on condition that we bought our own soap and toothpaste. A tube of toothpaste cost most of two weeks' allowance. Isobel and I were by then civilized enough to save for it. Ursula squandered her money.

Ursula always took the eccentric way, particularly over illness. The cardinal sin we could commit was to be ill. It meant that someone grudgingly had to cross the yard with meals for us. My mother usually made a special trip to our bedsides to point out what a nuisance we were being. Her immediate response to any symptom of sickness was to deny it. "It's only psychological," she would say. On these grounds I was sent to school with chicken pox, scarlet fever, German measles, and, for half a year, with appendicitis. Luckily the appendix never quite became acute. The local doctor, somewhat puzzled by my mother's assertion that there was nothing wrong with me, eventually took it out. He was an old military character, and in keeping with the rest of his life, he had only three fingers on his right hand. I still have a monster scar. I had the appendix in a bottle for years, partly to show my mother the boils on it and partly to live up to the title of semidelinquent. But Ursula, having concluded that "only psychological" meant the same as "purely imaginary," deduced that it was therefore no more wrong to pretend to be ill than to be really ill. She drew on her

Diana's sister Ursula

Diana's sister Isobel

strong acting talent, contrived to seem at death's door whenever she was tired of school, and spent many happy hours in bed.

I put some of the foregoing facts in *The Time of the Ghost*, but what I think I failed to get over in that book was how close we three sisters were. We spent many hours delightedly discussing one another's ideas, and looked after one another strenuously. For example, when I was fourteen, Isobel was told by the Royal Ballet School that she could never, ever make it as a ballet dancer. Her life fell to pieces. She had been told so firmly that she was a ballerina born that she did not know what she was any longer. She cried one entire night. After five hours, when we still could not calm her, I crossed the yard in my pajamas—it was raining—to get parental help. A mistake. My mother jumped violently and clutched her heart when I appeared. My father ordered me back to bed, despite my explanation and despite the fact that we had been ringing our recently installed emergency bell before I went over. I trudged back through the rain, belatedly remembering that my mother hated giving sympathy. "It damages me," she had explained over my appendix. Ursula and I sat up the rest of the night convincing Isobel that she had a brain as well as a body. We were close because we had to be.

This solidarity did not hold so well when our parents laughed at us. I became very clumsy in my teens and they laughed at anything I did that was not academic. Perhaps they needed the amusement, because, for the next year, my father sickened mysteriously. When I was fifteen, he was diagnosed as having intestinal cancer. To my misfortune, something painful went wrong with my left hip at the same time, so that I could only walk with a sailorlike roll, causing much mirth. It was the beginning of multiple back troubles which have plagued me the rest of my life, but no one knew about such things then. The natural assumption was that I was trying to be interesting because my father was ill. It is hard to express the guilt I felt.

My father, full of puritanical distaste, weathered that operation. He developed secondary cancer almost at once, but that was not apparent for the next three years or so. Once he had recovered, it occurred to him that I would need special tuition if I were to go to Oxford as planned. The Friends' School was not geared to university entrance. Academic ambition vied in him with stinginess. Eventually, he approached a professor of philosophy who had just come to live in Thaxted with his wife and small children and asked him to teach me Greek. In exchange, my father offered the philosopher a handmade doll's house that someone had given my sisters. My sisters loved the thing and had kept it in beautiful condition. But the philosopher accepted the deal, so no matter what their feelings, the doll's house was given away. In return, the philosopher gave me three lessons in Greek. Then he ran off with someone else's wife. I must surely be the only person in the world to have had three Greek lessons for a doll's house.

After that, pressure mounted on me to succeed academically. In my anxiety to oblige, I overworked. I did nothing like as well as was expected. I did scrape an interview at my mother's old college. There a majestic lady don said, "Miss Jones," shuddering at my plebeian name, "you are the candidate who uses a lot of slang." She so demoralized me that, when she went on to ask me what I usually read, I looked wildly round her shelves and answered, "Books." I failed. At the eleventh hour, I applied for and got a place at St. Anne's College, Oxford, where I went in 1953.

It was not a happy time. When I got there, I found that John Ruskin had taken belated revenge for the rubbed-out drawings: I had to share a vast, cold studio (which Ruskin had once occupied) with a girl who required me to wait on her hand and foot. And my father died after my first term there. I had to stay at home to see to his funeral, and spent the rest of my time at Oxford in nagging anxiety for my sisters, who were not finding my mother easy to live with. However, C. S. Lewis and J. R. R. Tolkien were both lecturing then; Lewis booming to crowded halls and Tolkien mumbling to me and three others. Looking back, I see both of them had enormous influence on me, but it is hard to say how, except that they must have been equally influential to others too. I later discovered that almost

Diana's husband, John, with Diana looking on, 1955

everyone who went on to write children's books—Penelope Lively, Jill Paton Walsh, to name only two—was at Oxford at the same time as me; but I barely met them and we never at any time discussed fantasy. Oxford was very scornful of fantasy then. Everyone raised eyebrows at Lewis and Tolkien and said hastily, "But they're excellent scholars as well."

Let's go back now to the empty swatch of time before I went up to Oxford, when my father was periodically at home between times of being a guinea pig at an early and unsuccessful form of chemotherapy. I have not said much about the young people who came to Thaxted on courses, because most of them were mere transients, but there were some who came often, some my own age, with whom we became firm friends. One was in love with Isobel (many people were), and he was coming to the house with ten friends to relax after doing finals at Oxford. Now this was an occasion comparable to the time when I was eight and knew that I would be a writer. As soon as I heard they were coming, I was seized with unaccountable excitement. I raced round helping get ready for them and made the tea far too early. They arrived while I made it. In the small hall outside my father's office I ran into a cluster of them talking with my father. One of them said, "Diana, you know John Burrow, do you?"

I sort of looked. Not properly. All I got was a long beige streak of a man standing with them in front of the old Arthur Ransome cupboard. And instantly I knew I was going to marry this man. It was the same calm and absolute certainty that I had had when I was eight. And it rather irked me, because I hadn't even looked at him properly and I didn't know whether I *liked* him, let alone *loved* him.

Luckily both proved to be the case. The relationship survived two years at Oxford when John was a graduate student, and a third year when he was a lecturer at King's College, London. It also survived my mother's impulsive purchase, after my father died, of a private school in Beeston outside Nottingham, in a *very* haunted house. We moved there in the summer of 1956. I had been ill all that year, but after four months of listening to invisible footsteps pacing the end of my bedroom, I went to Granny, who was living in Sampford (near where the angel appeared to the gardener), in order to be married to John in Saffron Walden, in a thick fog, three days before Christmas 1956. There are no photographs of the wedding because, as my mother explained, her own wedding was more important. She married Arthur Hughes, a Cambridge scientist, the following summer.

John and I lived in London until September 1957, where I seemed unemployable. I used the time to read Dante, Gibbon, and Norse sagas. Then we moved back to Oxford to a flat in a large house on the Iffley Road, with another family downstairs who became our lifelong friends. Meanwhile, Ursula failed all her exams in protest against academic pressure and made it to drama school. She is now an actress. Isobel was at university in Leicester, working grimly for a good degree, when my stepfather turned her out of his house. She arrived on our doorstep, shattered, around the time I discovered I was pregnant, and was living with us when my son Richard was born in 1958. She stayed with us until my next son, Michael, was born in 1961, and was married from our flat. Her husband is an identical twin. John, who gave Isobel away, was mightily afraid of handing her to the wrong twin. She is now one of the

Diana with her Anglo-Saxon tutor, Elaine Griffiths, and John, 1955

few women professors in England. Ursula and I always think we did a good job of persuading her she had a brain.

My third son, Colin, was born in 1963. My aim, from this time forward, was to live a quiet life—not an easy ambition in a house full of small children, dogs, and puppies. During this time, to my undying gratitude, John and my children taught me more about ordinary human nature than I had learned up to then. I still had no idea what was normal, you see. After that I found the experiences of my childhood easier to assimilate and could start trying to write. To my dismay, I had to learn *how*—so I taught myself, doggedly. At first I assumed I would be writing for adults, but my children took a hand there. First Michael threatened to miscarry. I had to stay in bed and, while I did, I read *The Lord of the Rings*. It was suddenly clear to me after that that it was *possible* to write a long book that was fantasy. Then, as the children grew older, they gave me the opportunity to read all the children's books which I had never had as a child, and what was more, I could watch their reactions while we read them. Very vigorous those were too. They liked exactly the kind of books—full of humor and fantasy, but firmly referred to real life—which I had craved for in Thaxted. Somewhere here it dawned on me that I was going to have to write fantasy anyway, because I was not able to believe in most people's version of normal life. I started trying. What I wrote was rejected by publishers and agents with shock and puzzlement.

In 1966 we moved briefly to a cold, cold farmhouse in Eynsham while we waited for my husband's college, Jesus College, to have a house built that we could rent. There Colin started having febrile convulsions and almost everything else went wrong too. I wrote *Changeover*, my only published adult novel,[2] to counteract the general awfulness.

In 1967, the new house was ready. It had a roof that was soluble in water, toilets that boiled periodically, rising damp, a south-facing window in the food cupboard, and any number of other peculiarities. So much for my wish for a quiet life. We lived there, contending with electric fountains in the living room, cardboard doors, and so forth, until 1976, except for 1968–9, which year we spent in America, at Yale. Yale, like Oxford, was full of people who thought far too well of themselves, lived very formally, and regarded the wives of academics as second-class citizens; but America, round the edges of it, I loved. I try to go back as often as I can. We went for a glorious time to

Diana's three sons—Richard, Colin, and Michael, 1964

Maine, and also visited the West Indian island of Nevis, where, to my astonishment, a number of people greeted me warmly, saying, "I'm so glad you've come back!" I still don't know who they thought I was. But an old man on a donkey thought John was a ghost.

On our return, now all the children were at school, I started writing in earnest. A former pupil of John's introduced me to Laura Cecil, who was just starting as a literary agent for children's books. She became an instant firm friend. With her encouragement, I wrote *Wilkins' Tooth* in 1972, *Eight Days of Luke* in 1973, and *The Ogre Downstairs* the same year. I laughed so much writing that one that the boys kept putting their heads round the door to ask if I was all right. *Power of Three* came after that, then *Cart and Cwidder*, followed by *Dogsbody*, though they were not published in that order. *Charmed Life* and *Drowned Ammet* were both written in 1975.

Also on our return, we acquired a cottage in West Ilsley, Berkshire, as a refuge from the defects of the Oxford house. The chalk hills there, full of racehorses, filled my head with new things to write. It was at this cottage that John was formally asked to apply for the English professorship at Bristol University. He did so, and got the job. We moved here in 1976 and were involved in a nightmare car crash the following month. Despite this, I love Bristol. I love its hills, its gorge and harbors, its mad mixture of old and new, its friendly people, and even its constant rain. We have lived here ever since. All my other books have been written here; for although the car crash, followed by my astonishment at winning the 1978 *Guardian* Children's Fiction Prize, almost stopped me dead between them, I get unhappy if I don't write. Each book is an experiment, an attempt to write the ideal book, the book my children would like, the book I *didn't* have as a child myself.

I have still not, after twenty-odd books, written that book. But I keep trying. Nor do I manage to live a quiet life. I keep undertaking things, like visiting schools and teaching courses as a writer, or learning the cello, or doing amateur theatricals, or rashly agreeing to do all the cooking for Richard's wedding in 1984. Every one of those things has led to comic disasters— except the wedding: that was perfect. My aunt Muriel came to it just before she died, wearing a mink headdress like a cardinal's hat, and gave the couple her blessing. My mother also came. She was widowed again in 1975 and keeps on cordial terms with the rest of her family. She thinks John is marvelous.

Another thing that stops me living a quiet life is my travel jinx. This is hereditary: my mother has it and so does my son Colin. Mine works mostly on trains. Usually the engine breaks, but once an old man jumped off a moving train I was on and sent every train schedule in the country haywire for that day. And my books have developed an uncanny way of coming true. The most startling example of this was last year, when I was writing the end of *A Tale of Time City*. At the very moment when I was writing about all the buildings in Time City falling down, the roof of my study fell in, leaving most of it open to the sky.

Perhaps I don't need a quiet life as much as I think I do.

Diana with her faithful dog Caspian, who inspired *Dogsbody*, 1984

The Girl Jones

A humorous autobiographical anecdote, this story was previously published in Sisters, *edited by Miriam Hodgson (Mammoth, 1998) and in Diana's collection* Unexpected Magic *(Greenwillow, 2004).*

It was 1944. I was nine years old and fairly new to the village. They called me "the girl Jones." They called anyone "the girl this" or "the boy that" if they wanted to talk about them a lot. Neither of my sisters was ever called "the girl Jones." They were never notorious.

On this particular Saturday morning I was waiting in our yard with my sister Ursula because a girl called Jean had promised to come and play. My sister Isobel was also hanging around. She was not exactly with us, but I was the one she came to if anything went wrong and she liked to keep in touch. I had only met Jean at school before. I was thinking that she was going to be pretty fed up to find we were lumbered with two little ones.

When Jean turned up, rather late, she was accompanied by two little sisters, a five-year-old very like herself and a tiny three-year-old called Ellen. Ellen had white hair and a little brown stormy face with an expression on it that said she was going to bite anyone who gave her any trouble. She was alarming. All three girls were dressed in impeccable starched cotton frocks that made me feel rather shabby. I had dressed for the weekend. But then so had they, in a different way.

"Mum says I got to look after them," Jean told me dismally. "Can you have them for me for a bit while I do her shopping? Then we can play."

I looked at stormy Ellen with apprehension. "I'm not very good at looking after little ones," I said.

"Oh, go on!" Jean begged me. "I'll be much quicker without them. I'll be your friend if you do."

So far, Jean had shown a desire to play, but had never offered friendship. I gave in. Jean departed, merrily swinging her shopping bag.

Almost at once a girl called Eva turned up. She was an official friend. She wore special boots and one of her feet was just a sort of blob. Eva fascinated me, not because of the foot but because she was so proud of it. She used to recite the list of all her other relatives who had queer feet, ending with, "And my uncle has only one toe." She too carried a shopping bag and had a small one in tow, a brother in her case, a wicked five-year-old called Terry. "Let me dump him on you while I do the shopping," Eva bargained, "and then we can play. I won't be long."

"I don't know about looking after boys," I protested. But Eva was a friend and I agreed. Terry was left standing beside stormy Ellen, and Eva went away.

A girl I did not know so well, called Sybil, arrived next. She wore a fine blue cotton dress with a white pattern and was hauling along two small sisters, equally finely dressed. "Have these for me while I do the shopping and I'll be your friend."

She was followed by a rather older girl called Cathy, with a sister, and then a number of girls I only knew by sight. Each of them led a small sister or brother into our yard. News gets round in no time in a village. "What have you done with your sisters, Jean?" "Dumped them on the girl Jones." Some of these later arrivals were quite frank about it.

"I heard you're having children. Have these for me while I go down the rec."

"I'm not good at looking after children," I claimed each time before I gave in. I remember thinking this was rather odd of me. I had been in sole charge of Isobel for years. As soon as Ursula was four, she was in my charge too. I suppose I had by then realized I was being had for a sucker, and this was my way of warning all these older sisters. But I believed what I said. I was not good at looking after little ones.

In less than twenty minutes I was standing in the yard surrounded by small children. I never counted, but there were certainly more than ten of them. None of them came above my waist. They were all beautifully dressed because they all came from what were called the "clean families." The "dirty families" were the ones where the boys wore big black boots with metal in the soles and the girls had grubby frocks that were too long for them. These kids had starched creases in their clothes and clean socks and shiny shoes. But they were, all the same, skinny, knowing, village children. They knew their sisters had shamelessly dumped them and they were disposed to riot.

"Stop all that damned *noise*!" bellowed my father. "Get these children out of here!"

He was always angry. This sounded near to an explosion.

"We're going for a walk," I told the milling children. "Come along." And I said to Isobel, "Coming?"

She hovered away backward. "No." Isobel had a perfect instinct for this kind of thing. Some of my earliest memories are of Isobel's sturdy brown legs flashing round and round as she rode her bicycle for dear life away from a situation I had got her into. These days, she usually arranged things so that she had no need to run for her life. I was annoyed. I could have done with her help with all these kids. But not that annoyed. Her reaction told me that something interesting was going to happen.

"We're going to have an adventure," I told the children.

"There's no adventures nowadays," they told me. They were, as I said, knowing children, and no one, not even me, regarded the war that was at that time going on around us as any kind of adventure. This was a problem to me. I craved adventures of the sort people had in books, but nothing that had ever happened to me seemed to qualify. No spies made themselves available to be unmasked by me, no gangsters ever had nefarious dealings where I could catch them for the police.

But one did what one could. I led the crowd of them out into the street, feeling a little like the Pied Piper—or no: they were so little and I was so big that I felt really old, twenty at least, and rather like a nursery school teacher. And it seemed to me that since I was landed in this position I might as well do something I wanted to do.

"Where are we going?" they clamored at me.

"Down Water Lane," I said. Water Lane, being almost the only unpaved road in the area, fascinated me. It was like lanes in books. If anywhere led to adventure, it would be Water Lane.

It was a moist, mild, gray day, not adventurous weather, but I knew from books that the most unlikely conditions sometimes led to great things.

But my charges were not happy about this. "It's wet there. We'll get all muddy. My mum told me to keep my clothes clean," they said from all around me.

"You won't get muddy with me," I told them firmly. "We're only going as far as the elephants." There was a man who built life-sized mechanical elephants in a shed in Water Lane. These fascinated everyone. The children gave up objecting at once. Ellen actually put her hand trustingly in mine, and we crossed the main road like a great liner escorted by coracles.

Water Lane was indeed muddy. Wetness oozed up from its sandy surface and ran in dozens of streams across it. Mr. Hinkston's herd of cows had added their contributions. The children minced and yelled. "Walk along the very edge," I commanded them. "Be adventurous. If we're lucky, we'll get inside the yard and look at the elephants in the sheds."

Most of them obeyed me except Ursula. But she was my sister and I had charge of her shoes along with the rest of her. Although I was determined from the outset to treat her exactly like the other children, as if this was truly a class from a nursery school, or the Pied Piper leading the children of Hamelin Town, I decided to let her be. Ursula had times when she bit you if you crossed her. Besides, what were shoes? So, to cries of, "Ooh! Your sister's getting in all the pancakes!" we arrived outside the big black fence where the elephants were, to find it all locked and bolted. As this was a Saturday, the man who made the elephants had gone to make money with them at a fête or a fair somewhere.

There were loud cries of disappointment and derision at this, particularly from Terry, who was a very outspoken child. I looked up at the tall fence—it had barbed wire along the top—and contemplated boosting them all over it for an adventure inside. But there were their clothes to consider, it would be hard work, and it was not really what I had come down Water Lane to do.

"This means we have to go on," I told them, "to the really adventurous thing. We are going to the very end of Water Lane to see what's at the end of it."

"That's ever so far!" one of them whined.

"No, it's not," I said, not having the least idea. I had never had time to go much beyond the river. "Or we'll get to the river and then walk along it to see where it goes to."

"Rivers don't go anywhere," someone pronounced.

"Yes, they do," I asserted. "There's a bubbling fountain somewhere where it runs out of the ground. We're going to find it." I had been reading books about the source of the Nile, I think.

They liked the idea of the fountain. We went on. The cows had not been on this farther part, but it was still wet. I encouraged them to step from sandy strip to sandy island, and they liked that. They were all beginning to think of themselves as true adventurers. But Ursula, no doubt wanting to preserve her special status, walked straight through everything and got her shoes all wet and crusty. A number of the children drew my attention to this.

"She's not good like you are," I said.

We went on in fine style for a good quarter of a mile until we came to the place where the river broke out of the hedge and swilled across the lane in a ford. Here the expedition broke down utterly.

"It's water! I'll get wet! It's all muddy!"

"I'm *tired*!" said someone. Ellen stood by the river and grizzled, reflecting the general mood.

"This is where we can leave the lane and go up along the river," I said. But this found no favor. The banks would be muddy. We would have to get through the hedge. They would tear their clothes.

I was shocked and disgusted at their lack of spirit. The ford across the road had always struck me as the nearest and most romantic thing to a proper adventure. I loved the way the bright brown water ran so continuously there—in the mysterious way of rivers—in the shallow sandy dip.

"We're going on," I announced. "Take your shoes off and walk through in your bare feet."

This, for some reason, struck them all as highly adventurous. Shoes and socks were carefully removed. The quickest splashed into the water. "Ooh! Innit *cold*!"

"I'm paddling!" shouted Terry. "I'm going for a paddle." His feet, I was interested to see, were perfect. He must have felt rather left out in Eva's family.

I lost control of the expedition in this moment of inattention. Suddenly everyone was going in for a paddle. "All right," I said hastily. "We'll stay here and paddle."

Ursula, always fiercely loyal in her own way, walked out of the river and sat down to take her shoes off too. The rest splashed and screamed. Terry began throwing water about. Quite a number of them squatted down at the edge of the water and scooped up muddy sand. Brown stains began climbing up crisp cotton frocks; the seats of beautifully ironed shorts quickly acquired a black splotch. Even before this was pointed out to me, I saw this would not do. These were the "clean children." I made all the little girls come out of the water and spent some time trying to get the edges of their frocks tucked upward into their knickers. "The boys can take their trousers off," I announced.

But this did no good. The frocks just came tumbling down again and the boys' little white pants were no longer really white. No one paid any attention to my suggestion that it was time to go home now. The urge to paddle was upon them all.

"All right," I said, yielding to the inevitable. "Then you all have to take all your clothes off."

This caused the startled pause. "That ain't right," someone said uncertainly.

"Yes it is," I told them, somewhat pompously. "There is nothing whatsoever wrong with the sight of the naked human body." I had read that somewhere and found it quite convincing. "Besides," I added, more pragmatically, "you'll all get into trouble if you come home with dirty clothes."

That all but convinced them. The thought of what their mums would say was a powerful aid to nudity. "But won't we catch cold?" someone asked.

"Cavemen never wore clothes and they never caught cold," I informed them. "Besides, it's quite warm now." A mild and misty sunlight suddenly arrived and helped my cause. The brown river was flecked with sun and looked truly inviting. Without a word, everybody began undressing, even Ellen, who was quite good at it, considering how young she was. Back to nursery teacher mode again, I made folded piles of every

person's clothing, shoes underneath, and put them in a large
row along the bank under the hedge. True to my earlier resolve,
I made no exception for Ursula's clothes, although her dress
was an awful one my mother had made out of old curtains, and
thoroughly wet anyway.

There was a happy scramble into the water, mostly to the
slightly deeper end by the hedge. Terry was throwing water
instantly. But then there was another pause.

"*You* undress too." They were all saying it.

"I'm too big," I said.

"You *said* that didn't matter," Ursula pointed out. "You
undress too, or it isn't *fair*."

"Yeah," the rest chorused. "It ain't *fair*!"

I prided myself on my fairness, and on my rational, intellectual
approach to life, but . . .

"Or we'll all get dressed again," added Ursula.

The thought of all that trouble wasted was too much. "All
right," I said. I went over to the hedge and took off my battered
gray shorts and my old, pulled jersey and put them in a heap
at the end of the row. I knew as I did so why the rest had been
so doubtful. I had never been naked out of doors before. In
those days, nobody ever was. I felt shamed and rather wicked.
And I was so big, compared with the others. The fact that we
all now had no clothes on seemed to make my size much more
obvious. I felt like one of the man's mechanical elephants, and
sinful with it. But I told myself sternly that we were having
a rational adventurous experience, and joined the rest in the
river.

The water was cold, but not too cold, and the sun was just
strong enough. Just.

Ellen, for some reason, would not join the others over by the hedge. She sat on the other side of the road, on the opposite bank of the river where it sloped up to the road again, and diligently scraped river mud up into a long mountain between her legs. When the mountain was made, she smacked it heavily. It sounded like a wet child being hit.

She made me nervous. I decided to keep an eye on her and sat facing her, squatting in the water, scooping up piles of mud to form islands. From there, I could look across the road and make sure Terry did not get too wild. They were, I thought, somewhat artificially, a most romantic and angelic sight, a picture an artist might paint if he wanted to depict young angels (except Terry was not being angelic and I told him to *stop throwing mud*). They were all tubular and white and in energetic attitudes, and the only one not quite right for the picture was Ursula, with her chalk-white skin and wild black hair. The others all had smooth fair heads, ranging from near white in the young ones, through straw yellow, to honey in the older ones. My own hair had gone beyond the honey, since I was so much older, into dull brown.

Here I noticed how *big* I was again. My torso was thick, more like an oil drum than a tube, and my legs looked *fat* beside their skinny little limbs. I began to feel sinful again. I had to force myself to attend to the islands I was making. I gave them landscapes and invented people for them.

"What you doing?" asked Ellen.

"Making islands." I was feeling back-to-nature and at ease again.

"Stupid," she said.

More or less as she spoke, a tractor came up the lane behind her, going toward the village. The man driving it stopped it just in front of the water and stared. He had one of those oval narrow faces that always went with people who went to chapel in the village. I know I thought he was chapel. He was the sort of age you might expect someone to be who was a father of small children. He looked as if he had children. And he was deeply and utterly shocked. He looked at the brawling, naked little ones, he looked at Ellen, and he looked at me. Then he leaned down and said, quite mildly, "You didn't ought to do that."

"Their clothes were getting wet, you see," I said.

He just gave me another mild, shocked look and started the tractor and went through the river, making it all muddy. I never, ever saw him again.

"Told you so," said Ellen.

That was the end of the adventure. I felt deeply sinful. The little ones were suddenly not having fun anymore. Without making much fuss about it, we all quietly got our clothes and got dressed again. We retraced our steps to the village. It was just about lunchtime anyway.

As I said, word gets round in a village with amazing speed. "You know the girl Jones? She took thirty kids down Water Lane and encouraged them to do wrong there. They were all there, naked as the day they were born, sitting in the river there, and her along with them, as bold as brass. A big girl like the girl Jones did ought to know better! Whatever next!"

My parents interrogated me about it the next day. Isobel was there, backward hovering, wanting to check that her instinct had been right, I think, and fearful of the outcome. She looked relieved when the questions were mild and puzzled. I think my mother did not believe I had done anything so bizarre.

"There is nothing shameful about the naked human body," I reiterated.

Since my mother had given me the book that said so, there was very little she could reply. She turned to Ursula. But Ursula was stoically and fiercely loyal. She said nothing at all.

The only result of this adventure was that nobody ever suggested I should look after any children except my own sisters (who were strange anyway). Jean kept her promise to be my friend. The next year, when the Americans came to England, Jean and I spent many happy hours sitting on the church wall watching young GIs stagger out of the pub to be sick. But Jean never brought her sisters with her. I think her mother had forbidden it.

When I look back, I rather admire my nine-year-old self. I had been handed the baby several times over that morning. I took the most harmless possible way to disqualify myself as a child minder. Nobody got hurt. Everyone had fun. And I never had to do it again.

The Origins of *Changeover*

This introduction was specially written for the 2004 reprint by Moondust Books of Diana's first published novel. An oddity in Diana's body of work, Changeover *is neither fantasy nor written for children. Instead, it is a satire set in a small African nation that is about to achieve independence from Britain.* Changeover *displays all Diana's trademark quirky humor and intelligence.*

I wrote *Changeover* in the mid-1960s, mostly to keep my sanity. In—I think—1965,[1] we moved into the coldest house in Oxfordshire. It was four hundred years old, it was large, and it had stone floors and three-foot-thick stone walls; and, after my help's fiendish small daughter had carefully strung a metal chain between the terminals of our only heater and blown it up, the only way to get warm was to light a fire in one of the two grates in the house. In one grate, a fire simply would not burn. The other involved my squatting—in three sweaters and a dressing gown—doing careful Boy Scout work for an hour every morning. *Changeover* was set in Africa because Africa is *warm.* The name of the country, Nmkwami, derives from the Latin word "numquam," meaning "never." That is, Neverland.

We were only supposed to be in this house for a few months, until the new one being built for us was ready, but this extended itself to a year, and during this time, misfortunes multiplied. My husband caught jaundice and, besides being ill for a long time, required a special fat-free diet. My two-year-old started having febrile convulsions. My five-year-old so hated school that he regressed to wetting himself. My eldest became madly accident-prone and was liable to be found—after long, vain search—hanging in a tree by the seat of his trousers. My father-in-law died and my mother-in-law came to stay, hating everything in her grief. My sister turned up, so ill with the aftermath of flu that she couldn't be left alone. A friend also arrived to stay with her baby daughter, fleeing the husband she was divorcing and hysterical with fear that he would find her living with us. In addition, we acquired a singularly bloodthirsty cat whose sole aim in life was to kill things. Finding half a baby rabbit underfoot became commonplace (although it was worse if the rabbit was alive). Fag ends of mice we took in our stride, but I never became acclimatized to having birds slain under our bed. Said cat crowned his achievements by falling into a pigsty one morning and turning up during (fat-free) lunch, dripping and reeking. In addition to all this, the Oxford college to which the house belonged kept trying to let the place over our heads, and would-be tenants kept turning up without notice and stumbling through the icy rooms among the half rabbits and bits of mice, crying out that the place was uninhabitable. My health began to deteriorate. My husband fell downstairs. . . .

This was the time when Britain was divesting itself of the last of its colonies. On the news, it seemed like every month we would hear that yet another small island or tiny country had been granted independence. It was as regular as the dead rabbits. Soon almost the only one left was Rhodesia (now Zimbabwe), and Britain, it seemed, wanted to hang on to that one. And did so, until Ian Smith, premier of Rhodesia, declared independence unilaterally. UDI,[2] it was called, and it caused a great furore. Ministers were sent to plead and cajole, without success. Smith stuck to his purpose and staged his coup. By this time I was actually writing *Changeover*. I felt as if the book were coming true as I wrote it.

The book itself owes its origin to my thoughts on the independence of colonies. We were in bed, trying to get back to sleep after the cat had killed a starling under our bed, and I began thinking that I could envisage how colonies were before independence (British rule) and see how it would be after independence (the inhabitants ruling themselves), but that I couldn't for the life of me visualize the actual *process*. How did they train people to take over? Where did they find the new politicians or the new civil servants? How did they get people to be sternly self-reliant? And so on. Out of these musings, I said to my husband, "How do they manage the change over?"

And he, already mostly asleep, said, "Who is Changeover?"

That did it, of course. I started writing the book the next morning. It was marvelous. I found I was oblivious to the half rabbits or the clouds of smoke from our one source of heat. I had something else to think of besides the next crisis. Thereafter, whenever a fresh crisis arose, *Changeover* was liable to acquire at least one more chapter. When we moved to the new house at last, the book was ready for typing.

A Conversation with Diana Wynne Jones

Diana Wynne Jones's home is set in the middle of a terrace of Regency houses between the Clifton and Hotwells areas of Bristol, on a steep and inaccessible hill that leaves taxi drivers scratching their heads and two-dimensional maps badly creased. It is not a particularly large building but is tall and thin, the gradient enabling its modest frontage to hide an implausible number of stories. On a first visit one approaches with some apprehension: thick wooden wind chimes bong apotropaically at the front door and a white-eyed Moorish face stares in grim challenge from the knocker. This slightly forbidding aspect is contradicted by a handwritten invitation to KNOCK FIRMLY, *however, and once inside one finds oneself in a welcoming and friendly home. Diana and her husband, the medievalist John Burrow, are ready with biscuits and excellent conversation, either in the kitchen-dining room or else on the floor above, where Diana's "writing" armchair sits near a large plush Calcifer—one of many mementoes from the film of* Howl's Moving Castle.

This conversation takes place in the kitchen, on a quiet day in February (February 15, 2011). Through the front window I can see that the terrace's communal lawn is deserted, but for a rabbit hutch belonging to one of the neighbors: at the back the view falls away toward Bristol's harborside, and the hills of Somerset recumbent against the horizon. An antique grandfather clock keeps time in a corner of the room, occasionally startling us to silence with its chimes. Though very ill, Diana speaks easily and with her usual sharpness of mind. Her appetite for the wonderful, the mysterious, and the absurd is undiminished, as is the laughter with which she celebrates their curious pas de trois. *Her eyes still gleam with their distinctive moon-silver. The coffee is very good.*

Charlie Butler (CB): *It's clear from* Reflections *that your childhood has had an important role not only in your life but in your writing. I wonder how you would summarize the relationship of your childhood experience to your work. Clearly it's given you a lot of material.*

DWJ: It's given me a lot of material, but I've never been able to use it directly. I don't know why, except that most of it was so extreme that most people wouldn't believe it. My problem was with realizing later that this was not normal. At the time it was going on, I thought it was entirely what ordinary life was like.

CB: *You had nothing to compare it with.*

DWJ: Well, I had loads of friends and people in the village. I did, actually, have quite a bit to compare it with, but it always struck me that they were strange and we weren't. That's how it struck me when I saw the dead man. Have I told you about the dead man?

CB: *Please do so.*

DWJ: I was cycling to see a friend, who lived in Wimbish, which was all of four and a half miles away, I think.

CB: *How old would you have been at this time?*

DWJ: I think I was thirteen. Nobody bothered about what I did—it was the holidays—so I cycled off. I was on the main road, but it was really very ill traveled in those days, and there was a bend and I came round the bend, and there was this fellow, lying on his side on his bicycle, with brown, trickly blood having come out of his head, but that had stopped quite a while ago. And it seemed to me fairly evident that he was dead. What do you do when you're thirteen, and on a bicycle and all alone? I had no idea. The only thing I could think of was to cycle madly to my friend's house. Her parents were very nice, very ordinary people—theirs was an ordinary life in a way, if you like, except that they were market gardeners and had greenhouses, which made them unordinary. And I arrived there, and immediately the father phoned friends, leaped in his van, roared off, and I thought, "Oh good, somebody's taking care of it." But what I really couldn't handle was my friend's mother, who sat me down and gave me strong, sweet tea and generally fussed over me. I thought, "Nobody does this kind of thing!" And at home nobody would. I almost couldn't handle it really: I thought, "What's going on here?" Then the father came back alone, and was terribly reassuring. He said the man was all right, he'd had fainting fits, he was perfectly well, he was alive—and I knew he was lying for my benefit. It was absolutely obvious that he was dead when I saw him. I said I'd better be going—I was still incredibly shaken—and I went cycling off, and inevitably passed this brown trickle on the road where the man no longer was, and wondered what they'd done with him, and got home. And I thought, well, this was a rather extraordinary thing to happen, I might tell my mother. So I went to tell my mother.

It seems to me nowadays that if one of my children came to me the color of cheese and shaking all over, saying, "Do you know what's happened?" you would tend to want to listen. She said, "No, not got any time for this," and walked away.

And that was really how our life was.

CB: *And that was normality? It seems pretty strange.*

DWJ: That was normality, yes.

CB: *That's an incident that I don't think has turned up in any of your books.*

DWJ: No, it hasn't. It was really blindingly startling, actually.

CB: *There was a huge cast of eccentrics in your village, as the pieces in this volume make clear. In a sense, when I said that your normality was strange, I was thinking not only of your family but of that wider community.*

DWJ: Yes, there were indeed. Almost everyone was a lunatic in some peculiar way. Mostly it was a tendency to sing madrigals in curious places, or to dance in the street—those were just the apparently normal people. Lots of Cecil Sharp folk dancing and that sort of thing. But the madder ones were the people who threw pots and the people who hand wove. And there was a woman who kept setting up cafés all over the place, potentially for the tourists, except that because it was a time of austerity there weren't any tourists, and besides they went away quite quickly when they realized there was no public lavatory in the place. She did all the cooking herself. We felt we ought to patronize this lady, because there she was with all these various handwoven cafés and nobody in them. So we went—and she served abominable coffee and rainbow cake, which was the same sort of consistency as ciabatta, which is not good for cake. It was dry and had a sort of tensile strength about it—very difficult to bite.

CB: *Something that was bad coffee by 1950s standards must have been pretty awful.*

DWJ: It was. I think she made it with real coffee, mind, because there were bits floating in it. And very weak, because of course she was hoping to make money.

CB: *So, thinking about this amazing cast of characters: in some respects you've drawn on it, perhaps toning things down a bit, but I was also wondering (without wanting to get too psychoanalytical about it) whether in a wider sense your childhood has provided, as well as material for mining, part of the impulse behind your writing.*

DWJ: Yes, I do agree, it has. It was quite clear that the world was mad, and that most adults were often entertainingly mad. You watched with wonder the man who thought he was a werewolf, the man who could polka sexily (I hadn't until I was fifteen realized that it was possible to polka sexily—he had a very big paunch, and he used to rub it against you as he gently polka'd about). And then there were the various people who said they were, and probably were, witches. Then there was the incredible amount of illegitimacy and incest that went on, and one just took it as a matter of course, really. But you realized that life was *not* like it was represented in the average children's book of the time. I rather yearned for the average children's book where life was straightforward, and Daddy sent telegrams saying "Don't be duffers" and things like that. My father would never have dreamed of sending telegrams saying "Don't be duffers." He would have rushed screaming at you and hit you, saying "You *are* a duffer!"

CB: *This despite his Ransome fixation?*

DWJ: Yes. Well, it wasn't a fixation actually. It was just that he was so mean, and he found this set of Ransome books going cheap in Cambridge. It was minus two volumes: that's why it was cut price. He knew we needed books, obviously—he'd been a schoolteacher—so he was going to give us books, one between the three of us every Christmas. And he did. Simple as that.

CB: *Do you think in any sense that writing was therapy for you, a way of working through or coming to terms with your experience?*

DWJ: I don't know. It probably was, actually, because I remember quite recently my doctor asked me, "What do you do when you're depressed?" and I said automatically, without thinking about it, "Write a book." So I suppose it was, yes. Because in a funny way it was very depressing, all this weird fandango of stuff. Oh and yes, there was the man who looked like Mr. Punch, who did photography—or at least he *didn't* do photography. He always hired a photographer, but he made very careful models to photograph, and these were sold as illustrations to books and for Christmas cards. He didn't make a living because he never paid any bills. At least, I think he didn't pay any bills because what living he did make he spent on drink. We knew his children very well, actually. They survived it, just as we were surviving our bit. But he once very much frightened my sister. She was in the Brownies, and he came in his van to collect the Brownies from some do, and he was terribly drunk, and he drove them into the middle of a cornfield and drove round and round in circles yelling and shouting and singing. And they were scared silly, actually. It wasn't very nice for them.

I suppose it was very lucky that there was more than one of us, because we could tell one another. I don't think I ever told my sisters about the dead man, oddly enough. That was too weird—my various reactions and people's reactions to me. I told you that because that's the sort of containing thing that seems to happen when I write, and why I don't actually directly use this autobiographical material—because it whams its way between two points, as it were, my reaction and other people's reactions to my reaction. And I don't find it very easy to break out of that.

CB: *You've got to refract it in some way?*

DWJ: Yes, that's right—or translate it, is what I think of it as, actually. I've got to take this particular incident or set of people or some kind of adventure, and say, "Yeah, but I can't do it like *that*, and besides no one would believe it anyway, so I will translate it into some other incident or set of people which are basically the same, but in some ways quite, quite different."

CB: *If we take the therapy idea a little further, do you find that performing that translation helps stop things whamming in your mind between your reaction and other people's reactions? Does it in any sense "lay" things that are otherwise troubling you?*

DWJ: I don't think it lays them; it makes me aware of them, which sometimes is good and sometimes bad. No, I think the therapeutic notion is a little easy: it doesn't lay them. It means that I probably have an overlay—the translation—above the constant video that I'm playing of these various peculiar incidents.

CB: *Given the fantastic (in one sense) nature of the environment you grew up in, it seems natural to turn to your choice of genre, or the genre that chose you. Actually, your very first book,* Changeover, *isn't a fantasy, although some pretty bizarre things happen in it. I wonder how you came to write that—and, given that you didn't go further down that road, how you came to move from writing that kind of comic novel for adults to writing fantasy for children.*

DWJ*:* It was like two different halves of the brain at work, actually. I wrote *Changeover*, to start with, because we were living in the coldest house in Oxfordshire. It really was absolutely appallingly cold: its walls were stone and they were three feet thick. In its original state it would have been a big, open hall, but somebody had constructed a nest of tiny, stone-walled rooms inside this. Each one seemed to be a freezing chamber. In order to get warm at all you had to light a fire, there was no other form of heating, and I got quite good at lighting fires and dealing with chimneys that wouldn't draw and so on, and also simply putting up with the cold. But when it got *really* cold I got fairly miserable. My kids were not at the time very happy, and the local school was not good. My youngest started having *petit mals*—like epilepsy except it isn't. It was quite alarming and the whole thing started getting me down. Curious things happened, like John ringing me up from Oxford (we were some way outside Oxford at this point) and saying it was the day of some big ceremony—St. Frideswide's[1] or something, and he had to go and parade there. And he rang up sounding a bit desperate and saying, "I fell downstairs and I broke my—" and stopped. And I went through every bone in his body, before he said, "glasses." Everything was a bit like that.

And I thought, well, let's do something different. Then it was the time when Ian Smith decided on UDI[2] for Rhodesia, which put Africa very much to the forefront of one's mind, and I just wrote and wrote and wrote—and laughed. And it was a sort of counterblast, rather than therapy, I think. It was something to be getting on with that didn't go wrong all the time and was in my control. Whereas with children's books, that seemed to be like a whole parallel chain of thinking. It was partly examining my own children's reactions to books, and finding that they obviously much more enjoyed fantasy. All the time, every book that they really, really liked turned out to be a fantasy, and I wondered what it did for them, and began to work it out. And I looked at the other books that were out there—there were loads around that were absolutely appalling—and considered what they were doing wrong, that the kids didn't like them at all. And in the end I decided, "Yes, I shall write fantasy for children." And I suppose one of the things was from childhood again, because both my parents were extremely opposed to the idea of fantasy, as I think I've mentioned in this book.

CB: *Was there in fact something slightly rebellious about writing fantasy?*

DWJ: I *suppose* there was. It was rebellious mostly against the *mores* of the time more than leftover parental stuff. The books were all so very do-goodery in those days, and very uneventful, and full of political correctness of a certain rather dismal kind.

CB: *I can see why you'd say somebody ought to write good fantasy books, because that's what your children and probably other children liked and there weren't enough of them. But having started, you kept on doing it. It clearly suited you.*

DWJ: I think the final thing that twitched me on was my oldest son Richard saying, "There aren't enough *funny* books." And I thought, well, *that* can be settled. So I wrote *Wilkins' Tooth*, which made me laugh, and then *The Ogre Downstairs,* which made me laugh even more. In fact *The Ogre Downstairs* made me laugh so much that people kept putting their head round the door and saying "Are you all right?" I was just sitting on a sofa, yelling with laughter. I always tend to do that with the funny bits of books actually.

CB: *You get quite drawn into them.*

DWJ: Oh goodness, yes.

CB: *You've talked about absentmindedly putting people's shoes in the oven when writing, which suggests somebody who's very much bound up in the experience.*

DWJ: They are terribly real to me, and I find this of other people's books too, if they're good, almost to the point that you can't criticize them. I always find it quite hard to write reviews, if it's a good book. It's like criticizing a piece of real living—it just happens, like life, you know?

CB: *I wonder what you feel about the lot of the children's writer today, who seems to be expected to keep a blog and make YouTube trailers, and basically do a lot of marketing, as well as writing the books.*

DWJ: That's the thing I feel that publishers are supposed to be doing. I don't know why they don't.

CB: *Although you've done your fair share of school visits over the years—*

DWJ: Lots. At one point I used to go at least once a month. But I don't think, except for one shining occasion, visiting schools ever repaid me, though I do hope they did something for the unfortunate kids. The exception was a visit on which, because of my travel jinx, I arrived two hours late anyway. We were drawing out of Bristol Parkway and a man in his sixties who was seeing his wife off (she was going to visit her sister in York) realized he was still on the train as it left. Luckily they don't gather speed very much leaving Bristol Parkway because there's a big bend, if you remember, and they go pretty slowly round it, but as it was attaining its maximum speed for the bend he rushed to the door and tried to open it. I was absolutely riveted to the spot. I thought, "I do not believe what this idiot is doing." I should have done something, I suppose, because I was the person nearest the door, but I just didn't believe it. And he opened the door and jumped out.

Everyone got out of the train afterward, except his wife, who was afraid of being left outside and the train going without her. They were obviously very neurotic about the whole business. Anyway, what happened was that the draft round the train caught him, and first of all he soared in the air—really odd, it was—and then he was sucked in toward the wheels. Somebody pulled the emergency cord, and there was a horrible grinding and rumbling, and I thought, "My God, we're running over him. This is awful." But no. In fact he was lying on the pebbles at the side of the rails. He was streaming with blood, but not really hurt. And of course that meant that we had to stop and the ambulance had to be called and he refused to go in the ambulance, and lots of argy-bargy. And the guard and the driver got out and argued with him, and people came out from the station and argued with him.

CB: *He felt he hadn't caused enough trouble yet?*

DWJ: Quite! And everybody ran round outside for at least an hour, which meant we had missed the train slot. So we were forced to wait until the next slot. And that meant all the trains were late going up north, where I was heading—I was going to the Midlands somewhere—and they were even worse on the way home. Anyway, I arrived two hours late, and there were all the kids, fortunately, and it was in the town hall and they'd had other things to occupy them. And it was there that a boy gave me the idea for *Howl's Moving Castle*. So it did pay off.

CB: *That was a good school visit, then?*

DWJ: It did make up for the idiocy. And I'll tell you a further outcome of this ridiculous man and his exit, which was that about a fortnight later I went to a school in quite the opposite direction, to Chippenham. Where I got lost, naturally, but I did eventually find the school and get talking, and I started talking about my travel jinx, which by then was really quite evident. And after a bit, people put their hands up and asked things, and a boy at the back put his hand up and said, "That person you were calling an idiot is my grandfather!"

CB: *That does seem most unfortunate! Was the boy upset?*

DWJ: Not really. He was slightly annoyed that I was calling his grandfather an idiot, but I suppose he had to admit that it was an idiotic thing to do.

CB: *Over the last fifteen years or so there's been a well-documented revival of fantasy. Before that you were writing fantasy, not quite as a voice in the wilderness but at a time when fantasy was not seen as particularly fashionable by publishers. Now, over the last few years, you've been writing in a world where suddenly publishers' lists are awash with fantasy.*

DWJ: Yes, isn't that nice?

CB: *Is it purely nice? Or do you find some negative aspects to it? Also, do you write differently because you have a different sense of what people will have in their heads before they pick up your book?*

DWJ: I don't think that's an issue, except that I do try to write differently with every book, but I do find that there are drawbacks, in that fantasy becomes almost a fetish, and you've got these fluffy werewolves—no, I don't mean werewolves . . .

CB: *Sparkly vampires? I'm sure there are fluffy werewolves too.*

DWJ: Yes, I'm sure there are. Pink ones. You know, it can get very, very silly. And then there was the thing I was complaining about in *The Tough Guide*, the Tolkien imitations, which were extant before the fifteen years actually, in huge numbers, though probably not accounted valid in the way they would be now. And they were all so similar! Most people felt that they had to do the same as the other person. I've never known why. This mass imitation and proliferation does upset me a bit. I don't read them, but I know about them, and I find it all a bit unnecessary and kitsch.

CB: *Is fantasy more like poetry than other narrative fiction? Is it more like play?*

DWJ: Yes to both, actually. Poetry tends to work with metaphors and ellipses and things, and so does fantasy. The beauty of fantasy is that it doesn't have to rhyme, it just has to have the right kind of plot, which you can actually draw a diagram of if you attend closely. What was the other thing?

CB: *Is it more like play? Is there some kind of freedom in fantasy which isn't available with other genres?*

DWJ: There is. Yes. You have a license to enjoy yourself thoroughly—if you want to get yourself thoroughly scared, get yourself thoroughly elated, get yourself thoroughly mystified, thoroughly awed, and all those other things that are rather splendid that you get from play.

CB: *To what extent does fantasy offer those kinds of freedoms in a way that other fiction doesn't? After all, it's not as if fantasy is without rules, and it's not as if other kinds of fiction don't allow you to make things up, by definition. So is there something about fantasy that offers peculiar freedoms, beyond those available to other fiction writers?*

DWJ: It's because it's not got to stick to the rather dreary tenor of ordinary life, which people are a bit serious about, aren't they? If you were to draw a graph of a mainline book you'd find it would just be smoothly wobbling up and down like ripples on a lake, whereas fantasy would have peaks and troughs and be generally bouncing about—sometimes a whole set of peaks and troughs, like on a seismograph.

CB: *Something you've drawn on quite a lot in writing fantasy, and very notably in your fairly recent book* The Game, *are different kinds of existing folktales and mythologies. You've made use of a wide range of them, in fact, from Norse mythology in* Eight Days of Luke, *to Greek mythology there in* The Game, *Celtic mythology in several places—*

DWJ: And Grimm's fairy tales, and various other things. All the European things, basically.

CB: *Yes. Of course, there's no reason one can't use mythology in non-fantasy fiction—there's* Ulysses, *for example—but it does seem to have a particular affinity with fantasy, doesn't it? Is that another attraction for you?*

DWJ: I don't know. Myth is, in its way, fantasy fiction itself, isn't it? It's just that myths were done so long ago that they've been honed down into a shape that makes a basic appeal to everybody, and you know that they're going to get there and resonate, you know? I don't think I've ever based a whole book on a particular myth, though you can correct me on that.

CB: *Well, not on one. You could say in a sense that* Fire and Hemlock *is based on* the *ballad of* "Tam Lin"—

DWJ: Yes, that's true. . . .

CB: *But even there it's only one of many myths that are in the mix. None of your books are retellings, or anything like that.*

DWJ: No, I wouldn't want to do a retelling. I think that would be very boring. You take it and run with it, basically, whatever it is.

CB: *If you know in advance exactly how it's going to turn out, then that is going to detract from the interest?*

DWJ: It is in a way, although it can sometimes work out very well. There are people who can tell a thing in such a way that it works even though you know what's going to happen. In Tolkien's case he tells you what's going to happen and it does, but it's still breathtaking. You're not sure it's going to come off, and you worry and wonder, and read on avidly.

CB: *You've long been big in Japan. There's Miyazaki's* Howl's Moving Castle *film,[3] of course, and many translations, but presumably they aren't able to draw on the same stockpot of myth that you use, or at least not with such ease.*

DWJ: No.

CB: *I wonder how they read you, given that?*

DWJ: I really don't know, but they seem to enjoy it. I think it is because, as I said, all these myths and legends and fairy stories and so forth, even though they're from a foreign source, have been honed into the right kind of shape anyway so that people pick up on them. I can only think that it's that. But I've been very lucky in Japan: the publishers that I have seem to be prepared to publish anything that I write, which is awfully good of them. They had tremendous trouble with *The Game* because their whole galaxy and mythology is quite, quite different, and I hadn't realized how different until they started sending me emails saying, "Jupiter doesn't mean this to us, it means something quite other. How are we going to handle that? And what about the two young men, one in the sun and one in the shade—are they supposed to be ruffians or high-born?" High-born? That's a Japanese concept. And I had to say, "You'll have to do them high-born, I think, if it's important." Oh, and all sorts of things. The Pleiades are different to the Japanese as well, of course.

CB: *Do they have their own astrology?*

DWJ: Oh, they do! Yes. But I only got glimpses of it. I got sent a summary of it by the main publishing lady, but it was so different from anything we have here that I almost couldn't take it in. So I really don't understand the popularity of things in Japan—but it does seem to work!

CB: *Are there any mythological figures or stories that you would steer clear of? I'm thinking of a preface that Garth Nix wrote to one of his stories, where in the first draft he'd used some kind of Aboriginal material and he'd been warned off because this was seen as trespassing on the cultural property, if not identity, of—[4]*

DWJ: The Aborigines warned him off?

CB: *His publisher did.*

DWJ: Yes, the Australians are very sensitive about that, I know. I would avoid Aboriginal myths because I don't really know them. Though you can see that the land is actually engorged with them, really. When I was in Perth, a whole road was closed and we had to take an enormous detour avoiding the river because apparently there was a river spirit in there, a very large one, and the Aborigines said it would be disturbed by cars thundering along the bank of the river. So every day there were huge traffic jams trying to get round the secondary roads.

CB: *The river spirit wasn't there all the time, then?*

DWJ: It had suddenly appeared and taken up its station. It seemed to occupy about an acre of river—quite a lot, anyway, and it may have had strands running off it, I don't know. Anyway, the Aborigines had brought caravans and camped by the place to warn people off. And the town council had said, "Yes, of course we will do what you want," because there was an awful lot of guilt, understandably, about the treatment of the Aborigines.

CB: *Perhaps we could talk a little about influence? You've mentioned in the book the impact Tolkien had on you, for example, but what does influence actually mean, for you? It's not the same as "taking ideas from," is it?*

DWJ: No, I think it's more about the way to do it. With Tolkien, as I say in this book, it was "Gosh, you can write a whole three-volume fantasy—this is marvelous, let's do this thing." With other influences like C. S. Lewis, the "how to do it" thing that grabbed me was that he was always so completely clear about what was happening. You are never in any doubt who is where, and doing what—and much more complicated things than that.

CB: *He had a very well-organized mind, I think.*

DWJ: Yes, though you wouldn't know it to look at him. And—let's see about other influences. . . .

CB: *When I interviewed you on a previous occasion, you mentioned*

George Meredith as an influence. Can you expand on that?

DWJ: Well, Meredith has this perfectly serious, and even overly serious emotional account of things in his books, but every so often they burst into—well, not exactly fantasy, but things that are so fantastic that you might think of them as fantasy. Also, they're very funny. It's the mingle, the seamless mingle that he does between things that are funny and things that are extremely serious. *The Egoist* is a very good example, but there are others. *Evan Harrington* is one. I shouldn't suppose anyone has read it. In that book, somebody is masquerading quite unintentionally as an aristocrat at a weekend country house party. It isn't sidesplittingly hilarious, it's just continuous-chuckle hilarious. It's also really very sensitive about this bloke's feelings. And then there's *Diana of the Crossways*, which again in its central parts is extremely serious, and it gives *me* a start of guilt when I think of what that woman did, but it still has these extraordinary comic bits, which are seamlessly plaited in. And that really is something I do find I like to do, and how I would want to do things. I wouldn't want to just tell a serious narrative, or just a hilariously silly one.

CB: *So it's not just "Here's a serious scene, and now it's time for a bit of light relief so let's have a comic scene," but somehow plaiting them more closely than that?*

DWJ: Much more closely, yes. And one's arriving out of the other.

CB: *I also remember your image of Langland's way of writing* Piers

Plowman *being like the tide creeping up the shore, one wave after another and a little higher each time, and that this lies behind the structure of* Fire and Hemlock *in some way.*

DWJ: Yes, it did. But it's very difficult to describe how.

CB: *What I've just described is fairly amorphous. You couldn't pin down a passage and say, "Yes, here's the page where she does that!"*

DWJ: I suppose it's the threat turning into more-than-threat that's gradually creeping in *Fire and Hemlock*.

CB: *Things that were merely translucent becoming opaque.*

DWJ: That's right. Which is one of the awful things that tends to happen to you in puberty, actually. Everything suddenly becomes opaque and confusing and too complicated to cope with. And you have to fight your way out of that. But never say that any of my books are about growing up!

CB: *No!*

DWJ: Or I shall reach for my gun!

CB: *Or about the necessity of coming to terms with it!*

DWJ: Quite, yes! As if anyone ever really does.

CB: *I know you're dyslexic and left-handed, and in both those ways you're coming at things from a slightly unusual angle, and I wonder if* *you feel that has had any relevance to the way you see and therefore write about the world?*

DWJ: It probably has, but the trouble is, you see, that it's normal for me. All it is is a struggle to try and keep level with right-handed ways of going on. I wouldn't know about that, because the way I see things is, to me, normal. But I think you're probably right and I think it probably does.

CB: *I was thinking of that part in* The Merlin Conspiracy *where it turns out that Grundo's magic is at ninety degrees to the magic of the universe he lives in.*

DWJ: Yes, he does everything back to front. Yes, that was the bit where I thought, "Well, there are quite a lot of people who are dyslexic; let's give them a champion, as it were."

One thing it's very good for, actually, being dyslexic, is solving anagrams. It ought to make me a past master at Scrabble, but it doesn't—but I'm very good at anagrams in crosswords, because I think my brain stores things scrambled as opposed to ordinary brains.

CB: *The unscrambling muscles must be quite well developed.*

DWJ: I think they are, yes. Though I did fail a driving test purely through dyslexia, because every time he told me to turn right I turned left. And we got lost. The examiner was furious, seething, and he failed me on the spot. Which was reasonable, of course. Goodness knows where we ended up. It was a completely strange part of Oxford to me, and obviously to the examiner as well. He couldn't wait to get out of the car when we finally worked our way back to civilization.

CB: *It's probably too big a question to take in one go, but it would be fascinating if you could talk through your writing process, from beginning to end. Is there a pattern which tends to repeat, or is the process with every book unique?*

DWJ: If it did repeat I'd get very bored. The only pattern that does repeat is that I write it out in longhand first and concentrate on getting the story down, and then do a very careful second draft, which is for publication, in which I've got all the wrong bits right and so forth.

CB: *And at that point has anyone else seen it? Editors? Members of your family?*

DWJ: No, I wait until there's a second draft available, because it's in longhand and nobody can really read my writing.

CB: *And do you talk about how it's going as you write? Do you discuss the plot, and so on?*

DWJ: Very rarely. I find that it kills it dead if I talk about it. I tried talking to my agent about plots early on, and I found that these were the things that just went "No, no, no," like that, and petered out. So I found that the best thing was to keep absolutely mum and let the book do its thing. It does in many ways feel like automatic writing. And *then* you can talk about it, afterward. But I know what I'm doing.

They start in all sorts of different ways, books. Two have been started by pictures. One is a photograph called "Intimate Landscapes," with a Judas tree in the foreground, and an inspissate woodland otherwise. That gave rise to *Hexwood*.

CB: *Really?*

DWJ: If you look at it there is no boundary to that wood. It just goes on. And I stared at it and stared at it and I knew that was going to produce something. *Fire and Hemlock* came from another photograph, which is *called* "Fire and Hemlock," a nighttime picture of some straw bales burning behind a whole row of hemlock heads, which is a gorgeous photograph, though it's faded a bit over the years. And the weird thing about that is that sometimes you look at it and you think there are people in there, and sometimes you look at it and you know there aren't, and it really does seem to change all the time. I thought when I'd written the book that maybe the people would vanish for good, but they haven't.

CB: *Are they in the flames, or in the—*

DWJ: No, in the shadowy bits around. Sometimes there are four or five of them. The *Hexwood* one has no people in at all.

I don't know what caused *Hexwood* to need to be written back-to-front and sideways, though I always knew it was going to be. It's just that they drop into your head in a certain shape and say, "This is how I'm going to be," and very often you get disappointed because they never are quite what they said they would be. I've got used to that now, but I try to get them as close as possible.

Various books were inspired by music. *The Magicians of Caprona* was one.

CB: *Which music was that?*

DWJ: "Vltava" by Smetana. That lovely river bit; there's a tune in there that absolutely cries out for words, and yet there are no words. And then *The Homeward Bounders* was inspired by train journeys at night, coming home from dreadful school visits. I would look out, and there would be several layers of reflections from the various windows, and you would get lights weaving about, and lights beyond that and reflections beyond that, and you would think this could be a transparent box of worlds, and so in the book they turned out to be.

CB: *I didn't know that.*

DWJ: None of these things are making the story—they're making the basic concept. The story is another matter, and that really wrestles itself.

CB: *And do you find when you send it finally to publishers and editors that you have a good experience? Do you enjoy being edited?*

DWJ: I *hate* being edited, because my second draft is as careful as I can get it. I try to get it absolutely mistake free, and absolutely as I feel the book needs to be. Then some editor comes along and says, "Change Chapter Eight to Chapter

Five, take a huge lump out of Chapter Nine, and let's cut Chapter One altogether." And you think, No, I'm going to hit the ceiling any moment. Then I call for my agent before I get my hands round this person's throat.

Editors were very majestic in the days when I first started writing. There was one who got hold of *The Ogre Downstairs*, and rewrote the ending entirely in her own purple prose, which was not in the least like mine, and I decided I was going to change publishers. "No, no, no," said my agent. "You mustn't do that. Carry on and see if you can manage to persuade her." And of course I couldn't persuade her. And then *Charmed Life*: I know by the time I'd done the second draft it was absolutely perfect, it really, really was, I mean just as it is at this moment, you know. And this woman rang me up and wrote to me and told me exactly this sort of thing: "You must take out this chunk and that chunk and rewrite this and alter that," and I was furious. And I thought surely we can do something about this. And thank God it was the days before computers. I said, "Send me the typescript back and I'll see what I can do." So she did, and I cut out the bits she told me to alter, in irregular jagged shapes, then stuck them back in exactly the same place with Sellotape, only crooked, so it looked as if I'd taken pieces out and put new pieces in. And then I sent it back to her, and she rang up and said, "Oh, your alterations have made *such* a difference." And I thought, "Right! Hereafter I will take no notice of anybody who tries to edit my books." And I don't. I make a frightful fuss if anybody tries to, now.

CB: *You've created a number of different universes and multiverses, some of which have several books set within them—the Chrestomanci* *books, for example, and the Dalemark series. In each case, the way the world is set up is quite distinct. Does that make a lot of difference to the kind of story you can tell, and to the kind of people who can inhabit that world?*

DWJ: It does. The extraordinary thing is what an enormous difference a very small change can make to a world and its inhabitants. It makes a totally different kind of story: if you were to set a Chrestomanci story in the Dalemark world, it would be quite different. The Chrestomanci world is more foursquare apart from anything else. More straightforward somehow.

CB: *Yes, I know what you mean. Dalemark is slightly more at an angle, isn't it?*

DWJ: Yes, it is. It's hard to express, but it ripples away sideways quite often. And there wouldn't be any room for gods, and Dalemark definitely needed gods.

CB: *True. I suppose there are gods in the Chrestomanci books, but in a way they're more . . . containable.*

DWJ: They are. They're the ones we're used to.

CB: *There's Millie, for a start!*

DWJ: Yes! But also they do go to church of a Sunday— though Gwendolen makes a riot of the church service. That was pure revenge actually, because when I was sent to boarding school we were marched off every Sunday—we had to wear gloves and hats and coats and all this Sunday stuff, and we were marched off in a crocodile, two by two, and we had to sit through all this incredibly boring church service. I spent my time grinding my teeth, and hating looking at crucifixes because they always make me feel terrible—I mean, fancy doing that to anyone!—and looking instead at the stained-glass windows, of which thank goodness there were many, and thinking, "Oh, if only they'd come alive and start running about." And finally I was able to get them to do that in *Charmed Life*. And it was somehow revenge—I wouldn't call it therapeutic, but it was revenge for many hours of extreme boredom. Not to speak of chill, because churches were very cold in those days.

CB: *In an upstairs room in your house there's a drawer that's jammed shut, which is full of manuscripts. Who knows what treasures lie therein? But I do know there are quite a few stories that you've started and not finished for one reason or another. Perhaps they didn't want to be written then, or they petered out, or whatever. What proportion of stories that get started make it to the finishing line, and how many of them get put away, or recycled later, or cannibalized?*

DWJ: Some of them are cannibalized, but mostly it's like cod spawn. You know, masses and masses of sperm and eggs, and only a small school resulting. There's that massive drawer, but I think what's in there is mostly the first drafts of things that did work. I've got another drawer in my study, which is actually two drawers deep, which is stuffed with beginnings. And they're certainly not all there were, either. I must have chucked quite a few out. Some of them I got quite a long way through, actually, and suddenly realized this is not working, this is swimming away into a swamp, this is simply losing shape, this is something I can't finish in anything shorter than the size of the Bible—or else things that were just two pages long and seemed like a frightfully good idea, a sort of seminal idea, and then just hit the buffers. There was no way to go on with them, and most of the time I don't know why. I occasionally take them out and read them, and think, "What was I even remotely intending to do with this? Where was it supposed to be going?" Because of course you do have that kind of idea—and most of the time I do not know. I know when I wrote *Enchanted Glass*, which did come from that drawer of half-started things, I'm pretty sure I hadn't intended it to go like it did when I fished it out and continued from Chapter One, where it had stopped. But I can't tell you what makes them stop, I really can't.

CB: *Well, I'm delighted that so many of them made it to the end.*

Two Family Views of Diana and Her Work

These two pieces were written by Diana's sons Colin and Richard after her death. They reflect on their mother's lasting legacy as a writer.

Fantasies for Children
Colin Burrow

This is the transcript of a fifteen-minute talk by Diana's son Colin Burrow that was broadcast on BBC Radio Three on July 4, 2011, as part of a series The Essay: Dark Arcadias. *The series explored the history of an idea, and other contributors offered essays on topics as varied as "Wild Nature" and "The Depiction of Poverty in the Renaissance."*

My mother died earlier this year. She was the children's author Diana Wynne Jones. She wrote more than thirty novels. Some of them are set in mythical worlds, which have their own completely convincing mythologies and histories, all of which she made up. Others blend magic into our own world. *Dogsbody*, which appeared in 1975, was perhaps the book in which she really worked out what she wanted to do as a writer. In *Dogsbody* the dog star Sirius is banished from the heavens and is born on earth as a puppy. He becomes an extremely doggy dog, who can't resist either a bitch in heat or a dustbin. He is unmistakably modeled on our own family dog at the time, who was a serial Lothario and bin raider. Sirius the dog, though, also happens to be a celestial hero on a quest to recover a tool for mending the stars.

That fusion of the completely ordinary and the completely magical was entirely typical of my mother's way of writing. It was also how she looked at reality. Normality could never just be normality. So if she got caught in traffic on the M25 it was not because it's one of the busiest roads in Europe. It was because she had her own particular travel jinx.

The obituaries all said nice things about her work, though I'm not sure they got her quite right. Most of them said that Diana Wynne Jones was the person who made Harry Potter possible. This is probably true, but she would hate to be remembered like that. She had a very low view of J. K. Rowling. Because my mother read English at Oxford while Tolkien and C. S. Lewis were lecturing there, the obituaries also said that they were the main influence on her writing.

Lewis and Tolkien played their parts, but the biggest literary influence on Diana Wynne Jones was, I think, a woman: E. Nesbit, whose books Mum read to us from a very early age. E. Nesbit was described by Bernard Shaw as "an audaciously unconventional lady." She smoked cigarettes and cut her hair short. She was a Fabian and a socialist and had a very odd love life. Her children's books wove together sand fairies and ginger beer, magic and experiences from her own life in a way that anticipates the mixture of magic and reality in a lot of contemporary children's fiction.

She was the main spirit behind Diana Wynne Jones's fiction. In my mother's best novel, *Fire and Hemlock*—which retells the story of "Tam Lin," but which is also about her own love for my father—the heroine, Polly, is sent a series of children's books which her admirer Thomas Lynn says nobody should grow up without reading. They include E. Nesbit's *Five Children and It* and *The Treasure Seekers*. When Thomas sends her *The Lord of the Rings* a bit later on, it's something of a disaster, since Polly starts to imitate Tolkien in her own writings, and Thomas tells her off for doing so.

Writing for children is often regarded as escapist, and fantasy in general is often sneered at as the simplest kind of utopian fiction. You create a world in which everything works out, as if by magic, and that's the end of it: Arcadia without darkness or death. Children's writing and fantasy in the line descended from E. Nesbit is not at all like that. E. Nesbit had an unhappy childhood. She often directly wrote about people she knew in her fiction. And her most utopian writing—particularly her late work *The Magic City*—is not simply escapist. It imagines a new and better world because of what is wrong with the present one. E. Nesbit created a kind of children's fiction which was always aware of the bad things it was trying to escape *from*— fathers in prison, or parents who are absent, or worlds that are wrecked. As a result her followers, including Diana Wynne Jones, created a kind of fantasy which does not simply run away into ideal or magical worlds, but which uses those ideal worlds to work out real problems from their own lives. This can make the worlds they describe serious and dark.

"Dark" is perhaps an odd word to use of Diana Wynne Jones's writing, since it is full of fun. Where else could you find a description of a griffin going to the vet, or indeed of a griffin cracking its way out of an egg? But her books are profoundly serious despite the jokes. They are quite consistently driven by rage against unfairness. Very often characters in her novels discover that they are being manipulated or controlled by people who have no right to do so, and they cry out (as my mother did, rather often and usually at high volume), "That's not *fair!*"

Diana Wynne Jones repeatedly embodied evil in people who are unfair in one particular way. She hated exploiters, people who tried to suck the magic and vitality from others. In *Charmed Life*, the central character Eric has a sister who steals his magic and stops him believing in himself. In *The Dark Lord of Derkholm*, a magical world parallel to our own is having the magic stolen from it by a cold entrepreneur who organizes fantasy tours through the countryside. He holds the whole world by the purse-strings: dragons are losing their luster, the Wizard's University is under threat, and the whole of Arcadia is being wrecked by commercial exploitation.

This sounds like a tract for our own times, though *The Dark Lord of Derkholm* was written in 1998. And it suggests that children's fiction about alternative worlds can be partly about politics. Diana Wynne Jones's magical worlds don't grow from politics in the sense of government policy or levels of taxation. They're much more about the politics of the spirit. Her books repeatedly represent acts of rebellion against anything or anyone that makes people ordinary and gray when they could be imaginative and alive.

Much of that comes from E. Nesbit. Some of it also comes from the poet Shelley, whom Diana Wynne Jones much admired. But her fiction was also underpinned by a profound sadness which was all her own. Many of Diana Wynne Jones's heroes and heroines are writers. Almost all of these have problems. Some have their words stolen by evil magicians who use them in nefarious magical ways (this happens in *Archer's Goon* as well as in *Fire and Hemlock*). Others have to give up the things they love in order to make the world better. The narrator of *The Homeward Bounders* is called Jamie. He discovers that a group of demons are playing an elaborate war game with the fates of all the worlds and all the people on them. For finding this out, he is ejected from his own world and is condemned to go seeking his home from universe to universe. Eventually, when he has given up all hope, he leads a rebellion against the demons who are destroying and exploiting the universes. The price of his victory is that he has to wander through the worlds for eternity on his own. It's from this position of profound loss that he relates his story.

In *Fire and Hemlock*, the heroine Polly also writes stories, and she eventually discovers that she can only win her true love back from the ice-cold queen of the fairies by giving him up. Repeatedly in the fiction of Diana Wynne Jones, a writer is a person who has to give up everything, and go through despair, in order to set other people free.

That's a profoundly strange idea. And anyone who saw Diana Wynne Jones actually writing a book would be particularly amazed by it. When she wrote she was a picture of complete happiness: she would sit with a cigarette in one hand and a pen in the other, a dog or a cat at her feet, and coffee nearby. She regarded the people and the worlds she created with real love. When she signed away the film rights to *Howl's Moving Castle* so that Hayao Miyazaki could make it into a wonderful animation, she said she felt like she was selling her characters into slavery. And yet clearly she regarded the process of imagining new and magical worlds as an exercise in loneliness so profound that it was almost a kind of sacrifice.

Many of the obituaries of Diana Wynne Jones dwelled on her early life—or rather her early life as she described it in "Something About the Author." This tells how she was brought up in the village of Thaxted in Essex. Thaxted was through the 1920s and beyond a center for communism, Morris dancing, hand-thrown pots, and eccentric living. She always said how much she hated the village, but her particular brand of utopian fiction is actually quite hard to imagine without that bizarre social and political background. Her autobiography also says that Diana Wynne Jones and her sisters spent much of their childhood living on their own in an annex with a concrete floor, where they were deprived of books, and were neglected by their parents. Her mother repeatedly called her a clever but ugly delinquent. Her sisters don't remember their childhood in the same way. I wasn't there, so I can only say that she needed to remember her childhood in this way, even if that wasn't quite how it was.

There is no doubt that this gives her fiction its characteristic darkness. Old women and failed mothers do not fare well in her stories. The central character of *Black Maria* is an elderly suburban lady of high respectability. She turns out to be a witch who uses magic to control a whole town full of zombielike conformist men. This particular witch is clearly based on my grandmothers. They are represented so cruelly that one of Diana Wynne Jones's own characters might well cry out, "It's not fair" if they read about them.

My mother's mother was herself a formidable woman. She grew up in a very modest background in Sheffield. She became a scholarship girl, went to Oxford, and transformed herself into a speaker of impeccably cultivated BBC English. She probably did not much want to be a mother. She certainly could be cruel, and very much liked to be admired by men. She runs through my mother's novels like a dark base note: she's there in the wicked Witch of the Waste in *Howl's Moving Castle*, who turns the young Sophie into a crone and who preserves her own beauty by magic. There is no doubt that my grandmother is the principal reason why Diana Wynne Jones's Arcadias are so dark, and why her fictions so often associate imaginative children with lonely defiance and with sadness.

One of the most obvious but most profound truths about fiction is that it does not paint things as they are. Fiction is often, as a result, not fair. People who make up imaginative worlds— Arcadias, utopias—often do so because they feel wronged, or because they feel that there is something wrong with the world around them. Fiction allows them to create a world with its own set of values, in which punishments can be handed out according to the rules of the imagination and emotion rather than the rule of law. People who knew Dante, and who saw him put people whom he hated into his representation of hell, probably had exactly the same response as I do to some of my mother's writing. Diana Wynne Jones used fiction partly to create worlds which were happier and more equal than our own, but she could also use fiction to take revenge on people she felt had injured or offended her.

I liked my grandmother, and I got punished for this in several of my mother's books. When I was a teenager I listened to The Doors and did a lot of photography. No doubt in my mother's eyes I was a chilly kind of thing. In *Fire and Hemlock* there is a chilly public schoolboy called Sebastian who likes The Doors and photography. He also happens to be in league with the glamorous and un-aging Queen of the Fairies, with whom he tries to erase the heroine's memories and perform a human sacrifice.

Well, thanks, Mum. But fiction is not meant to be fair. My mother needed to tap some of her darkest experiences in order to write, and she gave moral values to different characters according to a profoundly idiosyncratic emotional language. Her fictional worlds were not straight transcriptions of the world she saw, but of the world she felt. And she said what she felt about people more readily in fiction than she did in person.

I'm a literary critic by profession, and most of the people I write books about—Milton, Spenser, Sidney, and Shakespeare—lived around four centuries ago. It's therefore particularly odd for me to read my mother's novels and see at once where so much of the fiction comes from. My old dog Lily is effectively the hero of *House of Many Ways*, for example. This gives me a quite different perspective on the poems and plays I think about in my day job. Many of the writers I work on created dark Arcadias of one kind or another—pastoral or fantastical worlds which are marred by some problem. It's often said by literary critics that Shakespeare and Sidney and Spenser and Milton created Arcadian and pastoral fictions in order to reflect on their own worlds. If those Arcadias are dark—if kings are no good, or if queens are evil, if life in the forest becomes violent—critics usually end up saying that it's because Sir Philip Sidney (or whoever it might be) didn't like the foreign policy of Elizabeth I. We say that because we know a fair bit about the foreign policy of Elizabeth I, but we don't know much about the intimate lives and aversions of authors from that period. I learned many things from my mother and her books, but perhaps the principal thing I learned was that dark Arcadias, like all fictions, almost certainly come from places in the imagination which are very private. Fictions are so closely tied up in the lives and the emotions of their creators that readers—even the author's own children—can only see by glimpses where they really came from.

Address at Diana's Funeral
Richard Burrow

Mum had many good qualities, particularly her sense of humor and her extraordinary generosity. When I came to write down my thoughts, however, I discovered I didn't want to talk about these, but rather about her books and what they reveal about her as a person. This is because the real core of Mum is most evident in her books, for reasons that I hope to make clear. What follows then is not literary criticism, but an attempt to discover the person in the books.

I loved my mother desperately as a child. My fondest memories are of all three of us snuggling up to her for a bedtime story. She read very well and I often feel that she imagined her own books being read aloud as she wrote. They read aloud beautifully, as Neil Gaiman says in his obituary on the internet.[1] Later on I was to read all her books to my own children, and I discovered an almost poetic beauty at times, especially in the Dalemark books, which I always imagine being spoken by some bard who has scraped them together from various oral traditions.

It is in these books and a few others like *The Homeward Bounders*, *Hexwood*, and *Fire and Hemlock* that one discovers the real heart of this deeply shy and guarded person: as with Charles Dickens and Georgette Heyer, two of her favorite writers, her books are sustained by an enormous love; a childlike yearning to create a world that fully satisfies the human soul. As with Dickens, this yearning is so powerful that it creates an almost poetic language and rhythm which help to transform the everyday world. (Dickens, it is said, had constantly to guard against slipping into blank verse, and reading *Drowned Ammet*, one feels that same songlike quality; music, always the most immediately emotional of the arts, constantly threatens to take over.)

This yearning or elegiac quality that one finds in many of Mum's best books is partly a sign of the deep pain caused by her upbringing. At the heart of her books is a sense of loss. From this point of view, *The Homeward Bounders*, the most tragic of her books, is also the most honest. The main character is left literally creating worlds for others while never being able to return to his own. This book is atypical, however; more frequently the poetic beauty, the humor, and the sensuous vividness of the fantasy transport the reader away from this imperfect world. So many of the tweets that have flooded in recently have referred to one or other of Mum's books as the writer's "comfort book," read time and again in times of stress. The pain of her upbringing may have meant that she could only give and receive comfort sporadically in the "real world," but what she gave us is in a sense real in a deeper way: a direct line to that perfect world which all of us yearn for, whether we know it or not.

As I say, I read all her books aloud to Ruth particularly, who is dyslexic and was quite late learning to read. We had two copies of all of them, which meant that she could follow as I read. I remember solemnly forbidding her to read on by herself, knowing that she was so ornery that any encouragement would have backfired, and being secretly delighted the next night when I realized that she had read on a chapter, as well as disappointed at losing the pleasure of reading it aloud to her. It was in this cozy situation, reading aloud to my daughter, that Mum, like the incorporeal mother in *The Spellcoats*, came alive and spoke to me, offering me and anyone else who reads her books comfort.

Notes

Reflecting on *Reflections*
1. Virginia Woolf, *A Writer's Diary* (The Hogarth Press, 1953), p. 65.

The Shape of the Narrative in *The Lord of the Rings*
1. In 1925 Tolkien took up the Rawlinson and Bosworth Professorship of Anglo-Saxon at Oxford University, but in 1945 he became the Merton Professor of English Language and Literature at the same university. He retained this position until his retirement in 1959.
2. The page references are to the second edition in three volumes (*The Fellowship of the Ring*, *The Two Towers*, and *The Return of the King*) (Allen & Unwin, 1966).
3. D. S. Brewer, "*The Lord of the Rings* as Romance," in *J. R. R. Tolkien, Scholar and Storyteller: Essays in Memoriam*, edited by Mary Salu and Robert T. Farrell (Cornell University Press, 1979), pp. 249–64.

Two Kinds of Writing?
1. Diana's first published novel, *Changeover*, was for adults but was not fantasy. Here she is referring to her first adult fantasy/science fiction novel, *A Sudden Wild Magic*, which was published in 1992.

Reading C.S. Lewis's Narnia
1. *Prince Caspian*, published in 1951, was the second Narnia novel to be published.
2. Diana's son Michael points out that he actually preferred *Prince Caspian* and *The Silver Chair*.

Creating the Experience
1. When Johnny discovers how to use his magical chemistry set to become invisible, but as a side effect becomes a "sort of angry ghost."
2. In the 1988 US edition of *Eight Days of Luke*, published by Greenwillow, Diana provided an afterword explaining the Norse legends and gods she drew upon for the story. The god Loki, one of the major figures of Norse mythology, was associated with fire as well as with tricks and mischief.
3. This character is based on Tew (also Tiu or Tyr), the Norse god of strife and war. He gave his name to Tuesday.

Fantasy Books for Children
1. Diana's afterword explains that Brunhilde (also Brunhilda or Brynhild) was

one of the warrior women, the Valkyrie, and a daughter of Woden or Odin, the chief of the gods. When she disobeyed Woden, he sentenced her to sleep inside a ring of flames. The hero Siegfried (Sigurd) rescued her by braving the fire and waking her with a kiss, but when he betrayed her by marrying Gudrun (whose mother put him under a spell to forget Brunhilde), Brunhilde returned to her circle of fire. According to some legends, she killed Siegfried first, but in other stories she wreaked her revenge on him in a way that will eventually bring about Ragnarok, or the final battle of the gods.

Writing for Children: A Matter of Responsibility

1. In ancient British mythology the gods and heroes owned thirteen Treasures varying from an invisibility cloak to a chariot that magically transported its passengers anywhere they wished to go. The Treasures included a forerunner of a thermos flask in the shape of a horn that provided any drink that was desired. According to the legend, the magician Merlin took the Treasures with him into seclusion in a cave until such time as they are needed again.

2. After 2005, the Whitbread Book Awards were renamed the Costa Book Awards when Costa Coffee took over sponsorship.

The Heroic Ideal: A Personal Odyssey

1. In Greek legend, the priestess Hero lived in a tower on the one side of the strait of Dardanelles (formerly called the Hellespont) in what is now Turkey. Every night she would light a lamp in her tower room to guide her love, Leander, as he swam across from the other side of the strait. This worked well in the summer, but in a winter storm Hero's lamp blew out and Leander was blown off course. Leander drowned, and Hero threw herself from the tower to her death.

2. Originating in the Scottish Borders, the ballad of "Tam Lin" tells of the maiden Janet, who rescues her lover, Tam Lin, from the fairies by holding fast on to him although the fairies transform him into several dangerous animals.

3. The Goon is as big and dangerous as a gorilla, and he is also supposedly a debt collector sent by the mysterious Archer, who "farms" or controls part of the town.

4. T. S. Eliot, "Burnt Norton," *Four Quartets* (Houghton Mifflin Harcourt, 1936), 13.

5. T. S. Eliot, "The Dry Salvages," *Four Quartets* (Houghton Mifflin Harcourt, 1936), 35, 37, 38.

6. T. S. Eliot, "Burnt Norton," *Four Quartets* (Houghton Mifflin Harcourt, 1936), 14.

7. T. S. Eliot, "East Coker," *Four Quartets* (Houghton Mifflin Harcourt, 1936), 29.

8. T. S. Eliot, "Little Gidding," *Four Quartets* (Houghton Mifflin Harcourt, 1936), 58.

A Talk About Rules

1. Chris Bell was a close friend of Diana's who lived near Diana in Bristol. She is involved in British science fiction fandom.

2. John Clute and John Grant, *The Encyclopedia of Fantasy* (Orbit Books/St. Martin's Press, 1997). This award-winning book was compiled by several contributors, including Diana Wynne Jones and her friend Chris Bell.

3. In *Eight Days of Luke*, David can summon his friend Luke, who is really the Norse fire god Loki, by striking a match.

4. In Charles Dickens's *Hard Times*, Thomas Gradgrind is the founder of a practical, utilitarian educational system.

Answers to Some Questions

1. Twyford is a longstanding British manufacturer of bathroom equipment.

2. As her father was dying, a group of drunken male students besieged Diana and her sisters in the house by beating on the front door and roaring for women.

3. A common element in European folktales, seven-league boots transport the wearer seven leagues (twenty-one miles or nearly thirty-five kilometers) with each step. In *Howl's Moving Castle*, Sophie attempts to use one boot and ends up "zipping" all over the countryside when she keeps accidentally putting her foot down.

A Whirlwind Tour of Australia

1. The words "agony" and "action" are believed to have a common Proto-Indo-European linguistic root *ag*, meaning "to drive, draw out, draw forth, move." Agony developed from Greek, through *agein*, "to lead," through *agon*, "contest" to *agonia*, "a struggle for victory." Action developed from Latin, from *agree*, "to do" through *actionem*, "a putting in motion, a doing."

2. Fanny Cradock was a British restaurant critic, author of best-selling cookbooks, and a celebrity cook who presented a long-running television show from the mid-1950s through to the mid-1970s.

3. This book is unpublished.

Some Truths About Writing

1. The British newspaper the *Guardian*, founded in 1821 as the *Manchester Guardian*, is famous for its misprints. Because of this, it is often called the *Grauniad*.

2. See "The Heroic Ideal."

3. Libby was Elizabeth Shub, an editor at Greenwillow Books.

4. The "hero" of *Fire and Hemlock* is called Thomas Lynn, while one of the names of the villains is Leroy—"king."

5. See "Answers to Some Questions."

Freedom to Write

1. *Spindle's End.*

2. This is the sixth book in Terry Goodkind's Sword of Truth series (New York: Tor Books, 2000).

3. By James Barclay.

4. Diana's fantasy/science fiction books for adults are *A Sudden Wild Magic* (1992) and *Deep Secret* (1997). *The Dark Lord of Derkholm* (1998) and *Year of the Griffin* (2000) were published as adult novels in the UK and young adult novels in the US. The cluster around the turn of the millennium implies that this is the period she is referring to.

Our Hidden Gifts

1. Diana gave out the certificates first but was very nervous and forgot to shake the pupils' hands!

Something About the Author

1. Its real name is Peel Island.

2. Since this article appeared, Diana has published other adult novels.

The Origins of *Changeover*

1. In the "Something About the Author" autobiographical article, Diana says it was in 1966.

2. UDI, or Unilateral Declaration of Independence, was the proclamation made in 1965 by the white government of the British colony of Rhodesia (now Zimbabwe) that the country was cutting its links with the United Kingdom. The central issue was the refusal by the Rhodesian government, led by Ian Smith, to acknowledge the political rights of the African majority population of the country.

A Conversation with Diana Wynne Jones

1. St. Frideswide is the patron saint of Oxford. The priory she is thought to have founded in the late seventh or early eighth century was on the site of Christ Church, and the anniversary of her death is still commemorated every year on October 19.

2. See endnote 2 in "The Origins of *Changeover*" chapter.

3. The 2004 animated film directed by Hayao Miyazaki of Studio Ghibli, Tokyo, Japan. The Japanese title is *Hauru no Ugoku Shiro*, and it was nominated for an Oscar in the best animated feature film category in 2006.

4. Garth Nix, Introduction to "The Hill," in *Across the Wall* (HarperCollins, 2007), p. 167.

Two Family Views of Diana and Her Work

1. See Neil Gaiman's blog: http://journal.neilgaiman.com/2011/03/being-alive.html

Diana Wynne Jones Bibliography

ADULT BOOKS

Changeover, 1970

A Sudden Wild Magic, 1992

Deep Secret, 1997

STAND-ALONE CHILDREN'S BOOKS

Wilkins' Tooth (US: *Witch's Business*), 1973

The Ogre Downstairs, 1974

Eight Days of Luke, 1975

Dogsbody, 1975

Power of Three, 1976

Time of the Ghost, 1981

The Homeward Bounders, 1981

Archer's Goon, 1984

Fire and Hemlock, 1985

A Tale of Time City, 1987

Black Maria (US: *Aunt Maria*), 1991

Hexwood, 1993

The Dark Lord of Derkholm, 1998

Year of the Griffin, 2000

The Merlin Conspiracy, 2003

The Game, 2007

Enchanted Glass, 2010

THE DALEMARK QUARTET

Cart and Cwidder, 1975

Drowned Ammet, 1977

The Spellcoats, 1979

The Crown of Dalemark, 1993

THE CHRESTOMANCI SERIES

Charmed Life, 1977

The Magicians of Caprona, 1980

Witch Week, 1982

The Lives of Christopher Chant, 1988

Mixed Magics, 2000

Stealer of Souls, 2002

Conrad's Fate, 2005

The Pinhoe Egg, 2006

The Chronicles of Chrestomanci, Volume I (contains *Charmed Life* and *The Lives of Christopher Chant*)

The Chronicles of Chrestomanci, Volume II (contains *The Magicians of Caprona* and *Witch Week*)

The Chronicles of Chrestomanci, Volume III (contains the short stories also found in *Mixed Magics*)

THE HOWL SERIES

Howl's Moving Castle, 1986

Castle in the Air, 1990

House of Many Ways, 2008

FOR YOUNGER READERS

Who Got Rid of Angus Flint?, 1978

The Four Grannies, 1980

Chair Person, 1989

Wild Robert, 1989

Yes, Dear, 1992

Stopping for a Spell (contains *Who Got Rid of Angus Flint?,*
The Four Grannies, and *Chair Person*), 1993

Puss in Boots, 1999

Earwig and the Witch, 2011

Short Story Anthologies

Warlock at the Wheel, 1984

Hidden Turnings (editor), 1989

Fantasy Stories (editor), (US: *Spellbound*), 1994

Everard's Ride, 1995

Minor Arcana, 1996

Believing Is Seeing, 1999

Unexpected Magic, 2004

NONFICTION/HUMOR

The Skiver's Guide, 1984

The Tough Guide to Fantasyland, 1996

PLAYS

The Batterpool Business, 1968

The King's Things, 1970

The Terrible Fisk Machine, 1972

Diana Wynne Jones also wrote several poems and short stories that
have been published in anthologies.

Index

Index